Read 4 Today

Grade 2

Frank Schaffer Publications®

Editor: Kim Bradford
Interior Designer: Lori Kibbey

Frank Schaffer Publications®

Printed in the United States of America. All rights reserved. Limited Reproduction Permission: Permission to duplicate these materials is limited to the person for whom they are purchased. Reproduction for an entire school or school district is unlawful and strictly prohibited. Frank Schaffer Publications is an imprint of School Specialty Publishing. Copyright © 2005 School Specialty Publishing.

Send all inquiries to:
Frank Schaffer Publications
8720 Orion Place
Columbus, Ohio 43240-2111

Read 4 Today—grade 2

ISBN: 0-7682-3212-0

3 4 5 6 7 8 9 10 PAT 12 11 10 09

Read 4 Today

Table of Contents

Introduction 4

Reading Skills and Standards for Second Grade 5

Building a Reading Environment 6

Skills and Concepts Chart 7

Scope and Sequence Chart 11

Daily Activities/Assessments 13

Answer Key 93

Introduction

Read 4 Today supplies predictable, patterned review and practice materials for students. Four questions a day for four days a week provide students with the opportunity to hone their skills. A separate assessment is included for the fifth day of each week. On odd-numbered weeks, students will work on decoding or word strategies, vocabulary, fluency, and comprehension. On even-numbered weeks, the activities focus on book titles and previewing, with students answering questions before, during, and after reading. This book covers a forty-week period, and each grade level includes some curricula from the previous and the following grade levels.

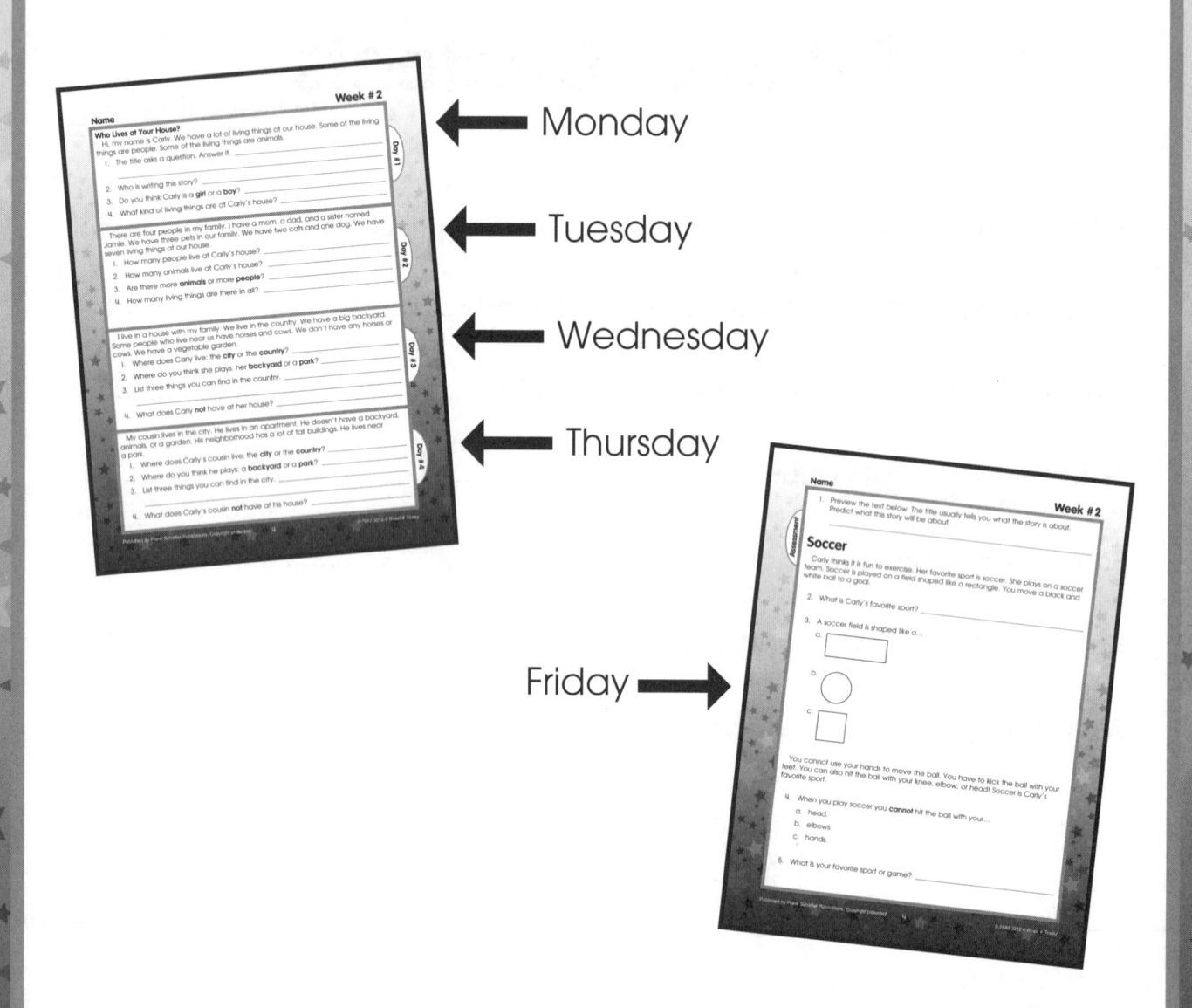

⬅ Monday

⬅ Tuesday

⬅ Wednesday

⬅ Thursday

Friday ➡

Skills and concepts are reinforced throughout the book, and it incorporates the style and syntax of standardized tests. The answer key reproduces each page, both daily practices and assessments, for ease in grading.

Reading Skills and Standards for Second Grade

Fluency

- read text aloud with appropriate pacing, intonation, and expression
- comprehend what is read as it is read (short time from reading to comprehension)
- repeated practice in reading text aloud from student's "independent" level (approximately 1 in 20 words difficult for the reader)

Vocabulary

- use word origins to find meaning of unknown words
- use context to find meaning of unknown words
- identify Greek and Latin roots, suffixes, and prefixes to analyze the meaning of complex words
- determine part of speech, pronunciation, and meaning of words using a dictionary

Comprehension

- establish purpose for reading
- identify main idea and supporting details
- make predictions based on evidence in text (inferencing)
- distinguish between fact and opinion
- identify and analyze organizational structures in text (cause and effect, compare and contrast, chronological order)
- summarize information
- answer literal, inferential, and evaluative questions
- identify the genre of a literary text
- identify story elements (characters, setting, plot, problem, solution)
- understand figurative language and its function in text (simile, metaphor, hyperbole, personification)
- self-monitor comprehension

Building a Reading Environment

The reading environment is essential to fostering successful readers. When building a positive reading environment, think of students' physical, emotional, and cognitive needs.

Physical Environment

- Make the physical reading environment inviting and comfortable. Create a reading corner with comfortable chairs, floor pillows, a rug, enticing lighting, and so on.
- Give students access to a variety of text by providing books, magazines, newspapers, and Internet access. Read signs, ads, posters, menus, pamphlets, labels, boxes, and more!
- Provide regularly scheduled independent reading time in class. Encourage students to read at home. They can read to a younger sibling, or read anything of interest, such as comic books, children's and sports magazines, chapter books, and so on.
- Set a positive example. Make sure students see you reading along with them!

Emotional Environment

- Learn about students' reading habits, preferences, strengths, and weaknesses, and then provide books that address these issues.
- Help students create connections with text. Facilitate connections by activating prior knowledge, examining personal meaning, and respecting personal reflections.
- Give students the opportunity to choose titles to read. This gives them a sense of ownership, helping to engage them in the text and sustain interest.
- Create a safe environment for exploring and trying new things. Foster a feeling of mutual respect for reading abilities and preferences.
- Require that students read at an appropriate reading level. Text in any content area, including leisure reading, should not be too easy or too difficult.
- Get all students to participate in reading, no matter what their reading level. Try not to alienate slower readers. Give them time to finish before moving on or asking questions.
- Be enthusiastic about reading! Talk about books you love, and share your reading experiences and habits. Your attitudes about reading are contagious!

Cognitive Environment

- No matter the grade level, read aloud to students every day. Reading aloud not only provides a good example but also lets students practice their listening skills.
- Help students build their vocabularies to make reading more successful. Create word walls, personal word lists, mini-dictionaries, and graphic organizers.
- Read for different purposes. Reading a novel requires different skills than reading an instructions manual. Teach students the strategies needed to comprehend these texts.
- Encourage students to talk about what and how they read. Use journal writing, literature circles, class discussions, conferences, conversations, workshops, seminars, and more.
- Writing and reading are inherently linked. Students can examine their own writing through reading and examine their reading skills by writing. Whenever possible, facilitate the link between reading and writing.

Skills and Concepts — Odd-numbered weeks

week 1—page 13
vowel sounds
vowel sounds—
short/long a, short/long e
silent letter
rhyme
synonym
antonym
detail
author's feelings
setting
cause and effect

week 3—page 17
vowel sounds
vowel sounds—short i,
short/long o, short u
synonym
antonym
detail
context clues
classify
math
character

week 5—page 21
letter sounds and blends
vowel sounds—long e
digraphs—th
synonym
detail
classifying
main idea
silent letters

week 7—page 25
character
vowel sounds—long a
blends—gr
rhyme
synonym
context clues
math
classification
problem

week 9—page 29
character
silent letters—w
compound words
rhyme
synonym
main idea
detail
predicting
problem

week 11—page 33
setting
vowel sound—long e
rhyme
synonym
details
context clues

week 13—page 37
main idea
vowel sounds—long/short i
rhyme
synonym
title
detail
true or false
character's feelings

week 15—page 41
main idea
vowel sounds—short/long u
rhyme
synonym
details

week 17—page 45
problem and solution
vowel sounds—long o
ea, oo
silent letter
rhyme
contraction
synonym
character
cause and effect

week 19—page 49
reality and fantasy
blends—st
rhyme
syllables
synonym
antonym
detail

week 21—page 53
sequencing
consonant sounds—s, c
rhyme
compound words
synonym
details
context clues
problem and solution
cause and effect

week 23—page 57
reality and fantasy
vowel sounds—long/short a, ow
compound word
synonym
antonym
title
detail
context clues
cause and effect
character's feelings

Published by Frank Schaffer Publications. Copyright protected. 0-7682-3212-0 Read 4 Today

Skills and Concepts — Odd-numbered weeks

week 25—page 61
summarizing
blends—ck, fl
rhyme
synonym
title
setting
details
character

week 27—page 65
summarizing
vowel sounds—short/long a, oo
consonant sound—g
rhyme
antonym
main idea
details

week 29—page 69
fact and opinion
consonant sounds—
hard g, hard c
synonym
math
main idea
detail

week 31—page 73
cause and effect
vowel sounds—long/short e
consonant sounds—le
silent letter—e
rhyme
antonym
math
context clues
character's feelings
detail

week 33—page 77
compare and contrast
vowel sound—short i
consonant sound—
hard/soft c, c (sh)
silent letter
syllables
synonym
antonym
problem and solution
context clues

week 35—page 81
compare and contrast
consonant sound—ck
diagraph—ch
synonym
antonym
details
math
cause and effect

week 37—page 85
context clues
vowel sounds—u, o
synonym
antonym
details
cause and effect
setting

week 39—page 89
inferencing
syllables
rhyme
antonym
details

Skills and Concepts   Even-numbered weeks

week 2—page 15
mixed story elements
title
character
setting
detail
context clues
math
compare and contrast

week 4—page 19
mixed story elements
details
context clues
characters
cause and effect
setting
reality and fantasy
problem and solution

week 6—page 23
mixed story elements
synonym
details
character
setting
context clues
title

week 8—page 27
character
detail
context clues
genre
true or false

week 10—page 31
setting
details
character
classification

week 12—page 35
setting
making predictions
details

week 14—page 39
main idea
details
context clues
setting

week 16—page 43
mixed story elements
character
setting
details
making predictions
author's purpose
context clues
characters feelings

week 18—page 47
classifying
details

week 20—page 51
making predictions
blends—qu
math
details
problem and solution

week 22—page 55
classifying
setting
details
compare and contrast

week 24—page 59
making predictions
character
setting
details

Skills and Concepts   Even-numbered weeks

week 26—page 63
summarizing
character
setting
details
context clues

week 28—page 67
fact and opinion
character
main idea
details
compare and contrast
sequencing
context clues

week 30—page 71
cause and effect
details
sequencing
context clues
compare and contrast

week 32—page 75
cause and effect
setting
details
compare and contrast
problem
character's feelings
prediction

week 34—page 79
compare and contrast
details
classifying

week 36—page 83
context clues
synonym
character

week 38—page 87
context clues
synonym
character
setting
true or false
title

week 40—page 91
inferencing
details
compare and contrast
title

Scope and Sequence

	1	2	3	4	5	6	7	8	9	10	11	12	13	14	15	16	17	18	19	20
vowel sounds:	•		•				•	•												
consonant sounds:					•		•													
blends:		•	•		•						•					•	•		•	•
silent letter:	•				•		•		•								•			
rhyme:	•						•				•		•				•		•	
syllables:											•						•		•	
compound words:																				
synonym	•		•		•		•		•				•						•	
(replacing words and phrases):																				
antonym (opposites):	•		•								•						•		•	
character:						•	•													
setting:	•				•	•														
main idea:	•				•	•			•	•		•	•	•	•	•	•	•	•	•
details:			•	•	•	•		•	•	•		•	•	•	•	•	•	•	•	•
problem and solution:																•				
classifying:			•							•										
reality and fantasy:				•				•					•							
true and false:																				
making predictions:							•					•				•			•	•
sequencing:																				
summarizing:																				
fact and opinion:	•			•											•					
cause and effect:		•		•		•	•	•	•	•	•						•			
compare and contrast:		•				•														•
context clues:																•				
inferencing:								•												
title:																				
genre:			•				•									•				•
math:																				
other:	•	•											•				•			

T = Weekly Test   • Indicates Skill or Concept Included and/or Tested

Scope and Sequence

	21	T 22	23	T 24	25	T 26	27	T 28	29	T 30	31	T 32	33	T 34	35	T 36	37	T 38	39	T 40	T
vowel sounds:			•								•		•				•					
consonant sounds:	•		•	•			•		•		•		•		•					•		
blends:					•		•				•											
silent letter:											•		•							•		
rhyme:	•										•									•		
syllables:	•												•				•		•			
compound words:																						
synonym	•		•																			
(replacing words and phrases):			•						•						•							
antonym (opposites):			•										•									
character:				•						•												
setting:	•		•		•				•			•	•	•		•		•				
main idea:	•			•	•	•		•	•		•	•	•	•		•	•	•	•	•	•	•
details:																						
problem and solution:		•						•							•							
classifying:						•										•						
reality and fantasy:			•																			
true and false:								•				•										
making predictions:	•							•														
sequencing:																						
summarizing:	•																					
fact and opinion:									•			•										
cause and effect:	•										•				•		•				•	•
compare and contrast:	•		•					•		•	•		•		•		•		•	•	•	•
context clues:					•								•		•		•		•	•	•	•
inferencing:																						
title:			•									•				•						
genre:																•						
math:																•						
other:																						

T = Weekly Test   • Indicates Skill or Concept Included and/or Tested

Name   Week #1

Day #1

Annie! Come here!
Look at this picture in the family album.
Look, it's you,
Eating apple pie.

1. Read or listen to the poem. Circle each letter **a** that makes the **short a** sound.
2. Circle the word **Eating**. Write another word for **Eating**. _____
3. What is in the family album: **pie** or **pictures**? _____
4. Is the writer of the poem excited or bored? _____

Day #2

On a day rainy and gray,
Amy and Kate stay inside to play.
They wear aprons and paint all day,
Until the rain goes away.

1. Read or listen to the poem. Circle each letter **a** that makes the **long a** sound.
2. What is the opposite of **inside**? _____
3. Put a line under all words that rhyme with **gray**.
4. Why can't they play outside? _____

Day #3

The elves like to do each exercise.
They touch their toes and reach for the skies.
So exhausted was Elmer Elf,
He couldn't even climb up to his shelf!

1. Read or listen to the poem. Circle each letter **e** that makes the **short e** sound.
2. Underline the word **exhausted**. Write another word for **exhausted**. _____
3. Do you hear the **b** at the end of **climb** or is it silent? _____
4. Where does Elmer Elf live? _____

Day #4

Paint a picture on an easel,
Of a single bee,
Or paint two, or even three,
By a leafy tree.

1. Read or listen to the poem. Circle each letter **e** that makes the **long e** sound.
2. How many bees is a **single** bee? _____
3. Which three words rhyme? _____
4. Where might the bees live? _____

Published by Frank Schaffer Publications. Copyright protected.   13   0-7682-3212-0 *Read 4 Today*

Week #1

Name

Assessment

Carly's Play Dough Recipe

Mix 1 cup flour and $\frac{1}{4}$ cup salt.
Add 1 cup water.
Add 1 teaspoon cooking oil.
Add 2 teaspoons cream of tartar.
Mix well. Ask parent to heat it on the stove.
Let it get cold.
Play!

1. Draw a line to match the type of sound with the word that has that sound.

    ask   long e
    heat   short a
    well   short e
    play   long a

2. What is the opposite of **cold**? _____

3. Where would be a good place to make this recipe? _____

4. How will parents help with this recipe? _____
   _____

5. Does the writer of this recipe think the last step is exciting or boring? _____
   _____

Name **Week #2**

Who Lives at Your House?

Hi, my name is Carly. We have a lot of living things at our house. Some of the living things are people. Some of the living things are animals.

1. The title asks a question. Answer it. _____
_____
2. Who is writing this story? _____
3. Do you think Carly is a **girl** or a **boy**? _____
4. What kind of living things are at Carly's house? _____

Day #1

There are four people in my family. I have a mom, a dad, and a sister named Jamie. We have three pets in our family. We have two cats and one dog. We have seven living things at our house.

1. How many people live at Carly's house? _____
2. How many animals live at Carly's house? _____
3. Are there more **animals** or more **people**? _____
4. How many living things are there in all? _____

Day #2

I live in a house with my family. We live in the country. We have a big backyard. Some people who live near us have horses and cows. We don't have any horses or cows. We have a vegetable garden.

1. Where does Carly live: the **city** or the **country**? _____
2. Where do you think she plays: her **backyard** or a **park**? _____
3. List three things you can find in the country. _____
_____
4. What does Carly **not** have at her house? _____

Day #3

My cousin lives in the city. He lives in an apartment. He doesn't have a backyard, animals, or a garden. His neighborhood has a lot of tall buildings. He lives near a park.

1. Where does Carly's cousin live: the **city** or the **country**? _____
2. Where do you think he plays: a **backyard** or a **park**? _____
3. List three things you can find in the city. _____
_____
4. What does Carly's cousin **not** have at his house? _____

Day #4

Published by Frank Schaffer Publications. Copyright protected. 0-7682-3212-0 Read 4 Today

Name

Week # 2

1. Preview the text below. The title usually tells you what the story is about. Predict what this story will be about.

_____

Soccer

Carly thinks it is fun to exercise. Her favorite sport is soccer. She plays on a soccer team. Soccer is played on a field shaped like a rectangle. You move a black and white ball to a goal.

2. What is Carly's favorite sport? _____

3. A soccer field is shaped like a...

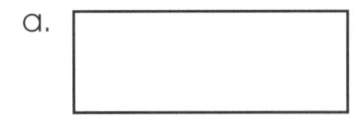

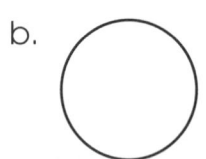

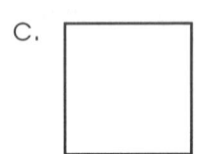

   a. ▭

   b. ○

   c. ☐

You cannot use your hands to move the ball. You have to kick the ball with your feet. You can also hit the ball with your knee, elbow, or head! Soccer is Carly's favorite sport.

4. When you play soccer you **cannot** hit the ball with your...

   a. head.
   b. elbows.
   c. hands.

5. What is your favorite sport or game? _____

Name   Week #3

Day #1

In an instant,
An inchworm inches near.
In an instant,
It can disappear.

1. Read or listen to the poem. Circle each letter **i** that makes the **short i** sound.
2. Write another word or two words for **disappear**. _____
3. About how long is an inchworm?   a. 1 inch   b. 1 foot   c. 1 mile
4. Is an **instant** a long time or a short time? _____

Day #2

Otter likes to play
With many things
Like olives, octagons,
And big, round rings.

1. Read or listen to the poem. Circle each letter **o** that makes the **short o** sound.
2. What is an **octagon**?   a. number   b. shape   c. car
3. What month starts with the **short o** sound? _____
4. Is Otter **serious** or **playful**? _____

Day #3

Oh, I like my overalls,
New or old, striped or bold.
Overalls are great to wear.
I own four pairs, and I won't share!

1. Read or listen to the poem. Circle each letter **o** that makes the **long o** sound.
2. What is the opposite of **like**? _____
3. Line 2 has two words that are opposites. What are they? _____
4. How many overalls does the writer own? _____

Day #4

An umbrella goes up.
An umbrella goes down.
People hide under umbrellas
All over town.

1. Read or listen to the poem. Circle each letter **u** that makes the **short u** sound.
2. What is the opposite of **under**? _____
3. This poem has two opposite words. What are they? _____
4. When do you put up an umbrella? _____

Name

Week #3

Weather Puzzle

Across

2. Strong wind with rain or snow
3. Drops of water that fall to the earth
5. Loud noise that comes after lightning
6. Moving air

Down

1. Very strong wind that makes a cloud shaped like a funnel
2. Light from the sun
4. Soft, white flakes

Word Bank
storm   rain   snow
sunshine   wind   thunder
tornado

1. Draw a line to match the type of sound with the word that has that sound.

   soft   long o
   funnel   short i
   snow   short o
   wind   short u

2. Which words in the Word Bank have a **short u**? _____

3. What kind of weather from the Word Bank is your favorite? _____

4. Which word from the Word Bank could be called a **funnel cloud**? _____

5. Use the clues and the words in the Word Bank to finish the puzzle.

Assessment

Name   **Week # 4**

A Picnic

One sunny day, Mrs. Ant said, "Let's go to the park for a picnic."

"Good idea," said Mr. Ant. "Families will be eating there."

1. What kind of animal is this story about? _____

2. The Ants went to the park for a picnic because…
   a. the park was pretty.
   b. families eat in the park.

3. What kind of weather is it? _____

4. Do ants really talk? _____ This clue tells us this story is not _____.

Day #1

"Can we go now?" asked Art Ant. "I am hungry."

"I don't want to go," said Amy Ant.

1. Who are the Ant kids? _____

2. Art Ant wanted to go because…
   a. he could play in the grass.
   b. he was hungry.

3. Do all the Ants want to go to the park? _____

4. Who does not want to go? _____

Day #2

"Why not?" asked Mrs. Ant.

"Last time we did not find any food," Amy said.

"This time we might find lots of food," said Art.

1. Does Amy say why she didn't want to go? _____

2. Amy Ant didn't want to go because…
   a. sometimes people don't leave food.
   b. sometimes people step on ants.

3. Has an ant ever crawled on your food? _____

4. What would you do to an ant on your food? _____

Day #3

Everyone followed Mrs. Ant to the park. They walked under a picnic table. The four ants sat down. Then they all looked up. They waited.

1. Did the Ants pack any food for the picnic? _____

2. The Ant family sat under the picnic table and looked up…
   a. to watch the sky.
   b. to wait for food to drop down.

3. So who packed the food the Ants will eat? _____

4. Do you think they got food this time? _____

Day #4

Name

Week # 4

1. Preview the text below. Are there any people or animal characters? _____

The Weather

The weather is strange,
Because it can change,
From hot to cold so fast.
The wind can blow,
Or it will snow,
But that will never last.

2. Why is the weather strange? _____

The weather is fun,
When up goes the sun,
But not when clouds fill the sky.
Snow and ice,
Are not so nice,
Coming down on the fly.

3. What kind of weather does the writer like? _____

Dry or wet,
You can bet,
The weather will
Always change!

4. Does the weather change a lot where you live? _____
5. What problems can weather cause? _____
_____

Name　　　　　　　　　　　　　　　　　　　　　　　　　　　　　　　　**Week # 5**

Turkeys

Turkeys are large birds. They have long tails. Wild turkeys are mostly brown.

1. Which word has an **e** with a **long e** sound?   a. turkeys   b. they
2. What is the opposite of **wild**: **tame** or **crazy**? _____
3. Have you ever seen a wild turkey? _____
4. What color are wild turkeys? _____

Day #1

Turkeys live in the woods. They sleep in trees at night. They eat berries, nuts, and seeds.

1. Which words have an **e** with a **long e** sound? _____
   _____
2. Berries, nuts, and seeds are all parts of **plants** or **animals**? _____
3. Listen to or read the paragraph. Is the **gh** in **night** silent? _____
4. What do turkeys do in trees? _____
   _____

Day #2

Mother turkeys are called hens. Hens build nests on the ground. They lay spotted eggs. The eggs hatch in about one month.

1. List all the **th** words in this paragraph. _____
2. What is a **hen**? _____
3. This paragraph is mostly about…
   a. hens and eggs.
   b. eggs and bacon.
   c. turkeys as parents.
4. How long before a turkey egg hatches? _____

Day #3

People like to eat turkey meat. They really like to eat turkey on Thanksgiving Day.

1. Circle all the words with a **th**.
2. Underline the words **really like**. Write another word for **really like**. _____
3. Do you like to eat turkey meat? _____
4. On what holiday do many people eat turkey? _____

Day #4

Published by Frank Schaffer Publications. Copyright protected.　　21　　0-7682-3212-0 *Read 4 Today*

Name: _____ Week # 5

Bird Beaks

All birds have beaks. The beaks of birds are shaped differently because of the food they eat.

The roseate spoonbill is a bird that has a spoon beak. It is shaped like a spoon to scoop up shellfish and water insects found in shallow water.

Birds such as sparrows and finches have cracker beaks. These are strong, short beaks that can crack the hard shells of seeds that they like to eat.

Herons have spear beaks. This beak is long and pointed so that the birds can catch fish and frogs along the shore.

Flamingos like to eat plants and shellfish. They have strainer beaks. These beaks are long and curved. They have combs that strain out the mud and keep the flamingos from swallowing it.

1. Circle all the **th** words in this story. Which one has a **long e** sound? _____

2. What is a **strainer beak**? _____

3. How many types of beaks are used to find food in the water? _____

4. Draw a line to match the type of beak a bird uses with the food it catches.

   cracker beak   fish and frogs

   strainer beak   seeds

   spoon beak   shellfish and water insects

   spear beak   shellfish and plants

5. Jayson does not live near water. Which kind of beak will he see most often?

   a. cracker beak
   b. strainer beak
   c. spoon beak
   d. spear beak

Name _____   # Week # 6

Manatees

Manatees are sometimes called sea cows. They are mammals. They must come to the water's surface to breathe air.

1. What does the title say this story is about? _____
2. What are **manatees**? _____
3. How do manatees get air? _____
4. What is another name for a manatee? _____

Day #1

The West Indian manatee lives along the coast of Florida. It is shy and gentle. Manatees are herbivores. This means that they eat only plants. Baby manatees are called calves. They drink their mother's milk like all mammals.

1. What word better describes a manatee: **mean** or **sweet**? _____
2. What is an **herbivore**? _____
3. What are baby manatees called? _____
4. What do manatee calves eat? _____

Day #2

Habitat is the place where something lives. Habitat is the space that has food, water, air, and shelter. The manatee habitat is changing so fast that manatees are in danger. They are on the endangered animals list.

1. What is a **habitat**? _____
2. What is your habitat? _____
3. What four things does a habitat need? _____
4. Is there a problem with the manatee's habitat? What? _____
_____

Day #3

Pollutants are harmful things that are sometimes in the water. They can cause manatees to become sick and weak. Manatees must have clean, warm water to live.

1. In this paragraph, what is a danger to manatees? _____
2. What happens to manatees when their water is polluted? _____
3. Who do you think puts pollutants in water: **people** or **plants**? _____
4. What can you do to help keep the water clean for manatees? _____
_____

Day #4

Week # 6

1. Preview the text below. What does the title say this story is about? _____

Wart Hogs

Wart hogs live in Africa. Wart hogs get their name from the **warts**, or bumps, on their faces. They look a lot like pigs.

2. How did the wart hog get its name? _____

Wart hogs have **tusks**, or long pointed teeth. The tusks stick out from the sides of their mouths. They use the tusks to **root**, or dig up the ground looking for food. They eat almost anything.

3. For each sentence, write a word from the paragraph that could take the place of the bold words.

   Wart hogs have **pointed teeth**. _____

   Wart hogs **dig for food in the ground**. _____

Wart hogs also use their tusks to fight. They usually do not choose to fight. They will **flee**, or run away, with their tails sticking up in the air. They hide in **thickets**, or bushes, in the day and come out at night to eat.

4. For each sentence, write a word from the paragraph that could take the place of the bold words.

   Wart hogs live in **bushes**. _____

   Wart hogs **run away** from danger. _____

5. Does a wart hog sound like a beautiful animal? Why or why not? _____

Name
Week #7

Trading Toys
John has three trucks, two balls, and one bear to trade. John wanted a car. Steve has one bear, seven balls, and two cars. John gave Steve two balls and one gray truck. Steve gave John one green car.

1. Circle words that start with **gr**. Which one has a **long a** sound? _____
2. What is another word for **trade**: **swap** or **sell**? _____
3. Who are the characters in this story? _____
   Are they boys or girls? _____
4. How many cars does Steve have at the end? _____

Day #1

Pat has four bears. She has one baseball and one jump rope. Terry has six dolls. She also brought five bears. Terry gave Pat two dolls. Pat gave Terry one baseball.

1. What word sounds like **two**: **toe** or **too**? _____
2. What kind of thing are the characters trading: **tools** or **toys**? _____
3. Who are the characters in this story? _____
   Are they boys or girls? _____
4. How many toys did Terry bring to trade? _____

Day #2

Name This Character
He climbed up and up the water spout. The rain fell and washed him out. Later, he climbed again.

1. Which word rhymes with **climbed**: **timed** or **bed**? _____
2. When the character is washed out, what does that mean?
   a. He fell off the water spout.   b. He had a nice bath.
3. Which character from a song is this about: the **Muffin Man** or the **Itsy Bitsy Spider**? _____
4. What is the character's problem? _____

Day #3

Name This Character
He was very hungry and very big. He wanted to eat three little pigs. He tried to blow their houses down.

1. Which word has **gr** in the middle? _____
2. Write one word that means the same as **very big**. _____
3. Which fairy-tale character is this about?
   a. the Big Bad Wolf   b. the Boy Who Cried Wolf
4. What is the character's problem? _____

Day #4

Week #7

The Lion and the Mouse

After eating a big meal, a lion took a nap. He woke up. Something ran across his back! He put out his big paw. It was a little mouse.

The mouse squeaked, "I am too small to be a good meal. Please let me go!"

"No!" roared the lion.

"Let me go. Someday I will help you," said the little mouse.

The lion laughed. "What could a tiny mouse do for a great big lion?" But he was not hungry, so he let the mouse go.

The next day, the mouse heard a roar for help.

Hunters had trapped the lion. He was in a big net. The little mouse ran to the lion. She chewed the net with her sharp teeth. She chewed and chewed. The lion was free!

"Thank you," said the lion.

The lion and the mouse became good friends.

1. Find one word that has a **gr** and a **long a** sound. Write it. _____

2. Find a word in the story that means the same thing as **little**. Write it. _____

3. Who are the characters in this story? _____
   Are they **kids** or **animals**? _____

4. Did the lion let the little mouse go because **he was kind** or because **he was not hungry**? _____

5. What was the mouse's problem? _____

   What was the lion's problem? _____

Name **Week # 8**

Farmer Mack

Mack is a farmer. He has an important job. He grows food that we eat. Mack grows wheat and oats. He also takes care of the animals on his farm. Mack works hard. He gets up early every day. He works until it is dark.

1. Who is this story about? _____
2. What does he do for a job? _____
3. What does he farm?   plants   animals   both
4. How do you know that Mack works hard?
   a. He grows wheat and oats.
   b. He gets up early and works late.

Day #1

Mack loves helping the young plants grow. He smiles as he works. In the fall, he harvests his crops. The wheat is made into bread. The oats are made into cereal.

1. When does Mack harvest his crops? _____
2. What do **you** do in the fall? _____
3. Does the wheat that Mack grows become **bread** or **lasagna**? _____
4. How do you know that Mack likes being a farmer?
   a. He smiles as he works.
   b. He harvests his crops.
   c. He grows oats for cereal.

Day #2

Little Miss Muffet sat on her tuffet,
Eating her curds and whey.
Along came a spider and sat down beside her,
And frightened Miss Muffet away.

1. What kind of writing is this: **poem** or **letter**? _____
2. Who is it about? _____
3. Is she eating pasta? _____
4. Circle **True** or **False**. Little Miss Muffet is not afraid of spiders.   **True**   **False**

Day #3

Mary Lou French sat on a bench,
Munching a sandwich and chips.
When Tarantula spied her and climbed up beside her,
She told him to take a long trip!

1. Who is in this poem? _____
2. What is Tarantula: **poisonous spider** or **fuzzy kitten**? _____
3. What is Mary Lou eating? _____
4. Circle **True** or **False**. Mary Lou French is not afraid of spiders.   **True**   **False**
   How do you know? _____

Day #4

Published by Frank Schaffer Publications. Copyright protected.   27   0-7682-3212-0 *Read 4 Today*

Name

Week # 8

1. Have you used a telephone before? _____ Do you know who invented the telephone?

_____

Alexander Graham Bell

Alexander Graham Bell did many great things. We know him most for inventing the telephone. But Alexander had many other talents. He could play music by ear when he was a very young boy. He taught music and speech. He also taught the deaf just as his father in Scotland did.

2. Was Alexander Graham Bell musical? _____

While Alexander was teaching, he became interested in electricity. He and his friend Thomas Watson did many experiments before he invented the telephone.

3. Did Alexander give up easily when he was trying to invent the telephone? _____
   Explain your answer. _____

Alexander stayed busy after inventing the telephone. He created a research laboratory for the deaf. He invented an electric probe used by doctors. He worked on ways to locate icebergs by using echoes. He did many experiments with kites.

4. Did Alexander work with the deaf his whole life, or only when he was young?

_____

5. Find the six words in the box that best describe Alexander. Circle them.

creative	clumsy	busy
afraid	strong	funny
talented	hard-working	mean
smart	musical	uncaring

Week #9

Barker's Big Problem

Barker wished she was the biggest dog on the block. Every time Barker saw Bruiser, she hung her head. "I'll never be that big," she thought. "What good is a little dog? A big dog can carry newspapers. She can chase away pesky cats."

Day #1

1. Which word is a compound word?   a. wished   b. biggest   c. newspapers
2. What other word could you write instead of **pesky**?   a. annoying   b. darling?
3. Is Barker **happy** or **jealous**? _____
4. What does Barker wish for? _____

One day, Barker padded along the sidewalk. "Help," someone cried. Barker ran to check out the problem. Bruiser stood nearby.

Day #2

1. Circle the compound words.

   sidewalk   problem   someone   nearby

2. In the story, what other word could you use instead of **padded**? _____
3. Barker runs to the sound of someone asking for help. What does that tell you about Barker's character? _____
4. Who does Barker see at the scene of the problem? _____

"A boy is caught in the bushes on the other side of the wall," Bruiser said. "There's a small hole, but I can't wriggle through."

Day #3

1. Do you pronounce the **w** at the beginning of **wriggled**? _____
2. What does it mean that the boy is caught in the bushes: has **he grabbed the bushes** or have **the bushes grabbed him**? _____
3. What is Bruiser's problem? _____
4. What do you think happens next? _____

Barker trotted through the hole. She tugged on the branches wrapped around the child's ankle. She got the boy free. "Thank you," cried the boy. The boy hugged Barker and patted her head.

Day #4

1. Do you pronounce the **w** at the beginning of **wrapped**? _____
2. What word could you use instead of **tugged**: **snipped** or **pulled**? _____
3. What is the main idea of this story?
   a. Barker learned only little dogs can help people.
   b. Barker learned both big and little dogs can help people.
4. How do you think Barker feels about her size now? _____

Name
Week #9

Jackie Joyner-Kersee

Who is Jackie Joyner-Kersee? Is she a wrestler? Is she a writer? No! She is a world class track star. Jackie Joyner-Kersee loves to compete in track events. She runs, jumps hurdles, throws a shot put (a metal ball), and throws the javelin (a long spear). She won many Olympic medals. She is a very good athlete.

Jackie has asthma. This is an illness that makes it hard for her to breathe. When you have asthma, it is hard to take a breath and get air in your lungs. Coughing and wheezing are also a part of asthma. Asthma makes it very hard for Jackie to run and jump. Jackie did not let asthma stop her from competing and winning races. She worked hard. She is known as the greatest multi-event athlete in women's track history!

1. Circle the words with a **w** you don't pronounce.

    wrestler   world   wheezing   writer

2. What is a **javelin**? _____

3. What is the main idea of this story?
    a. Some athletes have asthma.
    b. Track athletes work hard.
    c. Jackie Joyner-Kersee didn't let asthma stop her from competing and being the best.

4. Underline the two sentences that tell you why having asthma makes it hard to be a track athlete.

5. What does this story tell us about Jackie's character: that she is **determined** or that she is **lazy**? _____

Name _____   # Week #10

Day #1

The clock showed midnight. Two mice friends sat in their home. They talked about the things they wanted to do. One wanted to eat all the cheese in the world. The other wanted to break all the mice traps in the world.

1. Where does this story happen? _____
2. When does this story happen? _____
3. What do you call more than one mouse? _____
4. Do you think the mice can really do what they are talking about? _____
   Why or why not? _____

Day #2

Juan and Don went to school early in the morning. They sat at their desks. The teacher read a book about dolphins. Then Juan and Don wrote books of their own.

1. Where does this story happen? _____
2. When does this story happen? _____
3. Who are the people in this story? _____
4. Do you write books at school? _____
   What do you write about? _____

Day #3

The year is 3010. Rae and Raphael zoom into space. Their spaceship moves faster than the speed of light. They race toward the moon.

1. Where does this story happen? _____
2. When does this story happen? _____
3. Where are Rae and Raphael going? _____
4. Would you like to go to the moon? _____
   Why or why not? _____

Day #4

Chester was hungry. He ran down the tree trunk. He pawed at the dead leaves. He wanted the nut he had hid yesterday. He dug and dug. It wasn't there! He looked at all the other trees. Now, where did he hide that nut?

1. Where does this story happen? _____
2. When does this story happen? _____
3. What is Chester?   dog   bluejay   squirrel
4. What did Chester lose? _____

Published by Frank Schaffer Publications. Copyright protected.   0-7682-3212-0 Read 4 Today

Name

Week #10

1. Preview the text below. Where do you think this story will take place?
   _____

It's a Special Place

Maggie is at Grandma's house. She loves the kitchen.

2. What did you find out about the special place? _____
   _____

Pretty curtains with dots hang on the windows. The walls are bright yellow. There is a table with six chairs. Many cupboards hold dishes, pots and pans, and food.

3. What is pretty about the kitchen? _____

Grandma has magnets in her kitchen. They are so colorful. Maggie loves to look at them. She also loves to watch Grandma bake. She makes many good things. Right now Grandma is frosting a cake.

4. What two things does Maggie love to watch in the kitchen? _____
   _____

5. Describe a place that is special to you. (Example: I love my basement stairs because they are dark and have lots of spider webs.) _____
   _____

Name **Week # 11**

The Camping Trip
Aunt Maria and her niece went camping in the woods. First, they put up a tent under a big tree. Then they built a fire. As it got dark, they cooked dinner over the fire.

1. Does the **ie** in **niece** sound like the **ee** in **tree**? _____
2. What word could you use instead of **big**? _____
3. Underline the words that tell you what time of day they ate dinner.
4. Where do Maria and her niece camp: **by a stream** or **in the woods**?
   _____

Day #1

They ate marshmallows for dessert. It was warm by the fire. It was also cozy in the tent. Maria heard the crickets chirping before she fell asleep.

1. Circle the words that rhyme with **ate**.
   great   hate   eat   eight
2. What other word for **warm** does the writer use? _____
3. Underline the words that tell you where it was cozy.
4. What did Maria hear before she fell asleep: **crickets** or **frogs**? _____

Day #2

Icebergs
There are big sheets of ice on the South Pole and near the North Pole. Sometimes pieces break off from these sheets. The pieces float out in the ocean. They are called icebergs.

1. Does the **ie** in **pieces** sound the same as the **ee** in **sheets**? _____
2. What is an **iceberg**? a. a building made of ice b. a piece of ice floating in the ocean
3. If you were on an iceberg, would it be **cold and slippery** or **warm and cozy**?
   _____
4. Icebergs are formed when ice chunks break off at the…
   a. South Pole.   b. North Pole.   c. North and South Poles.

Day #3

If you were crossing the sea, you might see an iceberg. Some are as big as mountains. But often, only a tip of the iceberg can be seen above the water. Most of the iceberg is below water.

1. What two words in this paragraph rhyme with **be**? _____
2. How much is the **tip** of an iceberg: **a lot** or **a little**? _____
3. Will you always see icebergs if you cross the ocean? _____
4. To see an iceberg, should you be **on the beach** or **on a boat on the ocean**?
   _____

Day #4

Published by Frank Schaffer Publications. Copyright protected. 0-7682-3212-0 *Read 4 Today*

Week #11

The Arctic

The Arctic is an area located near the North Pole. The Arctic is very cold. It has dry winds but very little rain. The soil is always frozen because of the cold temperatures. Pieces of ice join together in winter to cover much of the water.

The highest part is closest to the North Pole. It does not have much plant or animal life. This is because of the extremely dry air, cold temperatures, and short growing season. The lower part is a little warmer. It is covered with plants and trees that can live in a cold and dry climate.

1. Does the **ie** in **pieces** sound like the **ee** in **trees**? _____

2. What other word could you write instead of **extremely** in **extremely dry**?
   _____

3. How many times does the writer describe the Arctic as **cold**? _____

4. Which area of the Arctic has more plant and animal life: the **high part** or the **low part**? _____

5. Write three words that describe the weather in the Arctic.
   _____
   _____
   _____

Name   Week #12

"Good morning, Mom," said Jaleel, as he raced down the stairs. "What time do we leave for vacation? I can hardly wait!"

1. What time of day does this story take place? _____
2. Where do you think it takes place? _____
3. Predict what is about to happen. _____
   _____
4. Does the story tell you if this is winter or summer? _____

Day #1

"The lake is the best!" said Anais. She leaned against a tree. "I really like it when the sun starts to go down. I'm ready to tell scary stories."

1. What time of day does this story take place? _____
2. Where does this story take place? _____
3. Predict what is about to happen. _____
   _____
4. Does the story tell you if Anais is staying in a tent or a cabin? _____

Day #2

The submarine moved deep in the ocean. Reggie saw fish and an octopus outside the window. He looked at his watch. "It's so dark down here, it does not seem like four o'clock," he thought.

1. What time of day does this story take place? _____
2. When is that time of day?   a. in the afternoon   b. the middle of the night
3. Where does this story take place? _____
4. What does Reggie see in this setting that he can't see at home? _____
   _____

Day #3

"Brrrr! It's so cold here on top of the mountain in the middle of the night." Shay pulled her hat down over her ears. Soon it would be time to go back down the mountain.

1. What time of day does this story take place? _____
2. Where does this story take place? _____
3. What is about to happen? _____
4. What other detail do we learn about the mountain? _____
   _____

Day #4

Name   **Week #12**

1. Preview the text below. Will this story be about a vacation? _____
   Why or why not? _____

All in a Day's Work

    Zookeepers care for the animals in the zoo every day. They make the animals' food and keep the animal homes clean. They spend a lot of time watching the animals to make sure they are healthy.

2. Where does this story take place? _____

    Zookeepers also have to keep the animals from being bored. In the wild, the animals' habitat is always changing. At the zoo, the animals' home stays the same. A good zookeeper will think of ways for the animals to have fun.

3. What is different for the animals about the zoo?
   a. They have other animals to talk to.
   b. The setting stays the same.
   c. The food is better.

    One way is to hide the food. The animals enjoy looking for their food because it is a little bit like hunting. Zookeepers also put safe plants from other places or different smells in the cages. These are some of the ways that zookeepers keep the animals in the zoo curious and happy.

4. What do zookeepers do to help the animals feel like they are hunting?
   _____

5. Would you like to be a zookeeper? _____ Why or why not?
   _____

Name _____   # Week # 13

The Loose Tooth Diaries

I have a loose tooth! This is my very first loose tooth! Today I spent a lot of time wiggling my very first loose tooth. I can't wait for it to come out!

1. Does the **oo** in **loose** have the same sound as the **oo** in **tooth**? _____
2. How do you wiggle a tooth: **move it back and forth** or **blow on it**?
   _____
3. How much time did Carly spend wiggling her tooth? _____
4. Circle **True** or **False**. Carly is scared to lose her tooth.   True   False
   Underline the sentence you used to figure this out.

Day #1

I can wiggle my tooth with my tongue! It is getting really loose! Today I tried to eat an apple. My loose tooth made it impossible! It really hurt. My mom cut the apple up into pieces for me.

1. What word rhymes with **tongue**: **song** or **sung**? _____
2. What does **impossible** mean? _____
3. What is this paragraph mostly about: **Carly's tooth has come out** or **Carly's tooth is getting really loose**? _____
4. Underline one sentence that helped you answer #3.

Day #2

Today I took a bite of my sandwich, and my tooth popped out! It hurt a little bit. I went into the bathroom. I rinsed my mouth with water. When I touch my space with my tongue, it feels funny! Tonight, I will put my tooth under my pillow. I can't wait!

1. Find one other word that has the same **i** sound as in **bite**. Write it. _____
2. When you rinse your mouth, do you **drink the water** or **spit it out**? _____
   _____
3. What is this paragraph mostly about: **how Carly's tooth came out** or **how to eat a sandwich**? _____
4. Underline one sentence that helped you answer #3.

Day #3

I woke up this morning and found a note under my pillow! It was from the Tooth Fairy! It said my tooth is nice and shiny. She also left me some money! I could get rich if I lose all of my teeth!

1. Does the **i** in **shiny** sound the same as the **i** in **nice** or the **i** in **rich**? _____
2. In the story, what other word could you use instead of **shiny**? _____
3. What is this paragraph mostly about: **what the Tooth Fairy leaves every child** or **what the Tooth Fairy left for Carly**? _____
4. Do you think Carly will get rich from her teeth falling out? _____
   Why or why not? _____

Day #4

Week # 13

Who Comes for the Teeth?

Many children around the world believe that a mouse comes to take their teeth when they lose them.

In South Africa, the children put their teeth in a slipper. They believe that a mouse comes into their room when they are sleeping. The mouse takes the tooth and leaves a small gift.

In Venezuela, children leave their teeth under their pillow. They believe that a mouse called El Ratón Miguelito takes the tooth and leaves money.

In Spain, children also put their teeth under their pillows. They believe that a mouse named Ratoncita Perez takes the teeth and leaves money or candy.

In Russia, mothers put the teeth in a mouse hole.

There are many customs around the world that use mice instead of a tooth fairy. Do you think a mouse comes for your teeth, too?

1. Circle the words where the letters in bold sound the same as the **i** in **into**.

   g**i**ft   **i**n   m**i**ce   sl**i**pper

2. What word from the story means "more than one mouse"? _____

3. What is the main idea of this story?
   a. Many children think that a mouse comes for their teeth.
   b. Some children put their teeth in a slipper.
   c. Some mothers put teeth in a mouse hole.

4. Which countries believe the rat or mouse will bring you money? _____
   _____

5. Circle true or false. America is the only country where kids get presents for lost teeth.   **True**   **False**

Name   Week #14

Animals on the Move

Many animals migrate. They move from one place to another. Some move because they cannot find food. Others move to find a better place to raise their young.

1. What does **migrate** mean?   a. move from one place to another   b. stay put

2. Does this paragraph talk about a specific animal? _____

3. Put an **X** next to the main idea of this paragraph.
    _____ Some animals move because it is cold where they live.
    _____ Many animals migrate.

4. Write one detail that supports the main idea. _____

Day #1

Many birds migrate south in the winter. They cannot find enough food where it is cold. They fly south where it is warm. There they find food for the winter. When winter is over, they fly back north.

1. Do all birds migrate south in the winter? _____

2. Fill in the blank. Warm weather = lots of food. Cold weather = _____

3. Put an **X** next to the main idea of this paragraph.
    _____ Birds migrate south so they can find food.
    _____ When winter is over, birds fly north.

4. Write one detail that supports the main idea. _____

Day #2

Some whales spend summers in the cold waters of the Arctic. When it begins to freeze, the whales swim to warmer seas. They have their babies in warm water because the babies do not have a thick layer of blubber to keep them warm.

1. Do all whales live in the Arctic? _____

2. When do whales have babies: **winter** or **summer**? _____

3. Put an **X** next to the main idea of this paragraph.
    _____ Some whales migrate to warm waters to raise their young.
    _____ Baby whales don't have blubber.

4. Write one detail that supports the main idea. _____

Day #3

Salmon are fish that are usually born in freshwater streams. They migrate to the ocean where they eat shrimp, squid, and small fish. When they are ready to lay eggs, they return to the streams where they were born.

1. What do salmon eat? _____

2. Do salmon lay eggs in the **ocean** or in their **home stream**? _____

3. Put an **X** next to the main idea of this paragraph.
    _____ Salmon migrate from fresh water to the ocean.
    _____ Salmon eat shrimp, squid, and small fish.

4. Write one detail that supports the main idea. _____

Day #4

Name   Week #14

1. Preview the text below. What do you think this story is mostly about?
   _____

Muscles Are Movers

Your body has more than 600 muscles. Exercise makes muscles bigger and stronger. Your muscles are at work all day long. They lift, push, and pull. Muscles work at night, too.

2. The main idea of this paragraph is: **Your muscles are at work.** Write two details from this paragraph that support the main idea.
   _____
   _____

Some muscles are called voluntary muscles. They move when you want them to move. Most movements use voluntary muscles. Raising your hand and stretching your legs to run are examples. The brain controls voluntary muscles.

3. The main idea of this paragraph is: **Voluntary muscles move when you want them to move.** Write two details from this paragraph that support the main idea.
   _____
   _____

Other muscles move or work for you. These are called involuntary muscles. Involuntary muscles work without you thinking about them. They work all of the time. Your heart pumps blood and your intestines help digest food. These are examples of involuntary muscles.

4. Underline the sentence that is the main idea of the paragraph above.

5. Imagine you just yawned. Is that an example of a voluntary or involuntary use of your muscles? _____

Name   # Week # 15

Airports
An airport is a busy place. It is where planes take off and land on runways. People line up to buy tickets for the planes. Their bags are driven to the plane in open trucks.

1. Circle the words with a **short u** sound.   runways   up   buy   trucks
2. What is a **runway**? _____
3. Underline the sentence that tells you the main idea of this paragraph.
4. List two details that support the main idea. _____
_____

Day #1

The airport has places where you can eat and buy things. Before your flight, you can buy a book from the gift shop. You might also get food from a restaurant.

1. Write a word that rhymes with **flight**. _____
2. Which place can you eat: **gift shop** or **restaurant**? _____
3. Underline the sentence that tells you the main idea of this paragraph.
4. Did the writer give any details about eating at the airport? If so, write them.
_____

Day #2

Animal Teams
Animals can work in teams. Some small fish eat food from the teeth of big fish. Then the big fish have clean teeth! Ants can get food from some small bugs. Then the ants keep the small bugs safe from other bugs.

1. Does **bugs** have a **long u** or a **short u** sound? _____
2. What is a **team**? _____
3. Underline the sentence that tells you the main idea of this paragraph.
4. What two pairs of animals are used as examples of animals that work in teams?
    a. small fish, big fish   b. ants, small fish   c. ants, small bugs

Day #3

Bike Rules
No matter how old you are, there are rules to follow when you ride your bike. These rules keep bikers safe. Riding a bike is fun, but you need to know the rules.

1. Which word has a **u** that is a **long u**? _____
2. What is a **rule**? _____
3. What is the main idea of this paragraph?
    a. Always know and follow the rules of bike riding.
    b. Older bike riders don't have to follow the rules of bike riding.
4. Why is it important to know and follow the rules? _____

Day #4

Grizzly Bears

Grizzly bears like to eat grass and berries. Some bears dig a den in the ground to hibernate. Hibernate means that bears rest a long time in winter. Others may hibernate in an old cave or a hollow tree. When the weather warms up, the bears will come out of hibernation. They like to eat small animals, too. Grizzly bears hibernate during the winter. At the end of the summer and in the fall, these huge bears spend a lot of time eating. They are trying to store enough food to get them through the long, cold winter. In one day, bears will eat as much as a person eats in 30 days!

1. Which story word has a **long u**? Circle it.

    up   summer   huge   much

2. Underline the sentence that tells you what it means to **hibernate**.

3. What is the main idea of this story?

    a. Grizzly bears eat a lot to get ready to hibernate.

    b. Bears are big and black.

    c. Bears hibernate.

4. Bears eat a lot during the summer and fall because…

    a. they are very hungry.

    b. they are getting ready to hibernate.

    c. they are very big.

5. Write three places where a bear can hibernate.

    _____

    _____

    _____

Week #16

Scary Sleepover

"Did you hear that noise?" Ellie asked.

"What was it?" asked Ava.

The girls pulled their sleeping bags up to their chins. Their hands shook with fright as they listened in the darkness.

Day #1

1. Who is in this story? _____
2. What time of day is it? a. 10 o'clock in the morning   b. 10 o'clock at night
3. How do the girls feel? _____
4. What makes them feel that way? _____

"There it is again. Do you think it's the troll from the scary story you told?" asked Ellie.

A light flashed outside the tent. The girls heard footsteps walking slowly toward them. The tent zipper slowly began to rise. The girls let out screams that could be heard for miles.

Day #2

1. What did the girls do that night? a. tell scary stories   b. read nursery rhymes
2. Where are they? _____
3. What do they do when the zipper goes up? _____
4. What would you do? _____

"What's all the noise?" asked Ava's mother. "Are you two all right?" She poked her head inside the tent. She moved her flashlight inside to see what was frightening the girls.

Day #3

1. What scared the girls: **a troll** or **Ava's mother**? _____
2. What is the setting of this story?
   a. Ava's bedroom   b. Ava's backyard   c. Ellie's backyard
3. How does Ava's mother feel: **worried about the girls** or **worried about her grass**? _____
4. Do you guess Ava and Ellie were happy to see Ava's mother? _____

Ava and Ellie sighed. "We told too many scary stories," said Ava. "I think we want to sleep in the house tonight after all! Camping in the backyard isn't as fun as we thought it would be."

Day #4

1. Predict what will happen next. _____
2. What would you have done if you were Ava or Ellie? _____
3. Why did the author write this story? a. to tell you about Ava and Ellie's camping trip
                                          b. to keep you from going camping
4. Would you like to go camping in a backyard? _____

Name

Week #16

Assessment

1. Preview the passage below. Predict what characters will be in this story.

_____

The Grasshopper and the Ant

A grasshopper was singing on a hot summer day. He watched a little ant drag a heavy piece of corn through the grass.

2. When does this story take place? _____

"Come play with me," the grasshopper called out. "It is much too pretty a day to work so hard."

"I do not have time to play," said the ant. "Winter is coming. It will be hard to find food then, so I am storing food now. Then I will have plenty to eat when there is snow on the ground."

The grasshopper laughed. "Why worry about winter now? It is so far away. There is lots of food to eat today." The ant just smiled and walked on.

3. What sentence could be added to the section above?
   a. Grasshoppers have long back legs they use for jumping.
   b. "You should store food for the winter, too," said the ant.
   c. Ants keep their food in special rooms in their underground homes.

When winter came, the grasshopper showed up at the ant's door.
"I am very hungry. Could you please give me some food?" he asked.
"I only have enough for me," said the ant. "You should have planned ahead."

4. What did the ant mean when it said, "You should have planned ahead"?

_____

5. Why did the author write this story?
   a. to make you feel sad for the grasshopper
   b. to tell you how ants store food for winter
   c. to teach an important lesson

Name **Week # 17**

Cat Problems

Each day the cat chased the mice. The mice had to hide in their nest. They could not hunt for food. They were very hungry.

1. When you say **each**, how many sounds does **ea** have? a. one (like in *ear*) b. two
2. What one word can you use instead of very hungry? a. full b. starving
3. Who are the characters in this story? _____
4. Why can't the mice hunt for food? _____
   _____

Day #1

"What can we do?" said Mother Mouse. "I don't know," said the biggest mouse. "I don't know," said the oldest mouse. "I don't know," said the tallest mouse.

1. Which word in this passage rhymes with **show** and has a silent letter? _____
2. What does **don't** mean: **donut** or **do not**? _____
3. How many mice are there in this story so far? _____
4. Do these mice come up with a solution to their problem? _____

Day #2

"I know," said the smallest mouse. "Let's hang a bell around the cat's neck. Then when we hear him coming, we can run."
   Everyone cheered. They told the smallest mouse how smart she was.

1. Does the **k** in **know** have a sound or is it a silent letter? _____
2. What does **let's** mean: **let us** or **lettuce**? _____
3. Who comes up with a solution to their problem? _____
4. What is the solution? _____
   _____

Day #3

Then the oldest mouse said, "That is a good idea, but we still have a problem. Who will put the bell on the cat?"

1. When you say **idea**, how many sounds does the **ea** have?
   a. one (like in *ear*)   b. two
2. Are there any mice older than the **oldest mouse**? _____
3. Was the smallest mouse's idea really a good solution to their problem? _____
4. What new problem does the solution cause? _____
   _____

Day #4

Published by Frank Schaffer Publications. Copyright protected.   0-7682-3212-0 *Read 4 Today*

Week # 17

Who's Lost?

Marla looked into her pet's cage. Henry should have been asleep in his nest. But he wasn't there! Then Marla saw the open cage door. Henry was gone! But where did he go?

Marla looked all around the cage. No Henry. She looked on the floor. Still no Henry. She looked under her bed. She did not find him. She did not know what to do.

Marla felt like crying as she got dressed for school. She sat down to put on her shoes. First she put on the left shoe. Then she picked up the right shoe. It felt heavy. Guess who she found in her shoe?

1. Circle the story words below that rhyme with **show**.

    shoe   go   no   know   who

    Which one has a silent letter? _____

2. Circle three words you could use when something was there and then it was gone.

    vanished   disappeared   underneath   missing

3. Who are the characters? _____

4. What is Marla's problem? _____

5. How is her problem solved? _____

Name

Week #18

Baby Animal Names

Many animals are called special names while they are young. A baby deer is called a fawn. A baby cat is called a kitten.

1. What is the name of a baby deer? _____
2. What is the name of a baby cat? _____
3. What is the name of a young person? _____
4. Have you ever seen a fawn or a kitten? _____

   Describe it. _____

Day #1

Some young animals have the same name as other kinds of baby animals. A baby elephant is a calf. A baby whale is a calf. A baby giraffe is a calf. A baby cow is a calf.

1. How many baby animals are called a calf? _____
2. Name the baby animals that are called a calf. _____
   _____
3. Which calves are wild animals? _____
4. Which calves live on a farm? _____

Day #2

Some baby animals are called cubs. A baby lion, a baby bear, a baby tiger, and a baby fox are all called cubs.

1. How many baby animals are called cubs? _____
2. Name the baby animals that are called cubs. _____
   _____
3. Which cubs are wild animals? _____
4. Which cubs are big cats? _____

Day #3

Some baby animals are called colts. A young horse is a colt. A baby zebra is a colt. A baby donkey is a colt.

1. How many baby animals are called colts? _____
2. Name the baby animals that are called colts. _____
3. Which colts are wild animals? _____
4. Use your answers to the last few days of questions to do the chart below. Write one animal that belongs with each special baby name.

calf	cub	colt

Day #4

Name   Week #18

Assessment

1. Preview the passage below. What do you think the setting of this story will be?

   _____

   # What's in My Room?

   Sometimes you want to put things in groups. One way to put things in groups is to sort them by how they are alike. When you put things together that are alike in some way, you classify them.

   2. Circle the words that also mean **classify**.

      group   sort   things

   You can classify the things in your room. In one group you can put toys and fun things. In the other group, you can put things that you wear.

   3. In the list below, circle all the things you can wear.

hat	doll	shirt
truck	mitten	shoe
ball	paints	shorts
sock	book	teddy bear

   4. Fill in the chart using the list of words.

THINGS I PLAY WITH	THINGS I WEAR

   5. Add something to each category that **you** have in **your** room.

Name **Week #19**

Zena's Game

Zena hurried. She didn't want to be late for her baseball game. All of a sudden, wings grew on her back. She flew all the way to the field.

1. List words from the story that rhyme with **new**. _____
   Circle the ones that have one syllable.

2. What word could you use instead of **all of a sudden**? a. quickly b. suddenly

3. Could this story really happen? _____

4. Underline the sentences that are not possible in the real world.

Day #1

Alex's Garden

The hot summer sun dried out the garden. Alex wanted his flowers to grow. He got the hose and watered his flowers.

1. Does the **ow** in **flowers** sound the same as the **ow** in **grow**? _____

2. What is the opposite of a **growing plant**? a. dead plant b. short plant

3. Could this story really happen? _____

4. Underline the sentences that are not possible in the real world.

Day #2

Keenan's Present

Keenan saved money all month. He wanted to buy a special gift for his grandfather. He bought a book about stereos. He knew his grandfather would love it.

1. List the words that have three syllables. _____

   Which one starts with **st**? _____

2. Cross out the word **gift**. Write another word for **gift**. _____

3. Could this story really happen? _____

4. Underline the sentences that are not possible in the real world.

Day #3

Michelle's Stairs

Michelle learned about the stars. She learned about Planet Mars. Michelle pulled stars from the sky. She made stairs from the stars. She walked all the way up her starry staircase to Mars.

1. List all the words that start with **st**. _____

   Which ones have two syllables? _____

2. Cross out **walked**. Write another way to go up a staircase. _____

3. Could this story really happen? _____

4. Underline the sentences that are not possible in the real world.

Day #4

Talk to the Animals

Can a gorilla talk? Gorillas don't form words the way humans do. But they can make known what they want to say. One gorilla, Koko, learned sign language. She talked with her hands. And she understood words humans said.

Dr. Penny Patterson is the scientist who taught sign language to Koko. She showed Koko a picture of the two of them together. Penny pointed to Koko in the picture and asked, "Who's that?"

Koko answered by signing her own name, Koko.

1. Write the words that have three syllables. _____
   _____

   Which one has an **st** in the middle? _____

2. What is another word for **humans**? _____

3. What is it called when you talk with your hands? _____

4. What is the name of the gorilla in this story? _____

5. Do you think this story really happened? _____
   Why or why not? _____

Week #20

Day #1

Joshua wants to be an actor more than anything. He takes acting classes. He has been in plays. He has a chance to be in another play. He has to try out this afternoon. The phone rings. Joshua's friend wants him to come over this afternoon.

1. What does Joshua love to do? _____
2. What does Joshua do about the thing he loves: **daydream about doing it** or **take classes and do it**? _____
3. What is Joshua's problem? _____
4. What will Joshua probably do?
   a. Joshua will go to his friend's house.   b. Joshua will go to try out for the play.

Day #2

All animals have to eat to stay alive. Squirrels eat nuts. Whales eat sea plants and animals. Other animals eat many different things. A squirrel is hungry. It sees a pile of sea plants and a pile of nuts.

1. If you caught a squirrel in a trap, which word with **qu** do you think would best describe the squirrel: **quiet** or **squirmy**? _____
2. What do squirrels eat? _____ What do whales eat? _____
3. What decision does the squirrel have to make? _____
4. Predict what the squirrel will do.
   a. The squirrel will eat the nuts.   b. The squirrel will eat the sea plants.

Day #3

Dalia has been racing on her bicycle after school for two years. She is tired of bicycle races. She wants to try something new. Dalia's teacher asks Dalia to swim on the swim team after school.

1. How long has Dalia been racing her bicycle? _____
2. How does she feel about bicycle racing now? _____
3. What decision does Dalia have to make? _____
4. What will Dalia probably do?
   a. Dalia will swim.   b. Dalia will race on her bicycle.

Day #4

Lucy has a favorite uncle. She wants to buy him a birthday present. He likes fishing, and she wants to buy him a fishing book. Lucy saves her money for two months. Finally, she has enough money for the book.

1. Who does Lucy want to buy a present for? _____
2. What does Lucy know about her uncle? _____
3. How long does Lucy save money? _____
4. Predict what Lucy will do with the money.
   a. Lucy will buy herself a new video game.   b. Lucy will buy a fishing book for her uncle.

Name

Week #20

1. Preview the story below. Predict what it will be about.

_____

Boa Constrictors

Boa constrictors are very big. They may grow up to 14 feet (4.3 meters) long. A boa kills its prey by squeezing it. Then the prey is swallowed.

2. Does the first paragraph tell you what kind of animal a boa constrictor is? _____ If so, what? _____

Boas do not eat cows or other large animals. They do eat animals that are larger than their own heads. The bones in their jaws stretch so they can swallow small animals such as rodents and birds.

3. The boa is hungry and hunting for food. Which type of prey will it most likely eat?

   a. cow

   b. panther

   c. mouse

Boa constrictors hunt while hanging from trees. They watch for their prey. Then they attack. After eating, they may sleep for a week. Boas do not need to eat often. They can live without food for many months.

Boas are not poisonous. They defend themselves by striking and biting with their sharp teeth.

Boa constrictors give birth to live baby snakes. They do not lay eggs. They may have up to fifty baby snakes at one time.

4. A boa constrictor is slithering through the grass. Out of the grass comes a hunter walking toward it. The boa will probably…

   a. strike the hunter with its teeth.

   b. slither up a tree to sleep.

   c. squeeze and kill the hunter.

5. Circle the paragraph where the writer finally tells you what type of animal a boa constrictor is.

Week # 21

The Lost Ring

Sadie Space Officer flew on her nightly patrol. She flew close to Mars. Tears rolled down Mars' craters and made huge pools. "What's the matter, Mars?" she asked. "How can I help?"

1. Which word rhymes with **blue**? _____
2. What is someone doing when they are "producing tears"? _____
3. Where does Sadie patrol? _____
4. What is the first thing Sadie does when she notices that Mars is upset? _____

Day #1

"One of my moons got a ring for a gift. But the ring is lost. My moon is so sad. Now it doesn't give any moonlight. My poor moon!" Mars sniffled.

1. What compound word in this paragraph has the same vowel sound as **blue** and **flew**? _____
2. What is **moonlight**? _____
3. Why is Mars's moon sad? _____
4. Why does Mars get upset? _____

Day #2

"I have an idea!" cried Sadie Space Officer. "I just need to race off to Saturn for a minute." She flew back carrying a sparkling ring. "Will this help?" she asked.

1. Find the two rhyming words in this paragraph. _____
   Which has an **s** and a **c** that make the same sound? _____
2. Does **race off** tell you that Sadie flew **quickly** or **slowly**? _____
3. Does **sparkling** tell you that the ring is **dull** or **bright**? _____
4. What two things does Sadie do in this paragraph? _____

Day #3

Mars smiled a smile that crossed all Mars' craters. Sadie threw the ring to Mars' moon. Instantly, the moon grew bright.

1. Which two words in this paragraph rhyme? _____
2. What other word could you write instead of **threw**? _____
3. Was Sadie's solution a good one? _____
4. What was the last thing Sadie did? _____

Day #4

Name

Week # 21

Assessment

Tim Teddy's Morning

Tim Teddy woke up. The sun was shining in his window. "Hello, new day!" he said. It was time to get up. He needed to find his clothes.

Tim found his blue shorts under his bed. He put them on. Tim put on his green shirt. Tim's shoes were in the dog's bed. Tim put on one shoe. Then the other.

Next, Tim Teddy brushed his teeth. He washed his face and combed his hair. Now Tim was hungry. Mama Bear called him to breakfast. After he ate his oatmeal, Tim cleaned his room. Tim Teddy had a busy morning.

1. Circle the words in the paragraph that rhyme with **grew**.

2. What word tells you that Tim Teddy did a lot that morning? _____

3. What order did Tim Teddy get dressed in?
   _____
   _____
   _____

4. Put the sentences in order. Write the number in front of each one.
   _____ Mama Bear called Tim to breakfast.
   _____ Tim Teddy got dressed.
   _____ Tim woke up.
   _____ Tim brushed his teeth.
   _____ Tim Teddy cleaned his room

5. Make a list of five things you did after you woke up this morning.
   _____
   _____
   _____
   _____

Name _____   **Week # 22**

Animal Picnic

It's spring! It's time for the big picnic. But how do all the animals get there? Carla Caterpillar crawls. Bubba Butterfly flies. Freida Fish swims. Bertha Bee flies.

1. What time of year is it in this story? _____
2. What event happens in this story? _____
3. Is the story about people, animals, or food? _____
4. Fill in the chart to show how each animal gets to the picnic.

animal				
how it moves				

Day #1

Fred Frog hops. Andrew Ant walks. Barsha Bunny hops. Willy Worm crawls.

1. How many animals do we learn about in this paragraph? _____
2. Which animal would make the best pet? _____
3. How many new ways to get to the picnic do you have to add to your chart? _____
4. Add the new animals to the chart below. Finish filling it out.

animal				
how it moves				

Day #2

Shrews

A shrew (SHROO) is a small animal. It looks like a mouse with a sharp, pointed nose. A shrew moves very fast. A shrew eats all day. The shrew's long, pointed nose can fit into tiny holes to find the insects and worms it eats.

1. What kind of thing is a shrew? _____
2. What other animal does the writer compare a shrew to? _____
3. Put an **X** on the word that does not describe a shrew.
   small   large   tiny
4. Put an **X** on the word that does not describe what a shrew eats.
   bugs   corn   insects

Day #3

The shrew lives in fields, woodlands, gardens, and marshes. Shrews are harmless to humans. They are helpful in gardens because they eat grubs and other insects. The smallest shrew weighs as little as a United States penny.

1. Where do shrews live? _____
2. Are any of those places near where you live? _____
3. Put an **X** on the word that does not describe where shrews live.
   gardens   fields   sun
4. Put an **X** on the word that does not describe shrews.
   rain   penny   harmless

Day #4

Name

Week # 22

1. Preview the story. What do you think the characters will be sorting? _____

Apple Picking Time

This family picks apples.

"This year, let's sort the apples by size," says Mom.

"Great idea," answers Jamie, "Then we can count them to see how many we have of each size."

"I bet there will be more big apples than any other size," says Dad.

2. Who is picking apples in this story? _____

3. How do they decide to sort the apples they have picked? _____

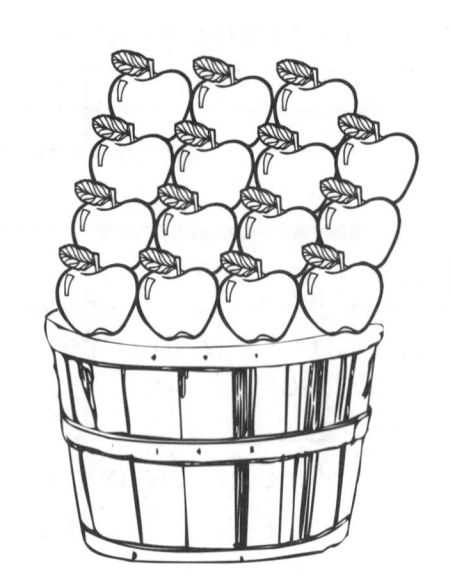

4. Look at the baskets. Which size has the most apples?
    a. small apples
    b. medium apples
    c. large apples

5. Was Dad right when he said, "I bet there will be more large apples than any other size"? _____ How can you tell? _____
_____

Name **Week # 23**

A long time ago, the sky was very close to the earth. When people were hungry, they just reached up and ate it. Sometimes the sky tasted like beef stew, corn, or pineapple. Everyone was happy because there was always plenty to eat.

1. Which compound word has a **short a** sound in it? _____
2. What is the opposite of **plenty**? _____
3. Did this story really happen or is it a fantasy? _____
4. According to the story, how did the people of long ago get their food?
    a. They hunted.   b. They grew crops.   c. They ate the sky.

Day #1

People began wasting the sky. They would break off big hunks and throw away the leftover pieces. The sky became angry.

"Do not waste me. Only break off what you can eat. If you don't take care of me I will go far away," said the sky.

1. Does the **ow** in **throw** sound like the **ow** in **now** or **own**? _____
2. When you **waste** something, are you throwing away **something you can use** or **just some garbage**? _____
3. Choose one sentence that you think is the most impossible. Underline it.
4. How does the sky feel? _____

Day #2

For a while, the people were careful not to waste the sky. After a time, the people began to waste the sky again. The sky became angry.

1. Which vowel sound is in **waste** and **became**?   short a   long a   long e
2. What does it mean to be **careful**?
    a. to pay attention   b. to be sad   c. to make a law
3. Why do the people start wasting the sky again? _____
4. Are you like the people in this story sometimes? _____ Do you forget things you've been told to do or not to do? _____

Day #3

"You are still wasting me. From now on you will have to hunt and grow your own food!" yelled the sky as he went very far away.

The people were sad. Now they had to grow and hunt for their food. They learned that it is not a good idea to waste the gifts of nature.

1. Does the **ow** in **grow** sound like the **ow** in **now** or in **own**? _____
2. What other word could you use instead of **far away**?   a. miles   b. distant
3. What is a better title for this story?   a. The Sky Gets Mad   b. Why the Sky Is Far Away
4. This is a folk tale from Nigeria. Folk tales have a lesson that is true, even if the story isn't. The true lesson in this story is "Do not _____."

Day #4

Published by Frank Schaffer Publications. Copyright protected.   57   0-7682-3212-0 Read 4 Today

A Warm Summer Day

(1) "What a beautiful day!" thought Trixie the Tree.

(2) "Hey! Let's go climb the apple tree. We'll see the whole park from the top," said James. "We can also smell the apple blossoms," said Sara.

(3) The children ran over to Trixie the Tree. They began to climb her huge branches.

(4) "Ha, ha, ha!" laughed Trixie to herself, "That tickles," she thought.

(5) The children climbed way up the tree. They spent the morning watching the other people in the park and whispering stories to each other.

(6) "Ahh!" sighed Trixie the Tree to herself. "I love when the children come out to play during the summer."

1. Does the **ow** in **low** sound like the **ow** in **now** or in **own**? _____

2. What other word could you use instead of **blossoms**? _____

3. Which paragraphs could really happen? Circle the numbers below.

   (1)   (2)   (3)   (4)   (5)   (6)

4. What does Trixie say to herself when the children climb her branches?

   a. "Ouch, that hurts."
   b. "Ha, ha, ha. That tickles."
   c. "I sure hope they don't pick my flowers."

5. Which paragraphs are fantasy? Circle the numbers below.

   (1)   (2)   (3)   (4)   (5)   (6)

Name

Week #24

What Would You Expect?

Isabel threw a little rock into a pond. Circles rippled out in the water around the little rock. More and more circles rippled until the ripples reached the shore.

1. Who is in this story? _____
2. Is Isabel a boy or a girl? _____
3. Where does this story happen? _____
4. What will happen if Isabel throws another little rock into the pond?
   a. Circles will ripple out into the water.
   b. An angry frog will throw the little rock at Isabel.

Day #1

Jamal never ate anything sweet. He went to Gina's party. Gina served sandwiches, popcorn, ice cream, and birthday cake. Jamal had fun.

1. Who is in this story? _____
2. What do you know about Jamal? _____
3. What kind of party is it? _____
4. What did Jamal eat?
   a. cake and popcorn
   b. sandwiches and popcorn

Day #2

The rain went on for hours and hours. Puddles formed on the streets. But the sun finally came out. The temperature rose to more than 100 degrees. The temperature stayed that hot for two days. There was no more rain.

1. What season is this? _____
2. Does the temperature often go above 100 degrees where you live? _____
3. Do you like very hot and sunny weather or rainy weather better? _____
4. What happened after two days in the story?
   a. The puddles were gone.
   b. The puddles were the same size.

Day #3

Chin loves to count. She counts everything. She counts leaves. She even counts clouds. The math test is tomorrow. Chin practices counting and adding all evening.

1. Who is in this story? _____
2. Is Chin a boy or a girl? _____
3. What does Chin love to do? _____
4. How will Chin do on the test?
   a. Chin will do poorly.
   b. Chin will not take the test.
   c. Chin will do well.

Day #4

Name

Week #24

Assessment

1. Preview the story below, and predict the characters.
   _____

Time for Dusty

Dusty wanted something. He ran to find Tyler. Tyler was reading a book. Dusty walked up the stairs to Holly's bedroom. She was playing a game. She did not look to see what Dusty wanted.

2. Who are the characters in this story? _____

Dusty ran back down the steps. He picked up his leash.

3. What is Dusty?
   a. a kid
   b. a dog
   c. a cat

He took the leash and went to Tyler. This time, Tyler put his book down. "What do you want, boy?" Tyler asked.

Dusty ran to the door. He wagged his tail.

Tyler pulled on his coat. He went to the steps and said, "Holly, do you want to go outside with us?"

"Yes," said Holly. She smiled.

4. What does Dusty want to do? _____
   _____

5. Predict what will happen next. _____
   _____

Week # 25

Day #1

Samantha stared into the tide pool. Tiny fish darted around among the rocks. Two sea stars were on the rocks. Four small crabs crawled in the sand. The tide came in and covered the rocky pool.

1. List all the words with **ck** in them. _____
2. What other word also means **stared**: **looked** or **poked**? _____
3. Where is Samantha: at the **beach** or at a **swimming pool**? _____
4. Use the underlined words from the story to complete this summary. This story is about a girl named _____ who was looking at a _____ She saw _____, _____, and _____.

Day #2

Sometimes a lizard is given a name because of the way it looks. A frilled lizard can spread the skin around its neck so it looks like a frilly fan. It has specks of blue, red, and yellow.

1. List all the words with **ck** in them. _____
2. Is a **speck** a **large spot** or a **small spot**? _____
3. What would be a good title for this? _____
4. Use the underlined words from the story to complete this summary. A _____ can be named for the way it _____. The _____ got its _____ because its neck skin can spread out to look like a very _____.

Day #3

Many people work in a school. Teachers help us learn. Custodians keep our school clean and safe. Bus drivers safely get us to school and back home again. Cooks make meals and help us to grow strong and healthy.

1. Does **learn** rhyme with **clean**? _____
2. Circle the word **meals**. What word means the same as **meals**? _____
3. Which two jobs include safety? _____
4. Use the underlined words from the story to complete the summary. Many people work in a _____. Some of these people are _____, _____, _____, and _____.

Day #4

Bertha Butterfly fluttered over a fence. She landed on a flower. She felt movement near her. Bertha looked up just as a kitten's paw reached for the flower. Away she flew! The kitten watched the empty flower move up and down.

1. Circle all the words that have **fl** in them.
2. What word means the same as **move up and down**: **spin** or **bounce**? _____
3. Who is in this story? _____
4. Use the information from the story to complete this summary. _____ landed on a _____. A _____ tried to catch her, but Bertha _____.

Helicopters

It's a helicopter! It flies up and down. It flies forward, backward, and even sideways. It can hover over just one spot. A helicopter is very useful. It can be used to help rescue people and report traffic and news. A helicopter can also lift huge pieces of equipment to the tops of tall buildings.

1. Circle all the words that have **ck** in them. List all the words that have **fl** in them. _____

2. What word also means **rescue**: **move** or **save**? _____

3. This paragraph is about a _____.

4. It can fly in. . .

   a. many directions

   b. one direction

   c. two directions

5. Use the answers to #3 and #4 to help complete the summary. This is a paragraph about a _____. It can fly in _____, so it is very useful.

Name _____   Week # 26

Life in the Midwest

Brittany is a second grader who lives in the part of the United States that is known as the Midwest. She lives on a farm in Nebraska.

1. Who is in this story? _____
2. Is this person a boy or a girl? _____
3. What state does he or she live in? _____
4. Which is a better summary of this paragraph: **Nebraska is in the Midwest** or **Brittany is a second grader from a farm in Nebraska**? Underline it.

Day #1

The Midwest is a very fertile part of the United States. This means that the Midwest is a place where it is easy to grow plants.

1. Do you live in the Midwest? _____
2. What does **fertile** mean? _____
3. Why is the Midwest a good place for a farm? _____
   _____
4. Which is a better summary of this paragraph: **the Midwest is a fertile place** or **there are fertile places in the United States**? Underline it.

Day #2

There is prairie land all around Brittany's farm. The prairie is a large open space of land. It is very flat and grassy. Many kinds of animals live on the prairie, such as prairie dogs, coyotes, buffalo, and wild mustangs.

1. List three words that describe the prairie. _____
2. Are the animals in the prairie **wild** or **tame**? _____
3. List three animals that live on the prairie. _____
4. Fill in words from the paragraph to complete the summary. Brittany's _____ is surrounded by prairie land that is very _____ and _____ Prairie dogs, _____, _____, and _____ live on the prairie.

Day #3

Brittany enjoys helping on the farm, in-line skating, and learning about science in her small class of only three children.

1. Does Brittany go to school with lots of other kids? _____
2. How many other children are in her class? _____
3. Would you like to live where Brittany does? _____
   Why or why not? _____
4. Write a summary of this paragraph in your own words. _____
   _____

Day #4

Published by Frank Schaffer Publications. Copyright protected.   0-7682-3212-0 *Read 4 Today*

Name

Week # 26

Assessment

1. Preview the story. What kind of writing is this? _____

A Rabbit Poem

2. What will the poem be about? _____

The rabbit is small and fast,
With a short and fluffy tail.
He has long ears that let him hear
Scary animals without fail.

3. Write a sentence to tell what rabbits look like. _____
_____

Rabbits love to eat and eat!
They love the green, green grass.
They love to munch on vegetables
In a farmer's garden patch.

4. What two things do rabbits love to eat? _____

5. Write one sentence to summarize the whole poem. _____
_____

Published by Frank Schaffer Publications. Copyright protected. 64 0-7682-3212-0 *Read 4 Today*

Name   Week # 27

Mantids

A mantid is an insect. We call it a praying mantis. When it hunts, it lifts its front legs and looks like it is praying.

1. Circle all the words with a **short a**.
2. What is a **mantid**? _____
3. What is this paragraph mostly about: **the name praying mantis** or **how the mantis hunts**? _____
4. Use the information in the paragraph to finish this sentence. A mantid is called a praying mantis because _____.

Day #1

A mantid can grow to be 2 to 5 inches (5 to 13 centimeters) long. It has front legs with sharp hooks to hold its prey. It has short, wide wings. Its body is long and thin.

1. Does **hooks** rhyme with **books** or with **boots**? _____
2. What is the opposite of **short and wide**? _____
3. What is this paragraph mostly about: **the mantid's front legs** or **what a mantid looks like**? _____
4. Use the information in the paragraph to finish this sentence. A mantid has sharp hooks on its front legs because _____.

Day #2

Mantid's are helpful to people because they eat harmful insects. A female mantid might even eat her mate if she is very hungry.

1. Is the **a** in **mantid** a **long a** or **short a**? _____
2. What word in this paragraph could be the opposite of **helpful**? _____
3. What is this paragraph mostly about: **what mantids eat** or **the mating habits of the mantid**? _____
4. Use the information in the paragraph to finish this sentence. Mantids eat insects that are harmful to people, but they will even eat _____.

Day #3

Mantids protect themselves by changing colors. If a mantid is on a green plant, its color might be green. If it is on a brown branch, its color might be brown.

1. Does **changing** rhyme with **hanging** or **ranging**? _____
2. A word for what the mantid is doing when it changes color to hide itself is: **peek-a-boo** or **camouflage**? _____
3. What is this paragraph mostly about: **how mantids turn green** or **how mantids protect themselves**? _____
4. Use the information in the paragraph to finish this sentence. A mantid protects itself by _____.

Day #4

Name

Week # 27

Marsupials

A <u>marsupial</u> is an animal that has a <u>pouch</u>. The pouch is mostly used to <u>carry</u> <u>babies</u>.

When a baby marsupial is born, the tiny animal must <u>crawl</u> into its mother's pouch. There it <u>drinks</u> its mother's milk and grows. When it is big enough to move on its own, it leaves the pouch. The baby stays close to its mother. If it is in danger, it goes back into her pouch.

A <u>kangaroo</u>, a <u>koala</u>, and an <u>opossum</u> are marsupials. These animals do not look alike. They do not eat the same kind of food, but they all have pouches.

1. Circle the words with a **short a**.

   that   back   animal   baby   danger

   Which word rhymes with stranger? _____

2. What is a **marsupial**? _____

3. What is this story mostly about: **kangaroos** or **what is different about marsupials**? _____

4. Name three animals that are marsupials. _____
   _____

5. Use words from the story to finish this summary.

   The story is about _____. A marsupial is an animal that has a _____. The pouch is used mostly to _____. When a baby is born, it must _____ into its mother's pouch. Inside the pouch, it _____ and grows.

Name _____   **Week # 28**

Baby Brother
My new baby brother, Ty, is the loudest baby in the world. It seems like he never stops crying. He cries all day long. He cries just as I am falling asleep at night. Mom has to guess what Ty wants, because he can't tell us.

1. How many people are in this story? _____
2. Who is this story about? _____
3. What is this paragraph mostly about? _____
4. Circle **F** for fact or **O** for opinion.
   F   O   Ty is the loudest baby in the world.
   F   O   Ty can't tell his family what he wants.

Day #1

Sometimes Ty stops crying. Then he is the cutest baby in the world! He has black hair and dark brown eyes. He likes to wave his hands in the air. He has a great smile.

1. Does Ty ever stop crying? _____
2. What is one thing Ty does when he is not crying? _____
3. What does Ty look like? _____
4. Circle **F** for fact or **O** for opinion.
   F   O   Ty has black hair and dark brown eyes.
   F   O   Ty is the cutest baby in the world.

Day #2

Tornado Scare
We looked out the window. A tornado was heading right for our house! We ran into the bathroom and closed the door. All three of us got into the bathtub. I could hear a loud roar. It sounded like a train. My heart was pounding.

1. What does the writer compare the tornado to? _____
2. What does the writer mean by **heart was pounding**? Is the author **exercising**, **afraid**, or **hammering**? _____
3. What is the first thing they did after they saw the tornado? _____
4. What is the last thing they did? _____

Day #3

Later, I found out that summer is the time when most tornadoes happen. These storms can knock down houses and other buildings. Sometimes, the tornado can pick up a car or a tree right off the ground.

1. Did the writer live through the tornado? _____
2. Was the writer right to be scared of the tornado? _____
3. Why should you be scared of a tornado? _____
4. Connect the two parts of the fact sentences. Draw lines.
   Tornados often happen   cars or trees.
   A tornado can knock down   in the summer.
   A tornado can pick up   houses and other buildings.

Day #4

Name

Week # 28

1. Preview the text below. What do you think this story is about?

_____

Vampire Bats

There are over 900 species of bats in the world. They are the only flying mammal in the world. One bat is the vampire bat. Vampire bats are found in Central and South America. I think they are the coolest and scariest bats.

2. Circle one fact sentence. Underline one opinion sentence.

Vampire bats are nocturnal. This means they sleep during the day and are active at night. When flying at night, bats use echolocation to help them "see" in the dark. Echolocation means that the bat sends out squeaks or clicks. When these sounds reach an object in the bat's path, they bounce off, and the sound echoes travel back to the bat. This lets the bat know where the object is, its size, and how fast it is moving.

3. What does nocturnal mean? _____

This is the cool part of how a vampire bat hunts. Vampire bats have heat sensors on their noses. This helps them find the area on their prey where the blood is close to the skin. Vampire bats usually feed on sleeping horses, cattle, chickens, or turkeys.

This is the yucky part of how a vampire bat hunts. The bat doesn't suck blood with sharp-pointed teeth called fangs, but licks the blood, from a small round cut, like a cat would drink milk. The saliva of the bat stops the blood from clotting so the bat can drink all it needs, which is about two tablespoons.

4. What does the writer compare a feeding bat to? _____
_____

5. Underline the two opinion sentences above.

Name   Week # 29

Figs

Fig is the name of a fruit and the plant the fruit grows on. The plant can look like a bush or like a tree. Fig plants grow where it is warm all year long.

1. List all the words that start with a **hard g** sound. _____
2. Which word describes a place where it is warm all year long? a. frosty b. tropical
3. Which word does **fruit** rhyme with: **hit** or **toot**? _____
4. Circle the sentence that is a fact. Underline the sentence that is an opinion.

   A fig is a plant and a fruit. The fig tree is very pretty.

Day #1

The fig fruit grows in bunches on the stems of fig plants. Some figs can be picked two times each year.

1. List all the words that have a **hard g** sound. _____
2. What word could you write instead of **bunches**? a. singles b. groups
3. What is the main idea of this paragraph: **how figs grow** or **what figs look like**?
   _____
4. Circle the sentence that is a fact. Underline the sentence that is an opinion.

   Figs remind me of a bunch of balloons. Figs grow in a bunch.

Day #2

They can be picked from old branches in June or July. They can be picked from new branches in August or September.

1. Circle all the words that have a **hard c** sound.
2. What other word could you write instead of **picked**? a. plucked b. bitten
3. How many months can you pick figs? _____
4. Circle the sentence that is a fact. Underline the sentence that is an opinion.

   Figs are hard to pick. You can pick figs mostly in the summer.

Day #3

Many people like to eat figs. They can be eaten in fig cookies or in fig bars. They can be canned or eaten fresh. Sometimes figs are dried.

1. Circle all the words that start with a **hard c**.
2. What other word could you use instead of **many**: **all** or **lots**? _____
3. What other food can be eaten fresh, canned, or dried? a. cherries b. broccoli
4. Circle the sentence that is a fact. Underline the sentence that is an opinion.

   The best way to eat a fig is in a fig cookie. You can eat figs in many ways.

Day #4

Name _____   Week # 29

Pilots

    A pilot is a person who can fly an airplane. Pilots go to special schools to learn how to fly planes. Some pilots fly planes for fun. Other pilots fly planes as their job. They carry people or cargo from city to city. Pilots have to learn how to fly in all kinds of weather. They have to work with people on the ground to land planes safely. Being a pilot is an important job.

1. List the story words that start with a **hard c**. _____

   List the story words that start with a **hard g**. _____

2. What is a **pilot**? _____

3. Draw lines to connect the two parts of the fact sentences together.

   Pilots go to special schools   for fun.

   Some pilots fly planes   of weather.

   Pilots have to fly in all kinds   to learn how to fly planes.

4. Circle the sentence that is a fact.

   a. Pilots must have a lot of fun flying planes.

   b. It must be scary to fly in a storm.

   c. Some pilots fly planes as their job.

5. Write your own opinion sentence about pilots. _____

Week #30

Chain Reaction

Terri dropped the marble. It hit the sleeping cat on the nose. The surprised cat jumped on the dog's tail. The dog yipped and chased the cat.

1. What happened first? _____
2. What happened second? _____
3. What happened third? _____
4. What happened fourth? _____

Day #1

The cat ran under the fish tank. The fish tank wobbled back and forth. Water and one small fish splashed out onto the floor. The happy cat ate the fish. The thirsty dog lapped up the water.

1. What was the last effect on the dog? _____
2. What was the last effect on the cat? _____
3. What caused the chain reaction? _____
4. Do you think Terri dropped the marble on the cat's nose **on purpose** or **by accident**? _____

Day #2

The Food Chain

Predators are animals that eat other animals. The animals they eat are called prey. Predators and prey do important jobs in nature. Prey animals are food for the animals that hunt them. But predators also help prey.

1. What do you call an animal that eats other animals? _____
2. What do you call an animal that is eaten by other animals? _____
3. How does the prey help the predator? _____
4. Are people predators or prey? _____

Day #3

Coyotes hunt rabbits. If coyotes did not eat some rabbits, there would be too many rabbits hopping around. There would not be enough food for all the rabbits to eat. Then the hungry rabbits would grow weak and sick. Some might even die.

1. Coyotes are called _____ because they eat other animals.
2. Rabbits are called _____ because they are animals that coyotes eat.
3. What would the effect be if coyotes stopped eating rabbits? _____
4. Does this paragraph tell you what rabbits eat? _____

Day #4

Name _____ Week # 30

Assessment

1. Based on the title below, predict what the story will be about.
   _____

Science Magic

Joe shared a magic science trick with his class. He said, "How can you tell a raw egg from a hard-boiled egg without cracking it open?"

Marta asked, "Shake it?"

"No," said Joe. "Watch this. One of these eggs is hard-boiled. The other one is raw."

Joe put the eggs on the table. He made each egg spin like a top. Then he gently touched the top of each egg with two fingers. One egg stopped. The other one kept spinning. Joe picked up the egg that stopped spinning.

2. What does Joe do first? _____

3. How are the two eggs different? _____

"This is the hard-boiled egg," Joe said. "The raw egg inside the shell keeps moving. That makes the raw egg keep spinning. The hard-boiled egg stops because nothing inside the shell is moving."

4. The raw egg kept moving because _____
   _____.

5. Why did Joe do this trick for his class? _____
   _____

Name _____   # Week # 31

Day #1

Jaleel and his brother made a sand castle. At the end of the day, the tide came in. The waves washed over the castle. It turned back into sand on the beach.

1. What word starts with a **short e**? _____
2. What is Jaleel's castle made of? _____
3. Underline the sentence that tells you what caused the sand castle to fall down.
4. What about the tide made the sand castle fall? _____
_____

Day #2

Neal liked walking. He walked in the woods near his home. It started raining. The ground got all wet. Neal stepped in a puddle. He looked down and saw that his shoes were muddy.

1. Do you pronounce the **e** in **puddle**? _____
2. What is mud made of: water with **dirt** or **sand**? _____
3. Why was the ground wet? _____
4. Did Neal's shoes get muddy **because he liked walking** or **because he stepped in a puddle**? _____

Day #3

Neal knew he would be in trouble. His shoes were new. Neal ran home and put them in the washing machine. He wanted to wash them before his mother came home.

1. Do you pronounce the **e** in **trouble**? _____
2. What is the opposite of **before**? _____
3. How do you think Neal's mother would feel about Neal's muddy shoes? _____
_____
4. Neal wanted to wash his shoes before _____.

Day #4

Did you ever think how it would feel
If nobody had invented the wheel?
No bikes, no wagons, no trucks or trains,
No cars to ride … not even planes!

1. Which two rhyming words have a **long e** sound? _____
2. What word is **planes** short for? _____
3. Circle all the vehicles in the poem you have ridden in. _____
4. Finish the sentence. There would be no wagons, bikes, cars, or planes if _____.

Name: Week # 31

Kito

    Kito is a seven-year old boy who lives in Ethiopia. Both of his parents died when he was young. He lives in a little orphanage. An orphanage is a place where children who have no family to take care of them live.

    Kito has been living in the orphanage since he was four. He lives in a large room. Many other children sleep there, too. He likes living in the orphanage. The children eat, sleep, play, live, and learn at the orphanage.

    Kito loves to go to school. He likes math, and he likes to read about faraway places. Kito wants to be a doctor when he grows up. He would like to help sick people in his country.

1. Match the word to the correct vowel sound.

    little   short e

    sleep   silent e

    when   long e

2. Underline the sentence that tells you what an orphanage is.

3. How old was Kito when he moved into the orphanage? _____

4. Kito is seven years old. How many years has he been living at the orphanage?
    a. two   b. three   c. six

5. There are two reasons why Kito lives in a orphanage. Circle the two causes.
    a. There was no other family to take care of him.
    b. Kito likes living with lots of other children.
    c. Kito's parents died when he was young.

Week #32

April Showers Bring Beauty

The class spent the morning on the playground. They were painting beautiful pictures of the warm, spring day. When the bell rang, the students went inside to eat lunch. The pictures were left outside on the playground to dry.

1. What season does the title tell you this story takes place in? _____
2. Where does this story take place? _____
3. What are the students doing in this paragraph? _____
4. What did they do with the pictures? _____

Day #1

During math the clouds opened up. Thunder could be heard clapping loudly. Lightning lit up the classroom.

"Our pictures!" yelled the students.

"Well, we can't go out and get them now," said the teacher.

1. What happens during math class? a. it rains lightly   b. there is a thunderstorm
2. When the author says **the clouds opened up** does that tell you that it **rained really hard** or it **sprinkled**? _____
3. What are the students worried about? _____
4. Have you ever had a thunderstorm during school? _____

Day #2

It continued raining through the entire math class. Then it stopped. The students went outside to look at their artwork.

"The paintings are beautiful!" exclaimed the students.

1. How do the students react to their wet paintings? _____
2. Did you expect them to be happy or upset? _____
3. What effect do you imagine the rain had on the paintings?
   a. It washed away the paint.
   b. It blended all the paint colors.
   c. The paintings floated away in a flood.
4. What other words do you think the students could be saying? _____

Day #3

The rain had washed the paint into pools of color over the playground. It looked like a giant rainbow in the sand.

"Your pictures were pretty," said the teacher, "but this April shower made them more beautiful."

1. What was the effect of the rain? _____
2. What does the writer compare the paint on the playground to? _____
3. What does the teacher think about the effect of the rain on the pictures? _____
4. Circle the sentence that helped you answer #3.

Day #4

Name Week # 32

1. What does the title below tell you this story is about?
   _____

Getting Mad

"Let's talk about how your body feels when you are angry or upset," said Ms. Porzio.

"My stomach hurts," said Lisa.

"I get tears in my eyes," said Michael.

"My face feels hot," said Steve.

"These are all ways that our bodies feel when we are upset," said Ms. Porzio. "Let's listen to our hearts and write down what we hear. This month, when you are angry or upset, you will listen to your heartbeat again to see if it sounds different."

2. What is the effect of anger on Steve's body? _____

3. Is being angry or upset the cause or the effect of Lisa's stomach hurting?
   _____

At the end of the month Michael said, "When I was upset, my heart beat very quickly."

"When I was mad, my heartbeat was loud," said Lisa.

"When I was embarrassed, my heartbeat was loud and fast," said Steve.

The students all learned that their heartbeats showed their feelings.

4. List the different effects of being upset on each kid's heartbeat.
   _____
   _____
   _____

5. How does your body feel when you are angry or upset? _____
   _____

Name _____ Week # 33

Farm or Beach?

"Let's plan our trip," said Lana. "I want to go see Aunt Linda. She lives by the Ocean City beach!"

"I want to go see Grandma," said Sammy. "Grandma lives on the farm!"

1. Which two-syllable word has a **soft c** and a **short i**? _____
2. What word could you use instead of **plan**: **forget** or **organize**? _____
3. Do Lana and Sammy agree about what to do? _____
4. What are Lana and Sammy's choices? _____

Day #1

"Both are fun trips," said Lana. "Let's go to the beach. We can swim in the ocean."

"Let's go to the farm," said Sammy. "We can milk the cows."

1. What sound does the **c** in **ocean** make: **hard c**, **soft c**, or **sh**? _____
2. What is the opposite of **both**: **some** or **neither**? _____
3. Compare what they can do at the beach and the farm. _____
   _____
   _____
4. Where do we get milk from? _____

Day #2

"At the beach we can build sand castles. We can see crabs," said Lana.

"At the farm we can see the baby chicks. We can feed the pigs," said Sammy.

1. Which two-syllable word has a **hard c** and a **silent t**? _____
2. A chick is a baby _____.
3. Compare what they can do at the beach and the farm. _____
   _____
   _____
4. Which has more animals: **beach** or **farm**? _____

Day #3

"At the beach we can ride on a boat. We can go fishing. We can collect shells," said Lana.

"At the farm we can ride on the tractor. We can dig up potatoes. We can collect the eggs," said Sammy.

1. What farm word has an **i** with a **short i** sound? _____
2. What word could you use instead of **collect**: **scatter** or **gather**? _____
3. Compare what they can collect at the beach and the farm. _____
   _____
4. Which one sounds more fun to you: **beach** or **farm**? _____

Day #4

Farm or Beach? (cont.)

Beach	Farm
Swim in the ocean	Milk the cows
Build sand castles	See baby chicks
Discover crabs	Feed the pigs
Ride on a boat	Ride on the tractor
Go fishing	Dig up potatoes
Collect shells	Collect the eggs

"We can do both!" said Lana. "Let's go to the beach to see Aunt Linda. Then we'll take Aunt Linda to see Grandma. We can do it all. And we can do it together."

1. Which word above has three syllables and a **short i**? _____

2. **Ant** sounds just like what word in the paragraph? _____

3. Compare what you could take home from the beach and what you could take home from the farm. _____
_____
_____

4. What solution does Lana come up with? _____
_____

5. Do you think Sammy will agree? _____
Would you agree? _____

Name   **Week #34**

Los Angeles and New York

Los Angeles and New York are alike because they are both cities. Many movies and television shows are filmed in both cities. Both cities can be fun to visit.

1. Which two cities does the writer compare here? Underline them.
2. How many ways does the writer say the two cities are alike? _____
3. What is the first way they are alike? _____
4. What is the last way they are alike? _____
   _____

Day #1

Los Angeles is on the West Coast. New York is on the East Coast. The winter weather stays warm in Los Angeles. The winter weather gets very cold in New York.

1. What is the difference between the weather in New York and Los Angeles?
   _____
2. What is another difference between New York and Los Angeles? _____
   _____
3. Do you live closer to Los Angeles or New York? _____
4. Which city would you rather live in? _____

Day #2

Sharks and Dolphins

A dolphin is like a shark in some ways. Both dolphins and sharks can swim. Both have fins. Sharks have teeth and so do dolphins.

1. Which two animals does the writer compare here? _____
2. Does the writer tell you where dolphins and sharks live? _____
   If so, where? _____
3. How many ways does the writer say the two animals are alike? _____
4. What is the last way they are alike? _____

Day #3

But a dolphin is different from a shark in other ways. A dolphin is a mammal. A shark is a fish. A shark uses gills to breathe. A dolphin has lungs for breathing. Dolphins live in family groups. Sharks mainly live alone.

1. What are two differences between dolphins and sharks? _____
   _____
2. Name any other animal you know is a mammal. _____
3. Would you rather be a dolphin or a shark? _____
   Why? _____

Day #4

Name

Week #34

Assessment

1. Preview the story below. Predict what will be compared in this story.
   _____

Where in the World?

What do the camel, the polar bear, the monkey, and the whale have in common? They are all mammals. But each of these mammals live in a different climate.

2. How are these animals alike? _____

3. Climate has to do with...
   a. what part of the world a place is in and what kind of weather it has.
   b. how many monkeys live in a place.
   c. how long it takes to climb a tree.

The camel lives in places that are dry and hot. The polar bear lives in snowy and cold places. The monkey lives in jungles and rain forests. And the whale lives in the ocean.

4. Which two animals live in a hot climate? _____

5. Which of the animal climates is closest to the climate where you live?
   _____

Name _____   # Week # 35

Birthdays around the World

Children around the world celebrate their birthdays in many different ways.

In Argentina, people pluck the earlobe of the birthday child. They give one tug for each year the child has been alive.

Day #1

1. Circle all the words that have a **ck** in them.
2. What other word means the same thing as **tug**: **poke** or **pull**? _____
3. Where is your **earlobe**?   a. top of your ear   b. bottom of your ear
4. How many tugs on your ear will you get on your next birthday? _____

People from Nova Scotia have an unusual tradition. Everyone puts butter on the birthday child's nose. They do this so that the child will have good luck. The tradition says that if the child's nose is slippery with butter, bad luck will not stick.

Day #2

1. List the words that have a **ck** in them. _____
   _____
2. What is the opposite of **unusual**: **strange** or **usual**? _____
3. What do people put on the birthday child's nose in Nova Scotia? _____
4. Why do they do that? _____

In China, family and friends meet for lunch. They eat noodles to ensure that the child will have a long life.

Day #3

1. Which words in this paragraph starts with **ch**? _____
   Which word ends with **ch**? _____
2. What does **ensure** mean: **to figure out** or **to make sure**? _____
3. What time of day do people in China celebrate birthdays? _____
4. Why do they eat noodles at birthday parties? _____
   _____

In England, objects are stuck in the birthday cake. The birthday child checks his or her cake. If a coin is found, this means that he or she will be rich.

Day #4

1. Which words in this paragraph have a **ck**? _____
2. What is a **coin**? _____
3. Do you think the birthday child always finds the coin in the cake? _____
4. Look back over the last few days of stories. Which one of the birthday celebrations would you like to try? _____ Why? _____
   _____

Week # 35

Jacks and Truyen

Nga moved to the United States from Vietnam when she was in the second grade. She met a girl named Denise. Nga and Denise were best friends. They enjoyed many of the same things.

"I want to teach you a game that I used to play with my friends in Vietnam," said Nga. "It is called Truyen. You play it with sticks and a piece of fruit. Do you want to try it?"

"Sure," answered Denise. "How do you play?"

"Well, first I lay one stick down. Then I lay the other sticks across. When I throw this small piece of fruit in the air, I pick up one stick. After that, I throw the fruit up again and pick up two sticks. I keep doing this, and each time I pick up one more stick," explained Nga.

"Hey! I know how to play this game. I call it Jacks. At home I have little metal things called jacks. I bounce a ball and I pick up the jacks one at a time. Then I pick up two at a time. It's just like Truyen!" exclaimed Denise excitedly.

Nga and Denise are from different countries. They still found ways they are alike.

1. List three words with **ck** in them. _____

2. What is a **jack**? _____

3. What game did Nga teach Denise: **Jacks** or **Truyen**? _____

4. How are Jacks and Truyen the same? _____
_____

5. How are Jacks and Truyen different? _____
_____

Name: _____   Week # 36

Up, Up, and Away
Tan and Sam went to the zoo. Whoops! Tan let go of her balloon. Tan's balloon _____ up into the sky. Sam shared his balloon with Tan. Tan said, "Thank you."

1. What does the title make you think of? _____
2. Who is in this story? _____
3. What is the setting of this story? _____
4. Which word is the best word for the blank?
   a. caught   b. floated   c. fell

Day #1

Sam dropped his ice cream cone. It _____ down to the ground. What a mess!

1. What is Sam eating? _____
2. Which word is the best word for the blank?
   a. popped   b. fell   c. floated
3. How do you think Sam felt? _____
4. Has this ever happened to you? _____

Day #2

Tan's grandpa held his balloon too close to the point on a fence. His balloon _____.

1. Which word is the best word for the blank?
   a. popped   b. caught   c. fell
2. Who are all the characters in this story? _____
3. Who is holding the balloon? _____
4. Is the point on that fence **sharp** or **dull**? _____

Day #3

Sam's brother had a long string on his balloon. The string got _____ in a tree. Sam's brother couldn't get it loose. He had to get another balloon.

1. Which word is the best word for the blank?
   a. fell   b. popped   c. caught
2. Who are all the characters in this story? _____
3. True or false: Sam's brother popped his balloon. _____
4. How did Sam's brother solve his balloon problem? _____

Day #4

Published by Frank Schaffer Publications. Copyright protected.   83   0-7682-3212-0 *Read 4 Today*

Name **Week # 36**

1. What does the title below tell you about the weather in this story?

   _____

It's Cold Outside

"Let's go outside to play," said Jada to her grandmother.
"It sure is cold," said Grandmother. "Do you have your mittens?"
"Yes," said Jada. She and Grandmother stepped outside.

2. What happened in this story? Circle **True** or **False** for each sentence.

The hot sun shone for many hours.	True	False
Jada played outside in her shorts.	True	False
They were bundled up in many layers.	True	False

Jada and her grandmother played in the tall white snowdrifts. They made big white balls and threw them.

3. What is another name for the **big white balls** Jada and her Grandmother threw?

   a. marshmallows

   b. snowballs

   c. stones

Little flakes began to fall. "Looks like we'll get a few more inches today," Jada said.

4. What season does this story take place in? _____

5. Do you have weather like this where you live? _____

   If yes, what is your favorite thing to do in cold weather? If no, what cold weather fun sounds the best to you? _____

Name _____ **Week # 37**

Day #1

The first snowball flies and hits a parent right in the back. Quickly the parents begin making snowballs as fast as they can. The children got a head start and already have their supply of snowballs. Cold, white balls of snow fly everywhere! Laughs and giggles can be heard everywhere.

1. Does the **u** in **supply** sound more like the **u** in **music** or the **u** in **mud**? _____
2. What is the opposite of **quickly**? _____
3. What season is it? _____
4. Are the parents angry at the children about the snowballs? _____

Day #2

As usual, the ice cream truck enters the park. The music can be heard all around. Because it is such a cold day, instead of ice cream, the ice cream man is selling hot chocolate to all of the families.

1. Does the **u** in **music** sound more like the **u** in **rude** or the **u** in **supply**? _____
2. What part of your body do you hear with? _____
3. Where does this story take place? _____
4. Why does the ice cream man have hot chocolate: **because he was out of ice cream** or **because it was cold outside**? _____

Day #3

Joseph is an Inuk boy who lives in Canada. His house was built on stilts so that it would be far above the deep winter snow. Joseph has special clothes to wear during the winter. He wears fur-lined boots, gloves, and a big coat.

1. Does the **o** in **Joseph** have the same sound as the **o** in **gloves**? _____
2. Does **deep snow** mean that **a lot of snow is piled on the ground** or **you can't see much snow on the ground**? _____
3. What kind of weather does Joseph have where he lives? _____
4. What does Joseph wear to keep warm in the winter? _____
_____

Day #4

Gabriel knew that soon, in the fall, the rivers around his town would freeze. He could already see patches of thin ice in the morning. By the time December rolled around, the rivers would be frozen solid. Children would be able to ice skate.

1. Does the **o** in **frozen** have the same sound as the **o** in **solid**? _____
2. What is another word for the season of **fall**: **winter** or **autumn**? _____
3. Circle what season it is in this story.   a. winter   b. late summer   c. fall
4. Do rivers get ice on them where you live? _____ If they do, what season does it happen in? _____

The Black Cat's Curse

    A left-handed pitcher for the New York Yankees, named Eddie Lopat, had beaten the Cleveland Indians 11 times in a row! When the two teams got together the twelfth time, something crazy happened. A rude man who was watching the game jumped out of his seat and ran onto the field. He had a black cat in his arms! Some people think that black cats are supposed to bring bad luck. The crazy fan dashed over to the pitcher's mound. He put the black cat right in front of Eddie's feet. Poor Eddie! He did not do a good job pitching. The New York Yankees lost the game.

1. Which word has a **u** that sounds like the **u** in **cup**?   a. jumped   b. rude

   Which word has an **o** that sounds like the **o** in **hose**?   a. solid   b. over

   Which word has both **short u** and **long o** sounds?   a. supposed   b. mound

2. Write **twelfth** as a number. _____

3. Why did the man put the black cat in front of Eddie?
   a. To give Eddie a sneezing fit.
   b. To give Eddie bad luck so his pitching would be bad.
   c. Because he promised Eddie he could take home a kitten.

4. What position did Eddie play?
   a. first base
   b. catcher
   c. pitcher

5. Eddie did not do a good job pitching in that game. Do you think Eddie believed that black cats bring bad luck? _____
   Why or why not? _____

Name   **Week # 38**

Day #1

Joe watched a busy little mammal climb up the tree. Then it raced down again, looking for nuts. Joe knew that it was hoarding nuts, storing them for winter.

1. What two creatures are in this story? _____
2. What is the mammal that Joe is watching: **squirrel** or **dog**? _____
3. What season does this story take place in? _____
4. What does **hoarding** mean: **climbing** or **storing**? _____

Day #2

A rowboat is a small boat that is moved with oars. Oars are long poles with wide, flat ends. Another kind of boat is a fireboat. It puts out fires with water and hoses.

1. Find the answer to this riddle: I help put out fires. What am I? _____
2. Which do you think is bigger, a **rowboat** or a **fireboat**? _____
3. What is an **oar**? _____
4. Answer this riddle: I am moved with oars. What am I? _____

Day #3

A sailboat is moved by the wind. It has sails, which are made from strong cloth. The wind fills the sails and moves the boat through the water. A houseboat is a wide, flat boat with rooms where people can live.

1. Find the answer to this riddle: I am moved by the wind. What am I? _____
2. What two things work together to make a sailboat move? _____
3. Answer this riddle: People can live in my rooms. What am I? _____
4. Would you like to live in a houseboat? _____
   Why or why not? _____

Day #4

Dear Grandma, I am glad you are having a good time on the beach. I bet it is warm there. I can't wait to get there during spring vacation! I want to swim and pick up shells on the beach.

1. Where does Grandma live? _____
2. What kind of weather does Grandma have? _____
3. What time of year is it? _____
4. What state could Grandma live in: **Florida** or **Maine**? _____

Name

Week # 38

1. Only read the title below. Who is the story about? _____

   What day is the story about?

   _____

Samantha's Birthday

I knew it would be a great day from the minute I woke up. Piled beside my bed was a stack of presents. I jumped out of bed. I was so excited. When I came downstairs carrying the presents, everyone shouted, "Happy birthday!"

2. Who do you think wrote this paragraph?
   a. Samantha's mother
   b. Samantha
   c. Samantha's brother

Before Samantha woke up, I left her presents beside her bed. I knew she would like the surprise from her father and me. When we saw Samantha on the stairs, we surprised her by saying, "Happy birthday!"

3. Who do you think wrote this paragraph?
   a. Samantha's mother
   b. Samantha
   c. Samantha's brother

I bought Samantha a book about dinosaurs for her birthday. Mom and Dad let me do extra chores to earn the money. I had to wake up early to surprise her but it was worth it to see her face when we all said, "Happy birthday!"

4. Who do you think wrote this paragraph?
   a. Samantha's mother
   b. Samantha
   c. Samantha's brother

5. Circle true or false: Samantha's family does not make a big deal about birthdays.   **True**   **False**

Name

Week #39

Day #1

Sam gathers lemons. His uncle cuts them. Sam squeezes the juice into a pitcher. He adds sugar and water. Sam puts in lemon slices and ice.

1. How many words have two syllables? _____
2. What is a lemon: **fruit** or **vegetable**? _____
3. What are Sam and his uncle making?
   a. ice cream   b. chocolate cake   c. lemonade
4. List what goes into Sam's recipe. _____

Day #2

Cela gets lettuce, tomatoes, and cucumbers from her garden. Her grandfather cuts them into pieces. Cela puts the pieces into a bowl.

1. What does **lettuce** sound more like: **let us** or **let ice**? _____
2. Before the grandfather cut the tomato, it was… **half** or **whole**? _____
3. What are Cela and her grandfather making?
   a. pasta   b. meatloaf   c. salad
4. List what goes into it. _____

Day #3

Ali and his mom buy a roll of dough at the grocery store. His mom cuts the dough into circles. Ali puts them on a long metal sheet. His mom puts them in the oven.

1. Which does **dough** sound more like: the word **do** or the **do** in **donut**? _____
2. What shape is a roll? _____
3. What are Ali and his mom doing?
   a. making cookies
   b. making Ali's bed
   c. making chocolate cake
4. How many steps do Ali and his mom take? _____

Day #4

Ana-Maria and her dad put flour, sugar, water, and an egg into a bowl. Ana-Maria adds melted chocolate. They stir the mixture. Then she puts the mixture in a pan. Ana-Maria's dad puts the pan in the oven. Frosting will come later.

1. Which word has three syllables? _____
2. What is the opposite of **add**? _____
3. What are Ana-Maria and her dad making?
   a. salad   b. chocolate cake   c. cherry pie
4. List what goes into Ana-Maria's creation. _____

Published by Frank Schaffer Publications. Copyright protected.   89   0-7682-3212-0 *Read 4 Today*

Astronauts

An astronaut is a person who travels in space. Only a few people can become astronauts. After a person is picked, he or she has to go to a special school. Astronauts can spend years learning everything they need to know for space travel. They must know all about their spaceships. They must be smart. They must be very healthy. Astronauts work hard to get ready for their jobs.

1. Which words have three syllables? _____

2. What is an **astronaut**? _____
   _____

3. Why does an astronaut have to go to a special school?
   a. because space travel is not taught in other schools
   b. because traveling in space is fun
   c. because astronauts must be healthy

4. Why do you think that an astronaut needs to be smart?
   a. to learn about the stars
   b. to help out if something goes wrong
   c. to be able to exercise

5. Which of these people do you think would make the best astronaut?
   a. a gardener
   b. a skater
   c. a scientist

Name _____ Week # 40

Day #1

Jen is having a party. She is going to wear a red costume. The napkins and plates for the party are black and orange. She is going to give everyone a little bag of candy corn to take home.

1. What kind of party is Jen giving: **birthday** or **Halloween**? _____
2. Which of these might be on the table: **a carved pumpkin** or **spring flowers**? _____
3. Which of these might be Jen's costume?   a. a brown bear   b. a firefighter
4. What kind of party would you like to give? _____

Day #2

Glassfish are small fish. You can see through a glassfish's skin. You can even see its bones! Some people have glassfish for pets. They are hard to raise in a tank.

1. Underline how you think the glassfish got its name: **because it is made from glass** or **because you can see through its skin**.
2. Have you ever seen fish bones? _____ Describe them. _____
3. What kind of fish is a glassfish?   a. medium   b. small   c. large
4. Do you have a fish tank at home? _____

Day #3

People have not always had cars. Long ago, a stagecoach was the best way to go from one town to another. This big coach needed four or six horses to pull it. Stagecoach trips could take days. The ride was bumpy and hard. But it was better than other ways of travel.

1. Why did people use stagecoaches? _____
2. Underline why you think riding in a stagecoach was bumpy and hard: because **the wheels were the wrong size** or because **the roads were not good**.
3. Underline one reason that a stagecoach would be better than riding a horse: because **riding a horse would be slower** or because **the stagecoach would protect you from rain and snow**.
4. Which would you rather ride in: a **car** or a **stagecoach**? _____

Day #4

When you read a riddle, you are playing a game to answer it. The riddle gives you clues. From the clues, you can guess what the riddle is about. **Dig me up from the ground. You can make fries from me!**

1. Is a riddle more like a **puzzle** or a **rhyme**? _____
2. Don't try to guess what the riddle is about. Name one thing you dig up from the ground. _____
3. What do you use to make French fries: **vegetables** or **fruits**? _____
4. What is this riddle talking about? _____

1. Does the title below tell you what kind of player the story will be about? If so, what? _____

Be a Talented and Healthy Player

"I want to be a star athlete like you," Chris said as he ate his candy bar.

"To be a good athlete, you need to be healthy," said Michael. "You need to eat healthy food, drink plenty of water, and exercise each day. It's also important to stretch your muscles before you play any sport. Drinking water while you play is also necessary," said Michael.

"Yeah, okay. If I do that, will I be like you?" asked Chris.

"To be a star, you have to be healthy and practice all the time," explained Michael.

2. What kind of player is this story about: **piano** or **sports**? _____

3. Do you think Chris was making a healthy choice when he was eating a candy bar? _____ Why or why not? _____

"You don't practice anymore, do you?" asked Chris.

"Are you kidding? This morning I jogged five miles. Then I worked on my free throws and jump shot for two hours. That doesn't even count my team practice later on this afternoon," said Michael.

Chris was speechless. He was surprised that Michael spent that much time practicing basketball.

"Gotta go!" said Chris. "I'm off to find a healthy lunch. Then I'm going to practice dribbling!"

"Have fun!" called Michael.

4. What made Chris speechless? _____

5. What makes a star athlete?

   a. They are born amazing athletes.

   b. A lightning bolt hits them and they can do amazing things.

   c. They work hard to get even better at the things they are good at.

Answer Key

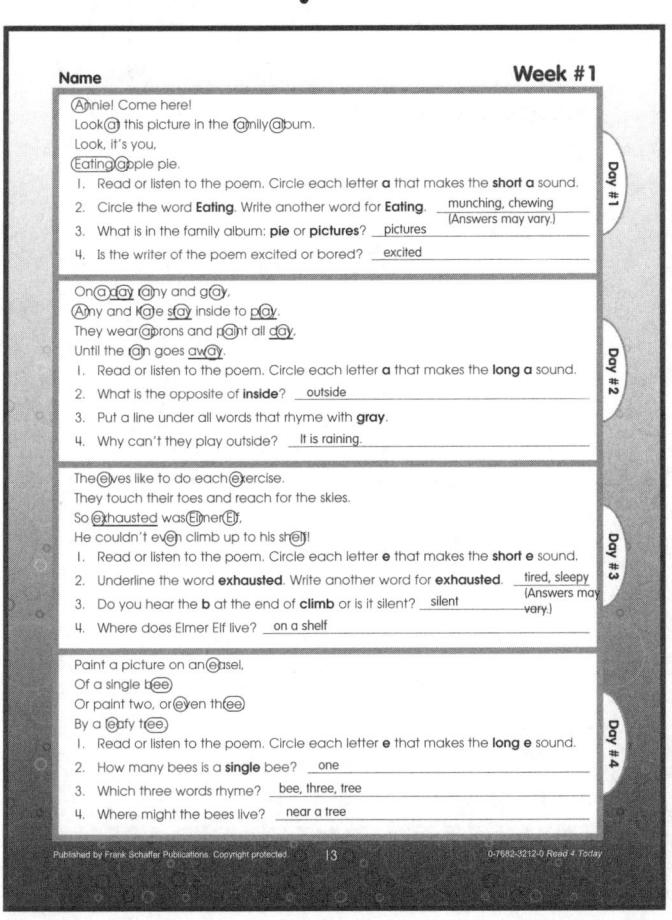

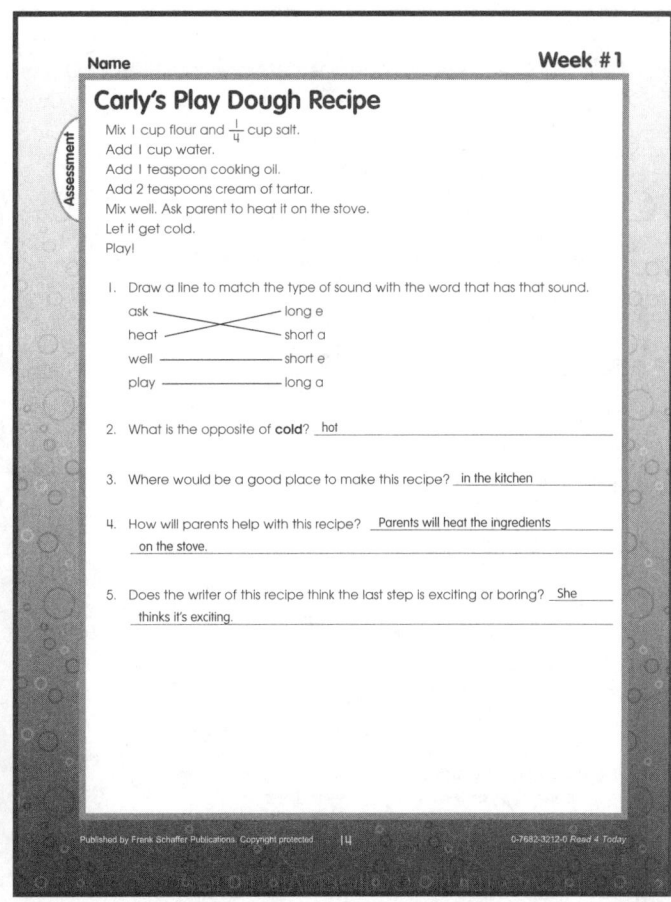

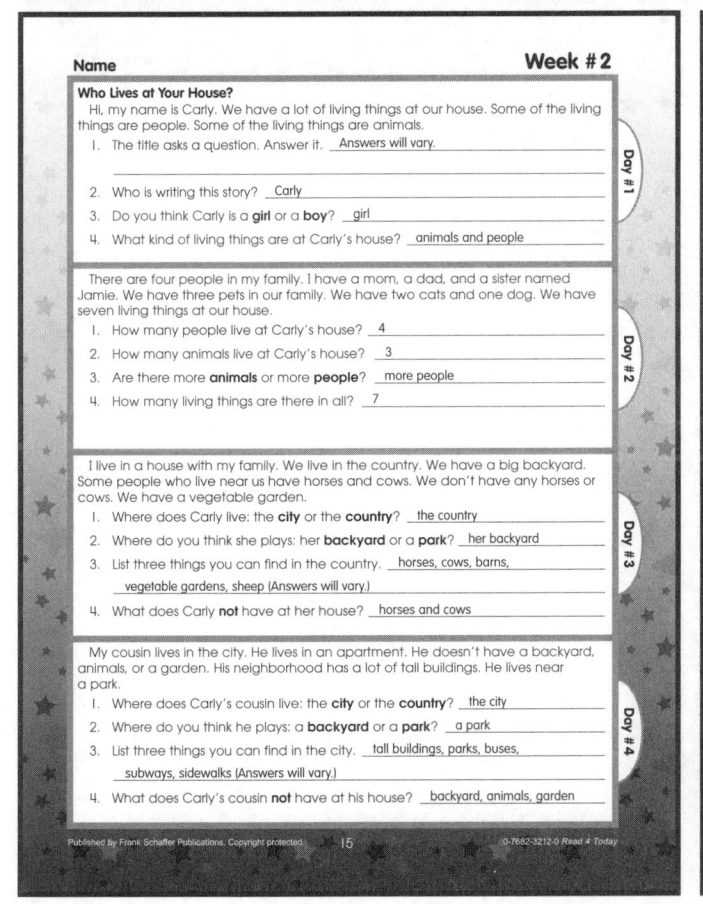

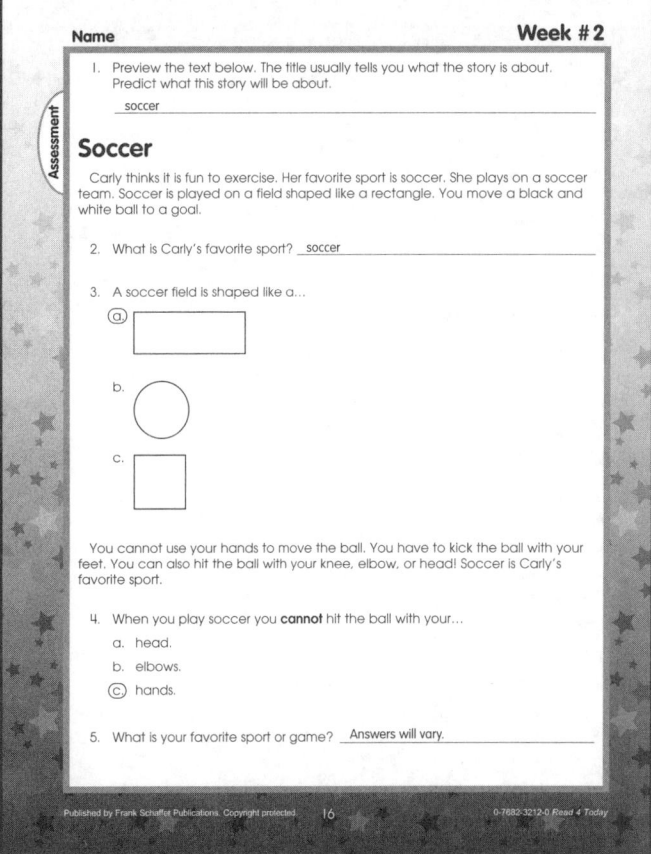

Week #1 — Day #1
A(nnie)! Come here!
Look (a)t this picture in the f(a)mily (a)lbum.
Look, it's you,
E(a)ting (a)pple pie.
1. Read or listen to the poem. Circle each letter **a** that makes the **short a** sound.
2. Circle the word **Eating**. Write another word for **Eating**. _munching, chewing_ (Answers may vary.)
3. What is in the family album: **pie** or **pictures**? _pictures_
4. Is the writer of the poem excited or bored? _excited_

Day #2
On (a) d(ay) (a)my and g(ay),
(A)my and K(a)te st(ay) inside to pl(ay).
They wear (a)prons and p(ai)nt all d(ay),
Until the r(ai)n goes (away).
1. Read or listen to the poem. Circle each letter **a** that makes the **long a** sound.
2. What is the opposite of **inside**? _outside_
3. Put a line under all words that rhyme with **gray**.
4. Why can't they play outside? _It is raining._

Day #3
Th(e) (e)lves like to do each (e)xercise.
They touch their toes and reach for the skies.
So (e)xhausted was (E)lmer (E)lf,
He couldn't ev(e)n climb up to his sh(e)lf!
1. Read or listen to the poem. Circle each letter **e** that makes the **short e** sound.
2. Underline the word **exhausted**. Write another word for **exhausted**. _tired, sleepy_ (Answers may vary.)
3. Do you hear the **b** at the end of **climb** or is it silent? _silent_
4. Where does Elmer Elf live? _on a shelf_

Day #4
Paint a picture on an (e)asel,
Of a single b(ee),
Or paint two, or (e)ven thr(ee)
By a l(ea)fy tr(ee).
1. Read or listen to the poem. Circle each letter **e** that makes the **long e** sound.
2. How many bees is a **single** bee? _one_
3. Which three words rhyme? _bee, three, tree_
4. Where might the bees live? _near a tree_

Week #1 — Assessment
Carly's Play Dough Recipe
Mix 1 cup flour and $\frac{1}{4}$ cup salt.
Add 1 cup water.
Add 1 teaspoon cooking oil.
Add 2 teaspoons cream of tartar.
Mix well. Ask parent to heat it on the stove.
Let it get cold.
Play!

1. Draw a line to match the type of sound with the word that has that sound.
   - ask — short a
   - heat — long e
   - well — short e
   - play — long a
2. What is the opposite of **cold**? _hot_
3. Where would be a good place to make this recipe? _in the kitchen_
4. How will parents help with this recipe? _Parents will heat the ingredients on the stove._
5. Does the writer of this recipe think the last step is exciting or boring? _She thinks it's exciting._

Week #2 — Day #1
Who Lives at Your House?
Hi, my name is Carly. We have a lot of living things at our house. Some of the living things are people. Some of the living things are animals.
1. The title asks a question. Answer it. _Answers will vary._
2. Who is writing this story? _Carly_
3. Do you think Carly is a **girl** or a **boy**? _girl_
4. What kind of living things are at Carly's house? _animals and people_

Day #2
There are four people in my family. I have a mom, a dad, and a sister named Jamie. We have three pets in our family. We have two cats and one dog. We have seven living things at our house.
1. How many people live at Carly's house? _4_
2. How many animals live at Carly's house? _3_
3. Are there more **animals** or more **people**? _more people_
4. How many living things are there in all? _7_

Day #3
I live in a house with my family. We live in the country. We have a big backyard. Some people who live near us have horses and cows. We don't have any horses or cows. We have a vegetable garden.
1. Where does Carly live: the **city** or the **country**? _the country_
2. Where do you think she plays: her **backyard** or a **park**? _her backyard_
3. List three things you can find in the country. _horses, cows, barns, vegetable gardens, sheep (Answers will vary.)_
4. What does Carly **not** have at her house? _horses and cows_

Day #4
My cousin lives in the city. He lives in an apartment. He doesn't have a backyard, animals, or a garden. His neighborhood has a lot of tall buildings. He lives near a park.
1. Where does Carly's cousin live: the **city** or the **country**? _the city_
2. Where do you think he plays: a **backyard** or a **park**? _a park_
3. List three things you can find in the city. _tall buildings, parks, buses, subways, sidewalks (Answers will vary.)_
4. What does Carly's cousin **not** have at his house? _backyard, animals, garden_

Week #2 — Assessment
1. Preview the text below. The title usually tells you what the story is about. Predict what this story will be about. _soccer_

Soccer
Carly thinks it is fun to exercise. Her favorite sport is soccer. She plays on a soccer team. Soccer is played on a field shaped like a rectangle. You move a black and white ball to a goal.

2. What is Carly's favorite sport? _soccer_
3. A soccer field is shaped like a...
   - (a) rectangle
   - b. circle
   - c. square

You cannot use your hands to move the ball. You have to kick the ball with your feet. You can also hit the ball with your knee, elbow, or head! Soccer is Carly's favorite sport.

4. When you play soccer you **cannot** hit the ball with your...
   - a. head.
   - b. elbows.
   - (c) hands.
5. What is your favorite sport or game? _Answers will vary._

Answer Key

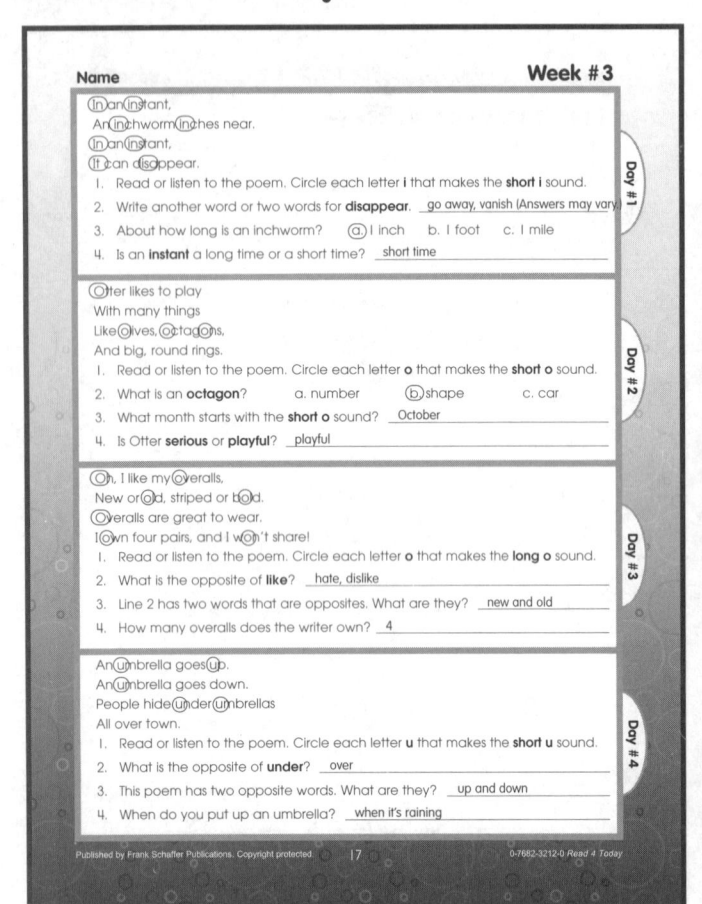

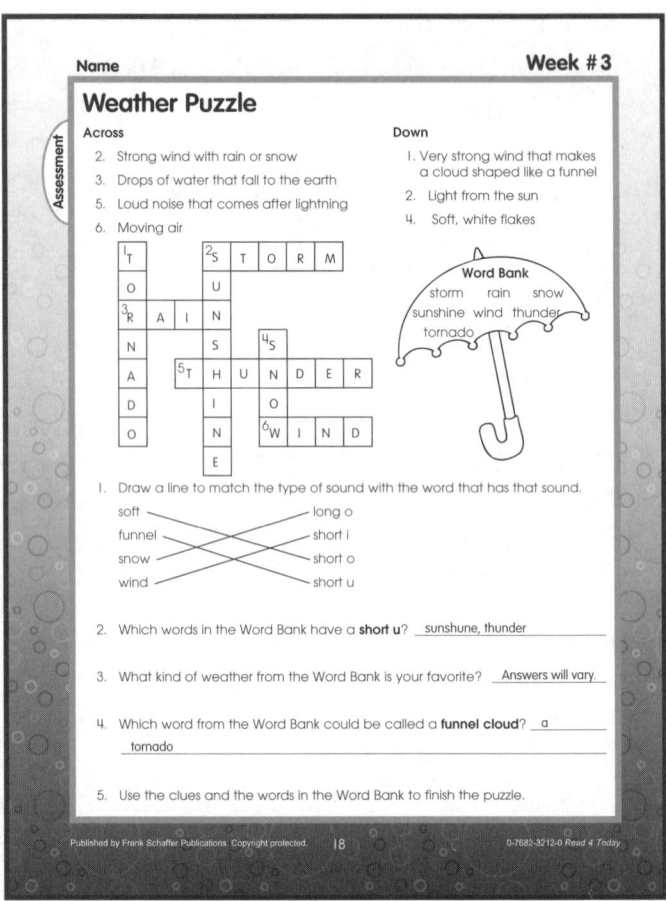

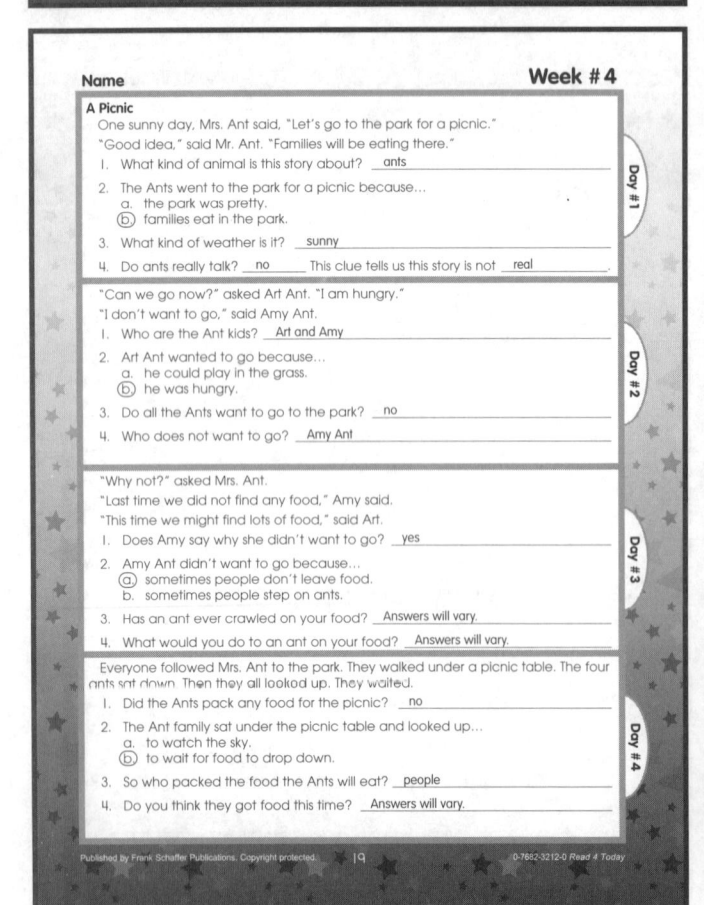

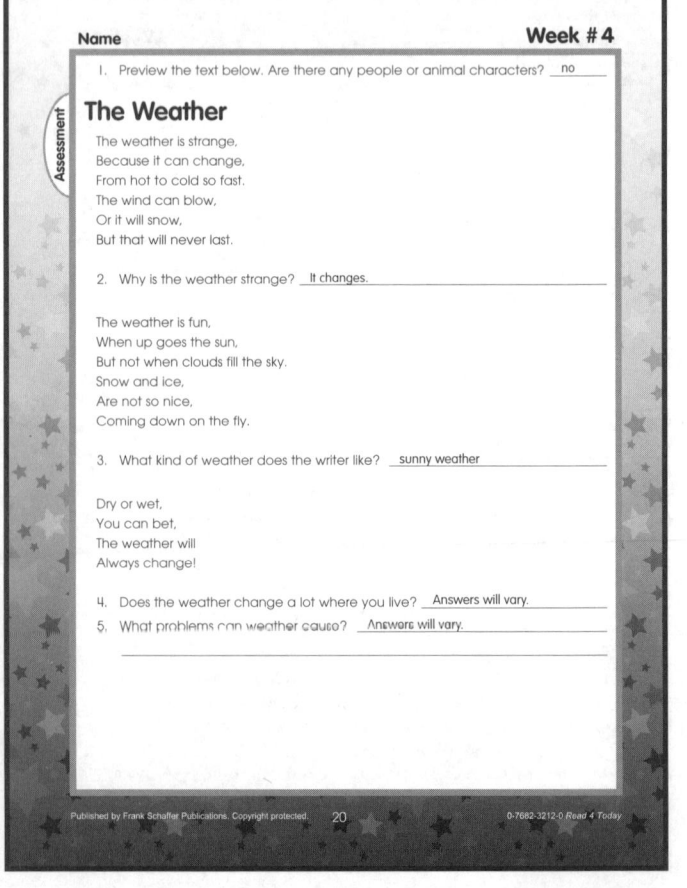

Week #3 — Day #1
(In) an (in)stant,
An (in)chworm (in)ches near.
(In) an (in)stant,
It can d(i)sappear.
1. Read or listen to the poem. Circle each letter **i** that makes the **short i** sound.
2. Write another word or two words for **disappear**. _go away, vanish (Answers may vary)_
3. About how long is an inchworm? (a.) 1 inch   b. 1 foot   c. 1 mile
4. Is an **instant** a long time or a short time? _short time_

Day #2
(O)tter likes to play
With many things
Like (o)lives, (o)ctag(o)ns,
And big, round rings.
1. Read or listen to the poem. Circle each letter **o** that makes the **short o** sound.
2. What is an **octagon**? a. number (b.) shape c. car
3. What month starts with the **short o** sound? _October_
4. Is Otter **serious** or **playful**? _playful_

Day #3
(O)h, I like my (o)veralls,
New or (o)ld, striped or b(o)ld.
(O)veralls are great to wear.
I (o)wn four pairs, and I w(o)n't share!
1. Read or listen to the poem. Circle each letter **o** that makes the **long o** sound.
2. What is the opposite of **like**? _hate, dislike_
3. Line 2 has two words that are opposites. What are they? _new and old_
4. How many overalls does the writer own? _4_

Day #4
An (u)mbrella goes (u)p.
An (u)mbrella goes down.
People hide (u)nder (u)mbrellas
All over town.
1. Read or listen to the poem. Circle each letter **u** that makes the **short u** sound.
2. What is the opposite of **under**? _over_
3. This poem has two opposite words. What are they? _up and down_
4. When do you put up an umbrella? _when it's raining_

Week #3 — Assessment: Weather Puzzle

Across
2. Strong wind with rain or snow
3. Drops of water that fall to the earth
5. Loud noise that comes after lightning
6. Moving air

Down
1. Very strong wind that makes a cloud shaped like a funnel
2. Light from the sun
4. Soft, white flakes

Crossword answers: 2 across STORM; 3 across RAIN; 5 across THUNDER; 6 across WIND; 1 down TORNADO; 2 down SUN; 4 down SNOW

Word Bank: storm, rain, snow, sunshine, wind, thunder, tornado

1. Draw a line to match the type of sound with the word that has that sound.
   soft — short o
   funnel — short u
   snow — long o
   wind — short i
2. Which words in the Word Bank have a **short u**? _sunshine, thunder_
3. What kind of weather from the Word Bank is your favorite? _Answers will vary._
4. Which word from the Word Bank could be called a **funnel cloud**? _a tornado_
5. Use the clues and the words in the Word Bank to finish the puzzle.

Week #4 — Day #1
A Picnic
One sunny day, Mrs. Ant said, "Let's go to the park for a picnic."
"Good idea," said Mr. Ant. "Families will be eating there."
1. What kind of animal is this story about? _ants_
2. The Ants went to the park for a picnic because…
   a. the park was pretty.
   (b.) families eat in the park.
3. What kind of weather is it? _sunny_
4. Do ants really talk? _no_ This clue tells us this story is not _real_

Day #2
"Can we go now?" asked Art Ant. "I am hungry."
"I don't want to go," said Amy Ant.
1. Who are the Ant kids? _Art and Amy_
2. Art Ant wanted to go because…
   a. he could play in the grass.
   (b.) he was hungry.
3. Do all the Ants want to go to the park? _no_
4. Who does not want to go? _Amy Ant_

Day #3
"Why not?" asked Mrs. Ant.
"Last time we did not find any food," Amy said.
"This time we might find lots of food," said Art.
1. Does Amy say why she didn't want to go? _yes_
2. Amy Ant didn't want to go because…
   (a.) sometimes people don't leave food.
   b. sometimes people step on ants.
3. Has an ant ever crawled on your food? _Answers will vary._
4. What would you do to an ant on your food? _Answers will vary._

Day #4
Everyone followed Mrs. Ant to the park. They walked under a picnic table. The four ants sat down. Then they all looked up. They waited.
1. Did the Ants pack any food for the picnic? _no_
2. The Ant family sat under the picnic table and looked up.
   a. to watch the sky.
   (b.) to wait for food to drop down.
3. So who packed the food the Ants will eat? _people_
4. Do you think they got food this time? _Answers will vary._

Week #4 — Assessment: The Weather

1. Preview the text below. Are there any people or animal characters? _no_

The weather is strange,
Because it can change,
From hot to cold so fast.
The wind can blow,
Or it will snow,
But that will never last.

2. Why is the weather strange? _It changes._

The weather is fun,
When up goes the sun,
But not when clouds fill the sky.
Snow and ice,
Are not so nice,
Coming down on the fly.

3. What kind of weather does the writer like? _sunny weather_

Dry or wet,
You can bet,
The weather will
Always change!

4. Does the weather change a lot where you live? _Answers will vary._
5. What problems can weather cause? _Answers will vary._

94

Answer Key

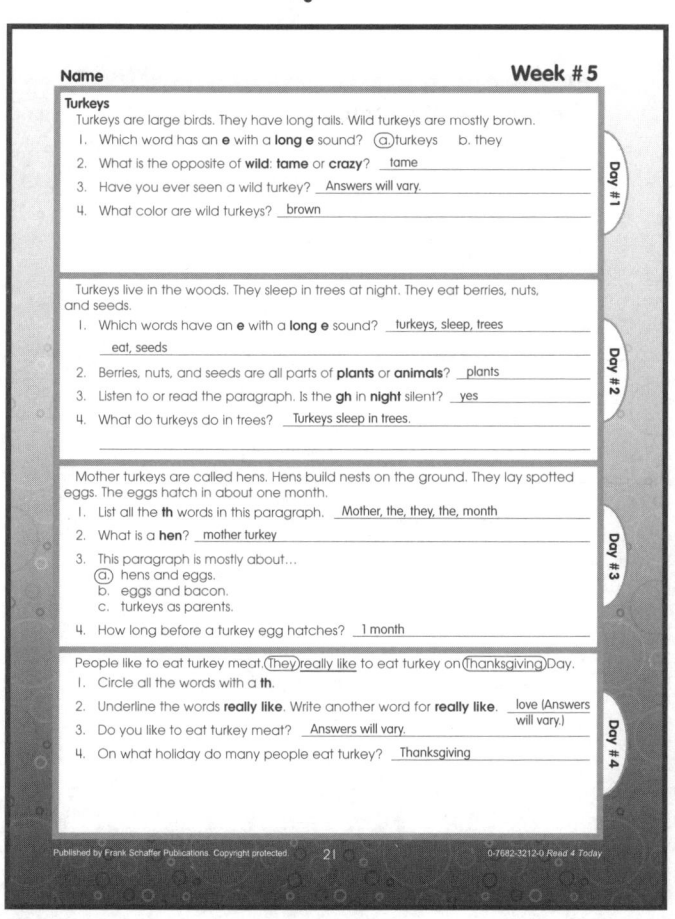

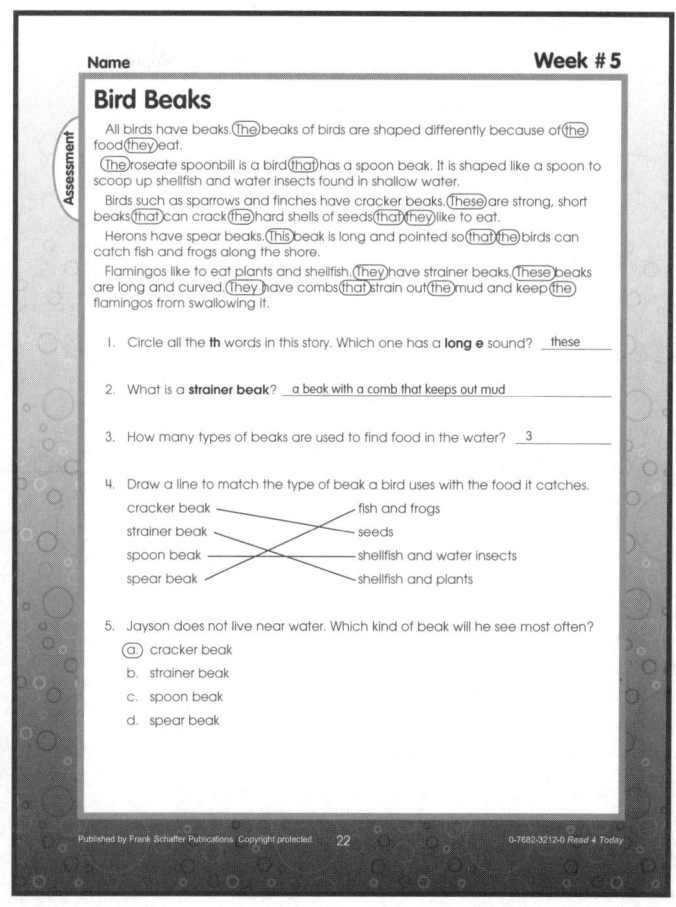

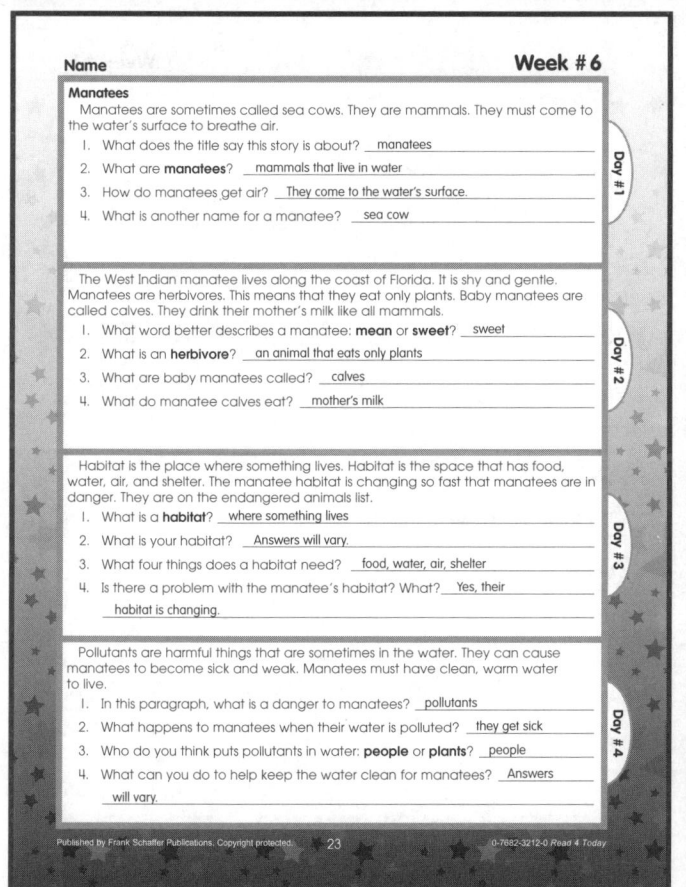

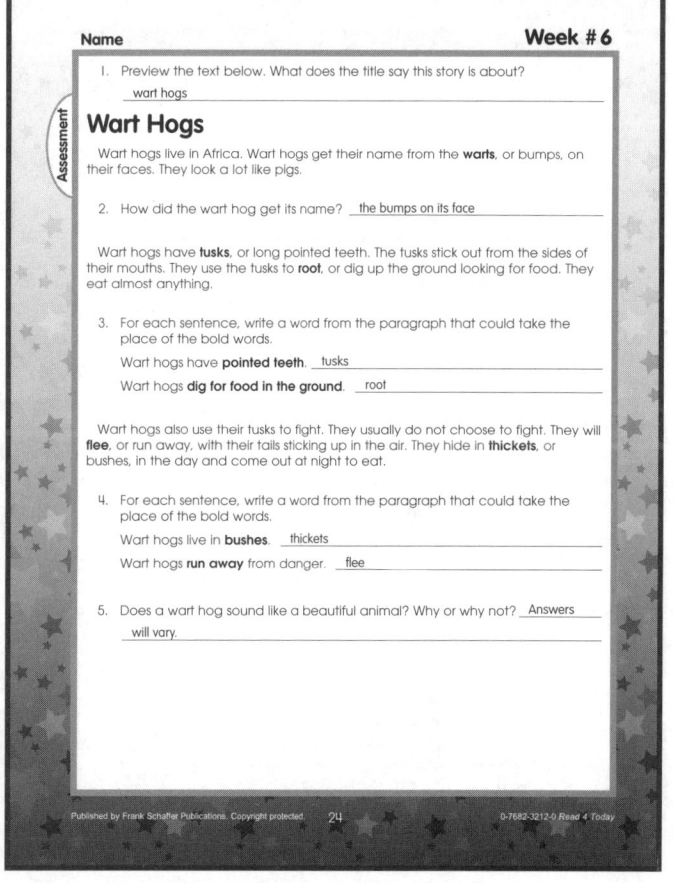

Week #5 — Turkeys

Turkeys are large birds. They have long tails. Wild turkeys are mostly brown.

Day #1
1. Which word has an **e** with a **long e** sound? (a) turkeys   b. they
2. What is the opposite of **wild**: **tame** or **crazy**? _tame_
3. Have you ever seen a wild turkey? _Answers will vary._
4. What color are wild turkeys? _brown_

Turkeys live in the woods. They sleep in trees at night. They eat berries, nuts, and seeds.

Day #2
1. Which words have an **e** with a **long e** sound? _turkeys, sleep, trees, eat, seeds_
2. Berries, nuts, and seeds are all parts of **plants** or **animals**? _plants_
3. Listen to or read the paragraph. Is the **gh** in **night** silent? _yes_
4. What do turkeys do in trees? _Turkeys sleep in trees._

Mother turkeys are called hens. Hens build nests on the ground. They lay spotted eggs. The eggs hatch in about one month.

Day #3
1. List all the **th** words in this paragraph. _Mother, the, they, the, month_
2. What is a **hen**? _mother turkey_
3. This paragraph is mostly about…
   (a) hens and eggs.
   b. eggs and bacon.
   c. turkeys as parents.
4. How long before a turkey egg hatches? _1 month_

People like to eat turkey meat. (They) really like to eat turkey on (Thanksgiving) Day.

Day #4
1. Circle all the words with a **th**.
2. Underline the words **really like**. Write another word for **really like**. _love (Answers will vary.)_
3. Do you like to eat turkey meat? _Answers will vary._
4. On what holiday do many people eat turkey? _Thanksgiving_

Week #5 — Bird Beaks (Assessment)

All birds have beaks. (The) beaks of birds are shaped differently because of (the) food (they) eat.
(The) roseate spoonbill is a bird (that) has a spoon beak. It is shaped like a spoon to scoop up shellfish and water insects found in shallow water.
Birds such as sparrows and finches have cracker beaks. (These) are strong, short beaks (that) can crack (the) hard shells of seeds (that) (they) like to eat.
Herons have spear beaks. (This) beak is long and pointed so (that) (the) birds can catch fish and frogs along the shore.
Flamingos like to eat plants and shellfish. (They) have strainer beaks. (These) beaks are long and curved. (They) have combs (that) strain out (the) mud and keep (the) flamingos from swallowing it.

1. Circle all the **th** words in this story. Which one has a **long e** sound? _these_
2. What is a **strainer beak**? _a beak with a comb that keeps out mud_
3. How many types of beaks are used to find food in the water? _3_
4. Draw a line to match the type of beak a bird uses with the food it catches.
   cracker beak — fish and frogs
   strainer beak — seeds
   spoon beak — shellfish and water insects
   spear beak — shellfish and plants
5. Jayson does not live near water. Which kind of beak will he see most often?
   (a) cracker beak
   b. strainer beak
   c. spoon beak
   d. spear beak

Week #6 — Manatees

Manatees are sometimes called sea cows. They are mammals. They must come to the water's surface to breathe air.

Day #1
1. What does the title say this story is about? _manatees_
2. What are **manatees**? _mammals that live in water_
3. How do manatees get air? _They come to the water's surface._
4. What is another name for a manatee? _sea cow_

The West Indian manatee lives along the coast of Florida. It is shy and gentle. Manatees are herbivores. This means that they eat only plants. Baby manatees are called calves. They drink their mother's milk like all mammals.

Day #2
1. What word better describes a manatee: **mean** or **sweet**? _sweet_
2. What is an **herbivore**? _an animal that eats only plants_
3. What are baby manatees called? _calves_
4. What do manatee calves eat? _mother's milk_

Habitat is the place where something lives. Habitat is the space that has food, water, air, and shelter. The manatee habitat is changing so fast that manatees are in danger. They are on the endangered animals list.

Day #3
1. What is a **habitat**? _where something lives_
2. What is your habitat? _Answers will vary._
3. What four things does a habitat need? _food, water, air, shelter_
4. Is there a problem with the manatee's habitat? What? _Yes, their habitat is changing._

Pollutants are harmful things that are sometimes in the water. They can cause manatees to become sick and weak. Manatees must have clean, warm water to live.

Day #4
1. In this paragraph, what is a danger to manatees? _pollutants_
2. What happens to manatees when their water is polluted? _they get sick_
3. Who do you think puts pollutants in water: **people** or **plants**? _people_
4. What can you do to help keep the water clean for manatees? _Answers will vary._

Week #6 — Wart Hogs (Assessment)

1. Preview the text below. What does the title say this story is about? _wart hogs_

Wart hogs live in Africa. Wart hogs get their name from the **warts**, or bumps, on their faces. They look a lot like pigs.

2. How did the wart hog get its name? _the bumps on its face_

Wart hogs have **tusks**, or long pointed teeth. The tusks stick out from the sides of their mouths. They use the tusks to **root**, or dig up the ground looking for food. They eat almost anything.

3. For each sentence, write a word from the paragraph that could take the place of the bold words.
   Wart hogs have **pointed teeth**. _tusks_
   Wart hogs **dig for food in the ground**. _root_

Wart hogs also use their tusks to fight. They usually do not choose to fight. They will **flee**, or run away, with their tails sticking up in the air. They hide in **thickets**, or bushes, in the day and come out at night to eat.

4. For each sentence, write a word from the paragraph that could take the place of the bold words.
   Wart hogs live in **bushes**. _thickets_
   Wart hogs **run away** from danger. _flee_

5. Does a wart hog sound like a beautiful animal? Why or why not? _Answers will vary._

Published by Frank Schaffer Publications. Copyright protected.   95   0-7682-3212-0 *Read 4 Today*

Answer Key

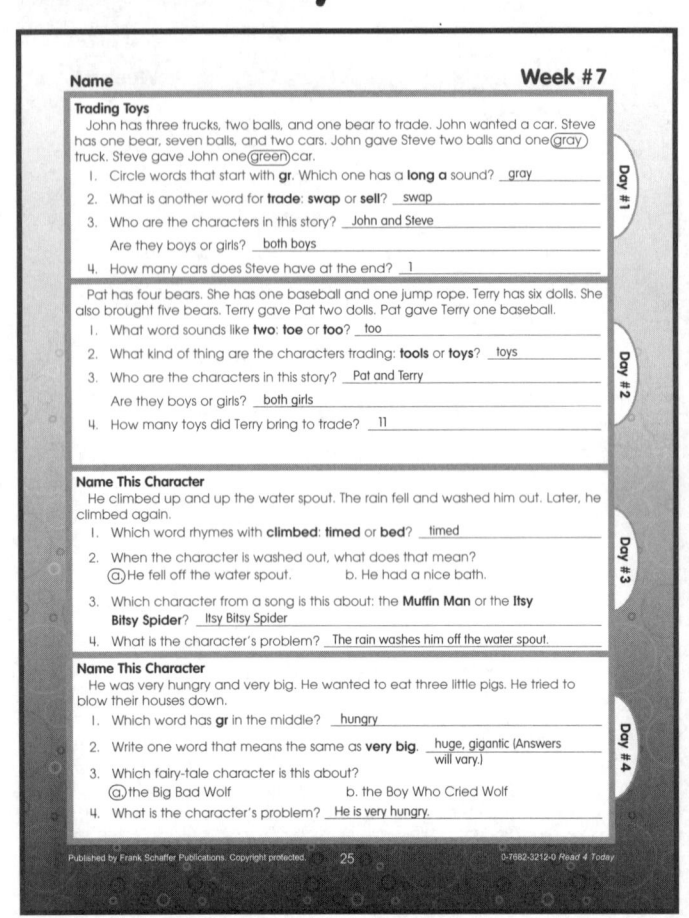

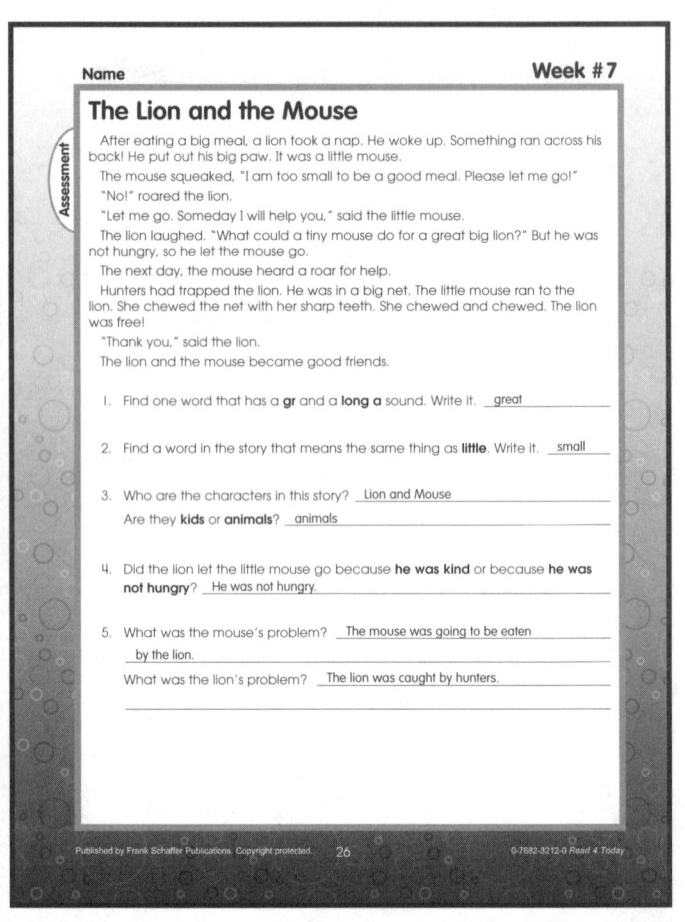

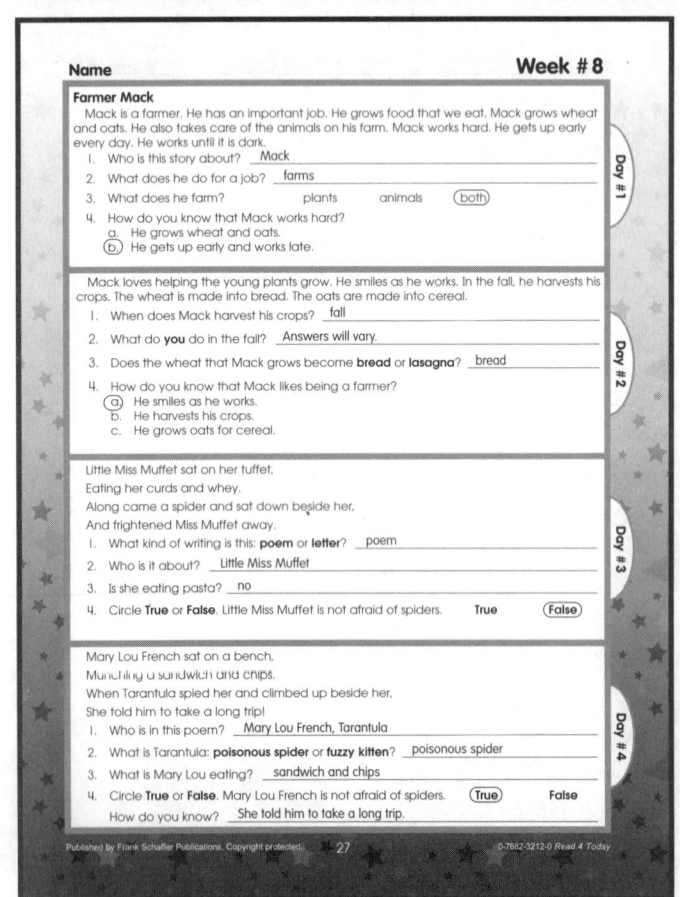

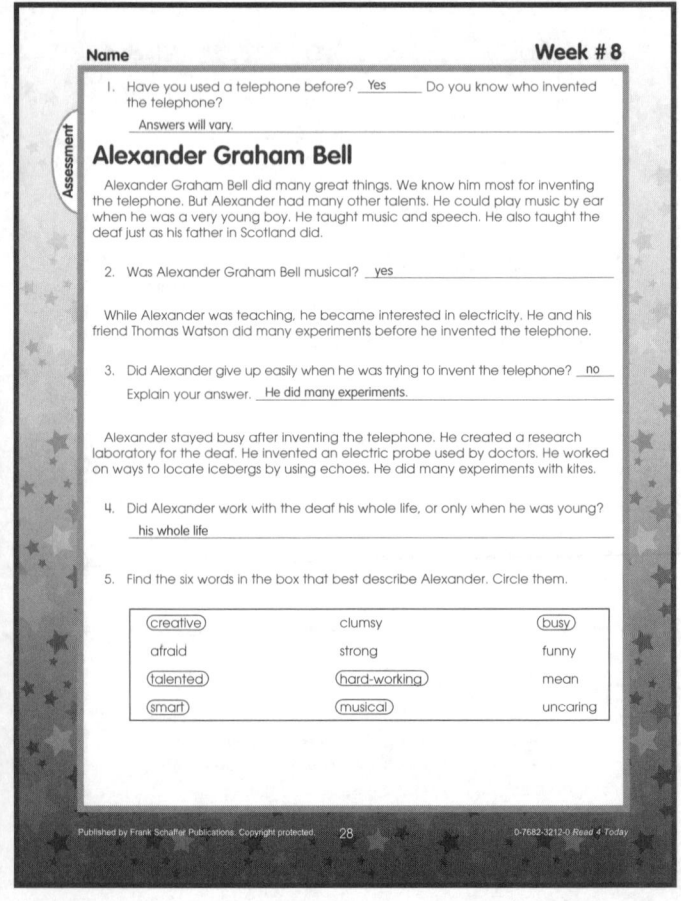

Week #7 — Trading Toys

John has three trucks, two balls, and one bear to trade. John wanted a car. Steve has one bear, seven balls, and two cars. John gave Steve two balls and one (gray) truck. Steve gave John one (green) car.

Day #1
1. Circle words that start with **gr**. Which one has a **long a** sound? __gray__
2. What is another word for **trade**: **swap** or **sell**? __swap__
3. Who are the characters in this story? __John and Steve__
   Are they boys or girls? __both boys__
4. How many cars does Steve have at the end? __1__

Pat has four bears. She has one baseball and one jump rope. Terry has six dolls. She also brought five bears. Terry gave Pat two dolls. Pat gave Terry one baseball.

Day #2
1. What word sounds like **two**: **toe** or **too**? __too__
2. What kind of thing are the characters trading: **tools** or **toys**? __toys__
3. Who are the characters in this story? __Pat and Terry__
   Are they boys or girls? __both girls__
4. How many toys did Terry bring to trade? __11__

Name This Character
He climbed up and up the water spout. The rain fell and washed him out. Later, he climbed again.

Day #3
1. Which word rhymes with **climbed**: **timed** or **bed**? __timed__
2. When the character is washed out, what does that mean?
   (a) He fell off the water spout.   b. He had a nice bath.
3. Which character from a song is this about: the **Muffin Man** or the **Itsy Bitsy Spider**? __Itsy Bitsy Spider__
4. What is the character's problem? __The rain washes him off the water spout.__

Name This Character
He was very hungry and very big. He wanted to eat three little pigs. He tried to blow their houses down.

Day #4
1. Which word has **gr** in the middle? __hungry__
2. Write one word that means the same as **very big**. __huge, gigantic (Answers will vary.)__
3. Which fairy-tale character is this about?
   (a) the Big Bad Wolf   b. the Boy Who Cried Wolf
4. What is the character's problem? __He is very hungry.__

Week #7 — Assessment — The Lion and the Mouse

After eating a big meal, a lion took a nap. He woke up. Something ran across his back! He put out his big paw. It was a little mouse.
The mouse squeaked, "I am too small to be a good meal. Please let me go!"
"No!" roared the lion.
"Let me go. Someday I will help you," said the little mouse.
The lion laughed. "What could a tiny mouse do for a great big lion?" But he was not hungry, so he let the mouse go.
The next day, the mouse heard a roar for help.
Hunters had trapped the lion. He was in a big net. The little mouse ran to the lion. She chewed the net with her sharp teeth. She chewed and chewed. The lion was free!
"Thank you," said the lion.
The lion and the mouse became good friends.

1. Find one word that has a **gr** and a **long a** sound. Write it. __great__
2. Find a word in the story that means the same thing as **little**. Write it. __small__
3. Who are the characters in this story? __Lion and Mouse__
   Are they **kids** or **animals**? __animals__
4. Did the lion let the little mouse go because **he was kind** or because **he was not hungry**? __He was not hungry.__
5. What was the mouse's problem? __The mouse was going to be eaten by the lion.__
   What was the lion's problem? __The lion was caught by hunters.__

Week #8 — Farmer Mack

Mack is a farmer. He has an important job. He grows food that we eat. Mack grows wheat and oats. He also takes care of the animals on his farm. Mack works hard. He gets up early every day. He works until it is dark.

Day #1
1. Who is this story about? __Mack__
2. What does he do for a job? __farms__
3. What does he farm?   plants   animals   (both)
4. How do you know that Mack works hard?
   a. He grows wheat and oats.
   (b) He gets up early and works late.

Mack loves helping the young plants grow. He smiles as he works. In the fall, he harvests his crops. The wheat is made into bread. The oats are made into cereal.

Day #2
1. When does Mack harvest his crops? __fall__
2. What do **you** do in the fall? __Answers will vary.__
3. Does the wheat that Mack grows become **bread** or **lasagna**? __bread__
4. How do you know that Mack likes being a farmer?
   (a) He smiles as he works.
   b. He harvests his crops.
   c. He grows oats for cereal.

Little Miss Muffet sat on her tuffet,
Eating her curds and whey.
Along came a spider and sat down beside her,
And frightened Miss Muffet away.

Day #3
1. What kind of writing is this: **poem** or **letter**? __poem__
2. Who is it about? __Little Miss Muffet__
3. Is she eating pasta? __no__
4. Circle **True** or **False**. Little Miss Muffet is not afraid of spiders.   True   (False)

Mary Lou French sat on a bench,
Munching a sandwich and chips.
When Tarantula spied her and climbed up beside her,
She told him to take a long trip!

Day #4
1. Who is in this poem? __Mary Lou French, Tarantula__
2. What is Tarantula: **poisonous spider** or **fuzzy kitten**? __poisonous spider__
3. What is Mary Lou eating? __sandwich and chips__
4. Circle **True** or **False**. Mary Lou French is not afraid of spiders.   (True)   False
   How do you know? __She told him to take a long trip.__

Week #8 — Assessment

1. Have you used a telephone before? __Yes__   Do you know who invented the telephone? __Answers will vary.__

Alexander Graham Bell

Alexander Graham Bell did many great things. We know him most for inventing the telephone. But Alexander had many other talents. He could play music by ear when he was a very young boy. He taught music and speech. He also taught the deaf just as his father in Scotland did.

2. Was Alexander Graham Bell musical? __yes__

While Alexander was teaching, he became interested in electricity. He and his friend Thomas Watson did many experiments before he invented the telephone.

3. Did Alexander give up easily when he was trying to invent the telephone? __no__
   Explain your answer. __He did many experiments.__

Alexander stayed busy after inventing the telephone. He created a research laboratory for the deaf. He invented an electric probe used by doctors. He worked on ways to locate icebergs by using echoes. He did many experiments with kites.

4. Did Alexander work with the deaf his whole life, or only when he was young? __his whole life__
5. Find the six words in the box that best describe Alexander. Circle them.

(creative)	clumsy	(busy)
afraid	strong	funny
(talented)	(hard-working)	mean
(smart)	(musical)	uncaring

Answer Key

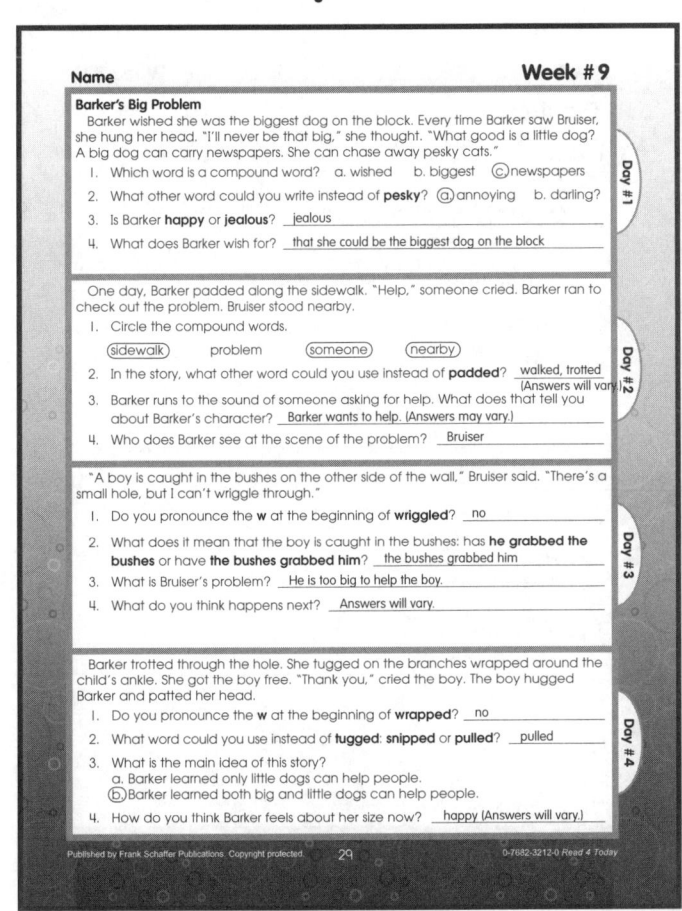

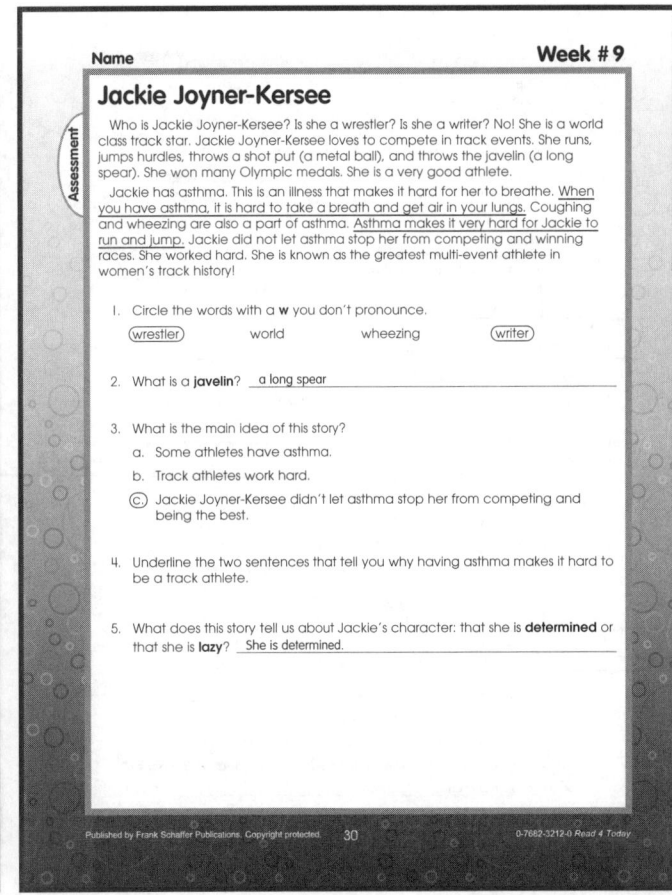

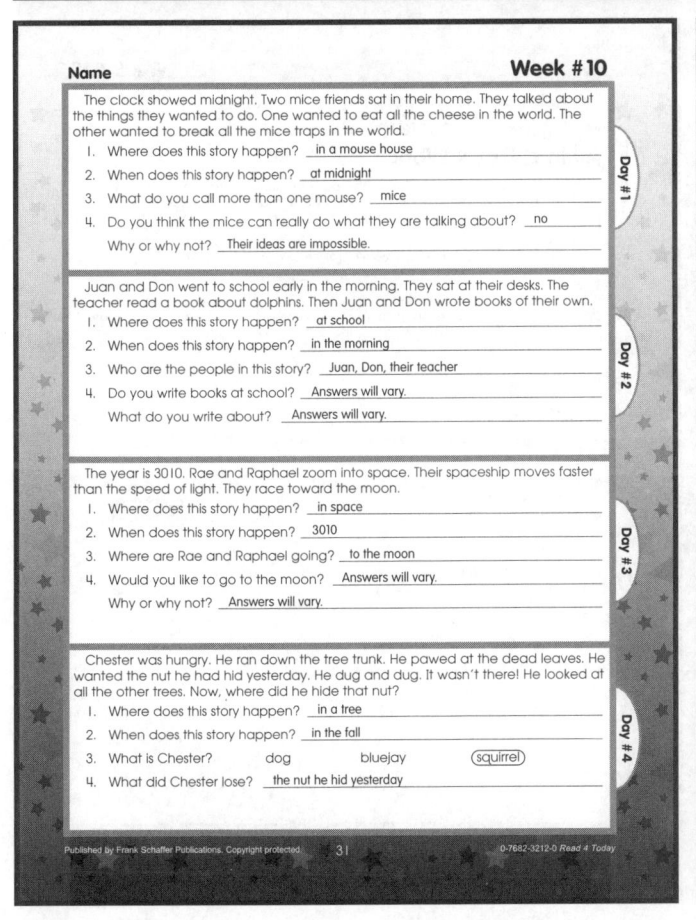

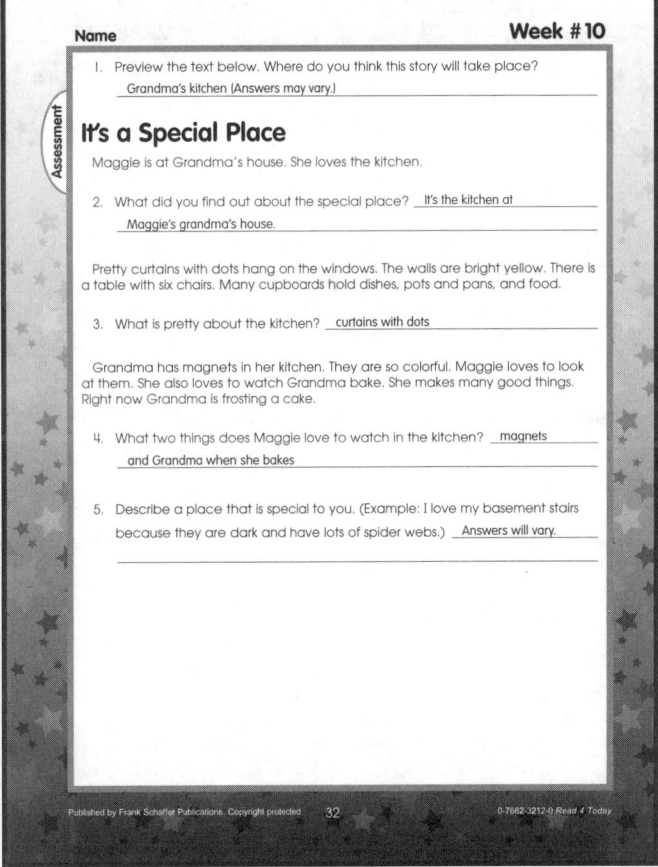

Week #9

Barker's Big Problem

Barker wished she was the biggest dog on the block. Every time Barker saw Bruiser, she hung her head. "I'll never be that big," she thought. "What good is a little dog? A big dog can carry newspapers. She can chase away pesky cats."

Day #1
1. Which word is a compound word? a. wished b. biggest (c.) newspapers
2. What other word could you write instead of **pesky**? (a.) annoying b. darling
3. Is Barker **happy** or **jealous**? __jealous__
4. What does Barker wish for? __that she could be the biggest dog on the block__

One day, Barker padded along the sidewalk. "Help," someone cried. Barker ran to check out the problem. Bruiser stood nearby.

Day #2
1. Circle the compound words.
   (sidewalk)   problem   (someone)   (nearby)
2. In the story, what other word could you use instead of **padded**? __walked, trotted (Answers will vary)__
3. Barker runs to the sound of someone asking for help. What does that tell you about Barker's character? __Barker wants to help. (Answers may vary.)__
4. Who does Barker see at the scene of the problem? __Bruiser__

"A boy is caught in the bushes on the other side of the wall," Bruiser said. "There's a small hole, but I can't wriggle through."

Day #3
1. Do you pronounce the **w** at the beginning of **wriggled**? __no__
2. What does it mean that the boy is caught in the bushes: has **he grabbed the bushes** or have **the bushes grabbed him**? __the bushes grabbed him__
3. What is Bruiser's problem? __He is too big to help the boy.__
4. What do you think happens next? __Answers will vary.__

Barker trotted through the hole. She tugged on the branches wrapped around the child's ankle. She got the boy free. "Thank you," cried the boy. The boy hugged Barker and patted her head.

Day #4
1. Do you pronounce the **w** at the beginning of **wrapped**? __no__
2. What word could you use instead of **tugged**: **snipped** or **pulled**? __pulled__
3. What is the main idea of this story?
   a. Barker learned only little dogs can help people.
   (b.) Barker learned both big and little dogs can help people.
4. How do you think Barker feels about her size now? __happy (Answers will vary.)__

Week #9 — Assessment

Jackie Joyner-Kersee

Who is Jackie Joyner-Kersee? Is she a wrestler? Is she a writer? No! She is a world class track star. Jackie Joyner-Kersee loves to compete in track events. She runs, jumps hurdles, throws a shot put (a metal ball), and throws the javelin (a long spear). She won many Olympic medals. She is a very good athlete.

Jackie has asthma. This is an illness that makes it hard for her to breathe. <u>When you have asthma, it is hard to take a breath and get air in your lungs.</u> Coughing and wheezing are also a part of asthma. <u>Asthma makes it very hard for Jackie to run and jump.</u> Jackie did not let asthma stop her from competing and winning races. She worked hard. She is known as the greatest multi-event athlete in women's track history!

1. Circle the words with a **w** you don't pronounce.
   (wrestler)   world   wheezing   (writer)

2. What is a **javelin**? __a long spear__

3. What is the main idea of this story?
   a. Some athletes have asthma.
   b. Track athletes work hard.
   (c.) Jackie Joyner-Kersee didn't let asthma stop her from competing and being the best.

4. Underline the two sentences that tell you why having asthma makes it hard to be a track athlete.

5. What does this story tell us about Jackie's character: that she is **determined** or that she is **lazy**? __She is determined.__

Week #10

The clock showed midnight. Two mice friends sat in their home. They talked about the things they wanted to do. One wanted to eat all the cheese in the world. The other wanted to break all the mice traps in the world.

Day #1
1. Where does this story happen? __in a mouse house__
2. When does this story happen? __at midnight__
3. What do you call more than one mouse? __mice__
4. Do you think the mice can really do what they are talking about? __no__
   Why or why not? __Their ideas are impossible.__

Juan and Don went to school early in the morning. They sat at their desks. The teacher read a book about dolphins. Then Juan and Don wrote books of their own.

Day #2
1. Where does this story happen? __at school__
2. When does this story happen? __in the morning__
3. Who are the people in this story? __Juan, Don, their teacher__
4. Do you write books at school? __Answers will vary.__
   What do you write about? __Answers will vary.__

The year is 3010. Rae and Raphael zoom into space. Their spaceship moves faster than the speed of light. They race toward the moon.

Day #3
1. Where does this story happen? __in space__
2. When does this story happen? __3010__
3. Where are Rae and Raphael going? __to the moon__
4. Would you like to go to the moon? __Answers will vary.__
   Why or why not? __Answers will vary.__

Chester was hungry. He ran down the tree trunk. He pawed at the dead leaves. He wanted the nut he had hid yesterday. He dug and dug. It wasn't there! He looked at all the other trees. Now, where did he hide that nut?

Day #4
1. Where does this story happen? __in a tree__
2. When does this story happen? __in the fall__
3. What is Chester?   dog   bluejay   (squirrel)
4. What did Chester lose? __the nut he hid yesterday__

Week #10 — Assessment

1. Preview the text below. Where do you think this story will take place? __Grandma's kitchen (Answers may vary.)__

It's a Special Place

Maggie is at Grandma's house. She loves the kitchen.

2. What did you find out about the special place? __It's the kitchen at Maggie's grandma's house.__

Pretty curtains with dots hang on the windows. The walls are bright yellow. There is a table with six chairs. Many cupboards hold dishes, pots and pans, and food.

3. What is pretty about the kitchen? __curtains with dots__

Grandma has magnets in her kitchen. They are so colorful. Maggie loves to look at them. She also loves to watch Grandma bake. She makes many good things. Right now Grandma is frosting a cake.

4. What two things does Maggie love to watch in the kitchen? __magnets and Grandma when she bakes__

5. Describe a place that is special to you. (Example: I love my basement stairs because they are dark and have lots of spider webs.) __Answers will vary.__

Answer Key

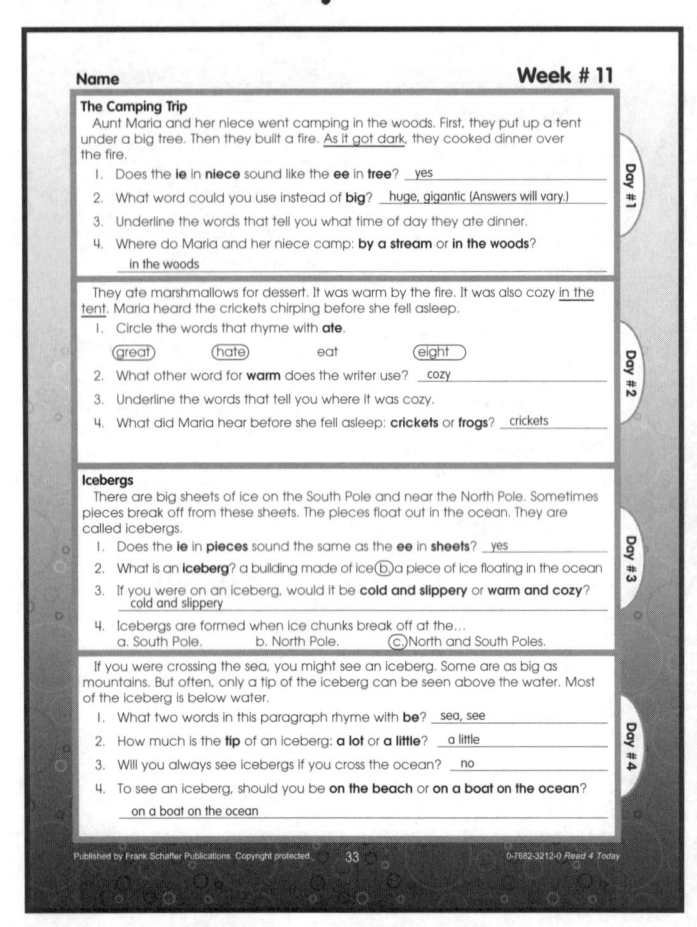

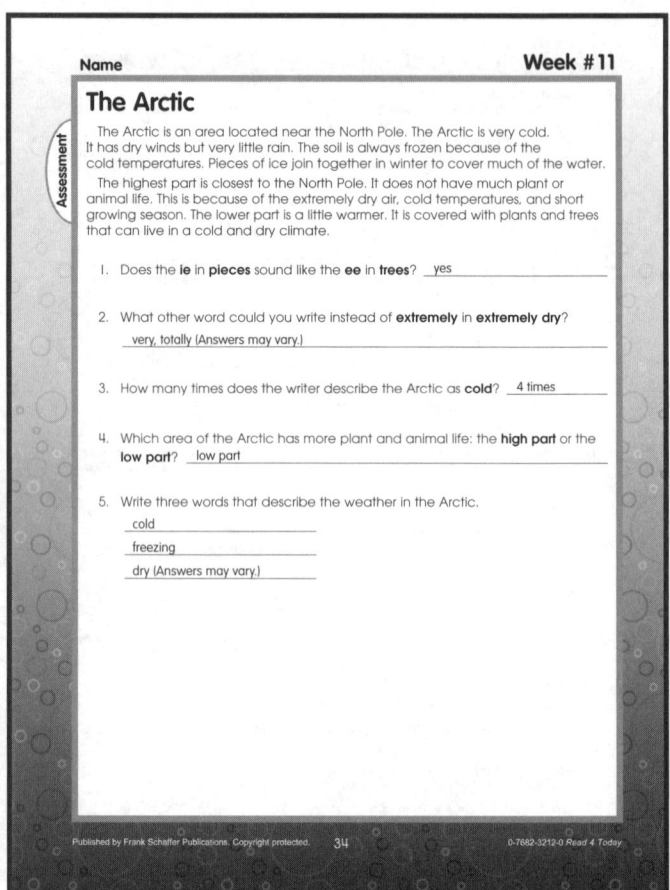

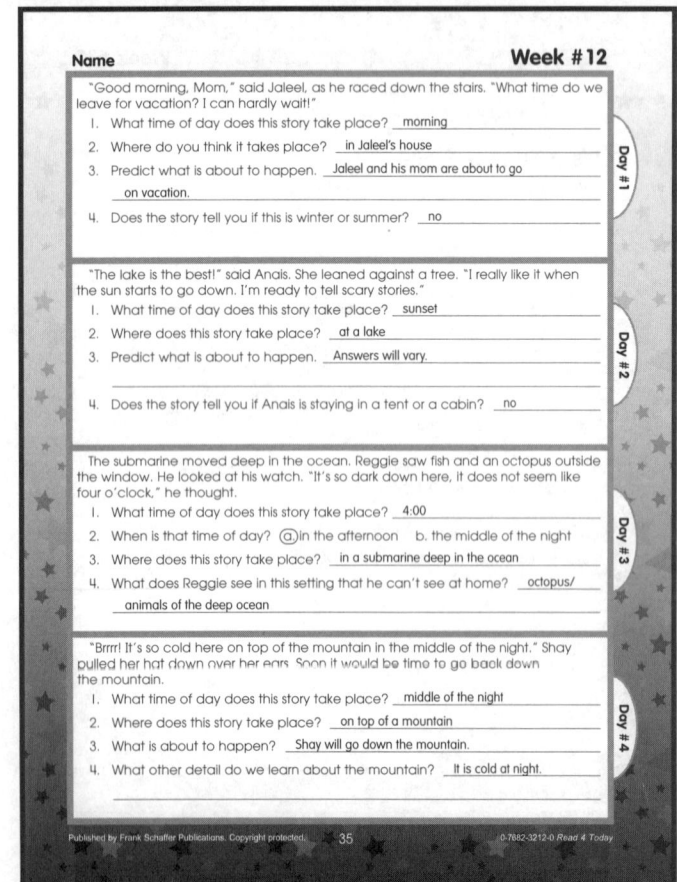

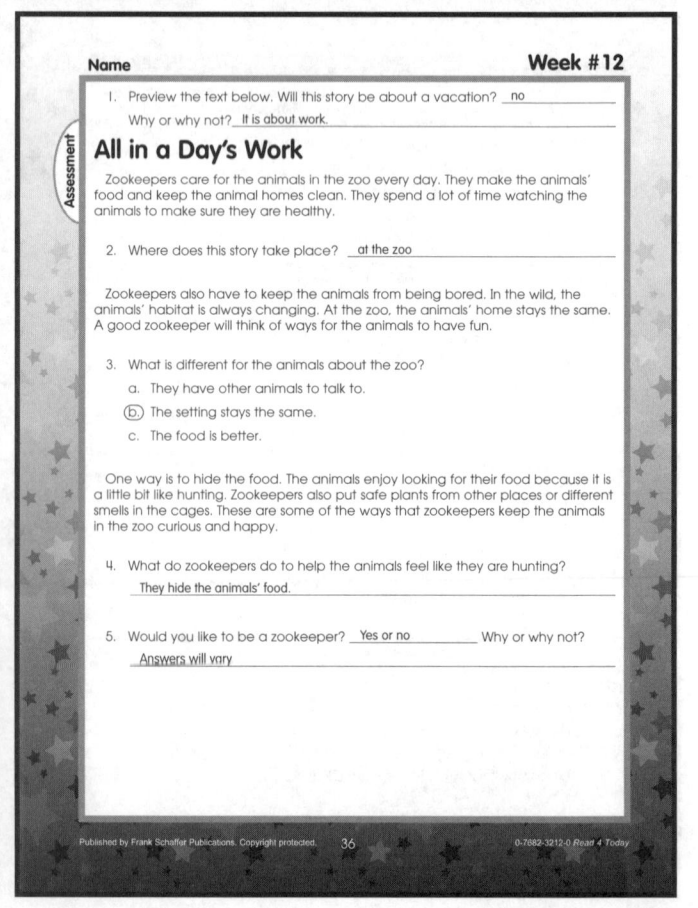

Week #11

The Camping Trip
Aunt Maria and her niece went camping in the woods. First, they put up a tent under a big tree. Then they built a fire. **As it got dark**, they cooked dinner over the fire.

Day #1
1. Does the **ie** in **niece** sound like the **ee** in **tree**? _yes_
2. What word could you use instead of **big**? _huge, gigantic (Answers will vary.)_
3. Underline the words that tell you what time of day they ate dinner.
4. Where do Maria and her niece camp: **by a stream** or **in the woods**? _in the woods_

They ate marshmallows for dessert. It was warm by the fire. It was also cozy **in the tent**. Maria heard the crickets chirping before she fell asleep.

Day #2
1. Circle the words that rhyme with **ate**.
   (great)   (hate)   eat   (eight)
2. What other word for **warm** does the writer use? _cozy_
3. Underline the words that tell you where it was cozy.
4. What did Maria hear before she fell asleep: **crickets** or **frogs**? _crickets_

Icebergs
There are big sheets of ice on the South Pole and near the North Pole. Sometimes pieces break off from these sheets. The pieces float out in the ocean. They are called icebergs.

Day #3
1. Does the **ie** in **pieces** sound the same as the **ee** in **sheets**? _yes_
2. What is an **iceberg**? a. a building made of ice (b.) a piece of ice floating in the ocean
3. If you were on an iceberg, would it be **cold and slippery** or **warm and cozy**? _cold and slippery_
4. Icebergs are formed when ice chunks break off at the…
   a. South Pole.   b. North Pole.   (c.) North and South Poles.

If you were crossing the sea, you might see an iceberg. Some are as big as mountains. But often, only a tip of the iceberg can be seen above the water. Most of the iceberg is below water.

Day #4
1. What two words in this paragraph rhyme with **be**? _sea, see_
2. How much is the **tip** of an iceberg: **a lot** or **a little**? _a little_
3. Will you always see icebergs if you cross the ocean? _no_
4. To see an iceberg, should you be **on the beach** or **on a boat on the ocean**? _on a boat on the ocean_

Week #11 — Assessment

The Arctic
The Arctic is an area located near the North Pole. The Arctic is very cold. It has dry winds but very little rain. The soil is always frozen because of the cold temperatures. Pieces of ice join together in winter to cover much of the water.

The highest part is closest to the North Pole. It does not have much plant or animal life. This is because of the extremely dry air, cold temperatures, and short growing season. The lower part is a little warmer. It is covered with plants and trees that can live in a cold and dry climate.

1. Does the **ie** in **pieces** sound like the **ee** in **trees**? _yes_
2. What other word could you write instead of **extremely** in **extremely dry**? _very, totally (Answers may vary.)_
3. How many times does the writer describe the Arctic as **cold**? _4 times_
4. Which area of the Arctic has more plant and animal life: the **high part** or the **low part**? _low part_
5. Write three words that describe the weather in the Arctic.
   cold
   freezing
   dry (Answers may vary.)

Week #12

"Good morning, Mom," said Jaleel, as he raced down the stairs. "What time do we leave for vacation? I can hardly wait!"

Day #1
1. What time of day does this story take place? _morning_
2. Where do you think it takes place? _in Jaleel's house_
3. Predict what is about to happen. _Jaleel and his mom are about to go on vacation._
4. Does the story tell you if this is winter or summer? _no_

"The lake is the best!" said Anais. She leaned against a tree. "I really like it when the sun starts to go down. I'm ready to tell scary stories."

Day #2
1. What time of day does this story take place? _sunset_
2. Where does this story take place? _at a lake_
3. Predict what is about to happen. _Answers will vary._
4. Does the story tell you if Anais is staying in a tent or a cabin? _no_

The submarine moved deep in the ocean. Reggie saw fish and an octopus outside the window. He looked at his watch. "It's so dark down here, it does not seem like four o'clock," he thought.

Day #3
1. What time of day does this story take place? _4:00_
2. When is that time of day? (a.) in the afternoon   b. the middle of the night
3. Where does this story take place? _in a submarine deep in the ocean_
4. What does Reggie see in this setting that he can't see at home? _octopus/animals of the deep ocean_

"Brrrr! It's so cold here on top of the mountain in the middle of the night," Shay pulled her hat down over her ears. Soon it would be time to go back down the mountain.

Day #4
1. What time of day does this story take place? _middle of the night_
2. Where does this story take place? _on top of a mountain_
3. What is about to happen? _Shay will go down the mountain._
4. What other detail do we learn about the mountain? _It is cold at night._

Week #12 — Assessment

1. Preview the text below. Will this story be about a vacation? _no_
   Why or why not? _It is about work._

All in a Day's Work
Zookeepers care for the animals in the zoo every day. They make the animals' food and keep the animal homes clean. They spend a lot of time watching the animals to make sure they are healthy.

2. Where does this story take place? _at the zoo_

Zookeepers also have to keep the animals from being bored. In the wild, the animals' habitat is always changing. At the zoo, the animals' home stays the same. A good zookeeper will think of ways for the animals to have fun.

3. What is different for the animals about the zoo?
   a. They have other animals to talk to.
   (b.) The setting stays the same.
   c. The food is better.

One way is to hide the food. The animals enjoy looking for their food because it is a little bit like hunting. Zookeepers also put safe plants from other places or different smells in the cages. These are some of the ways that zookeepers keep the animals in the zoo curious and happy.

4. What do zookeepers do to help the animals feel like they are hunting? _They hide the animals' food._
5. Would you like to be a zookeeper? _Yes or no_   Why or why not? _Answers will vary._

Answer Key

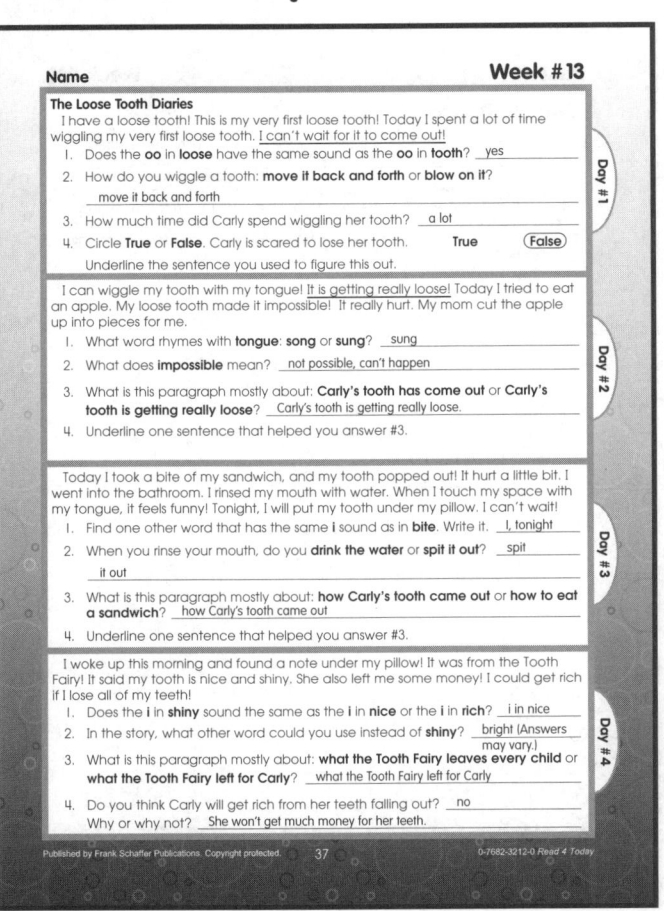

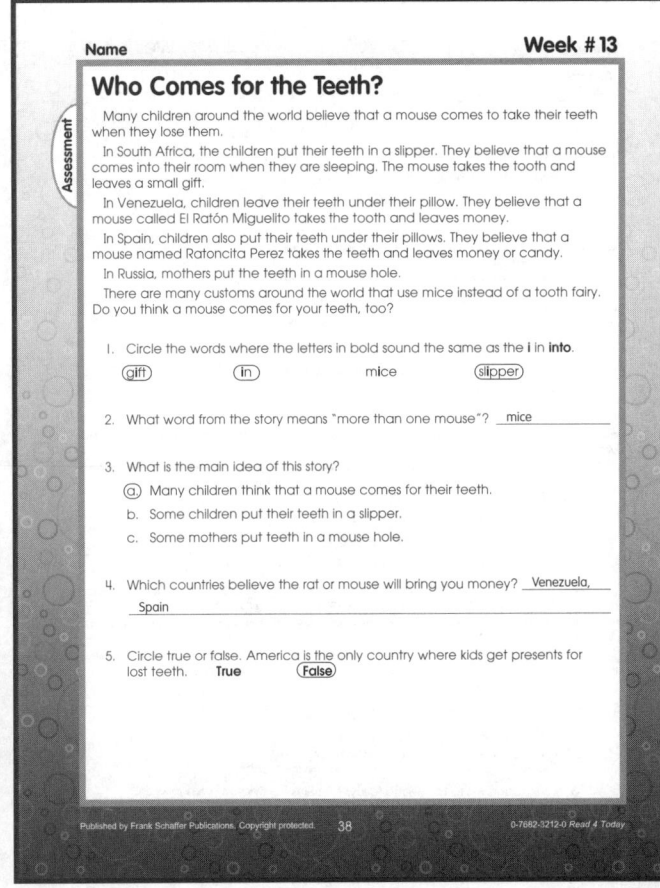

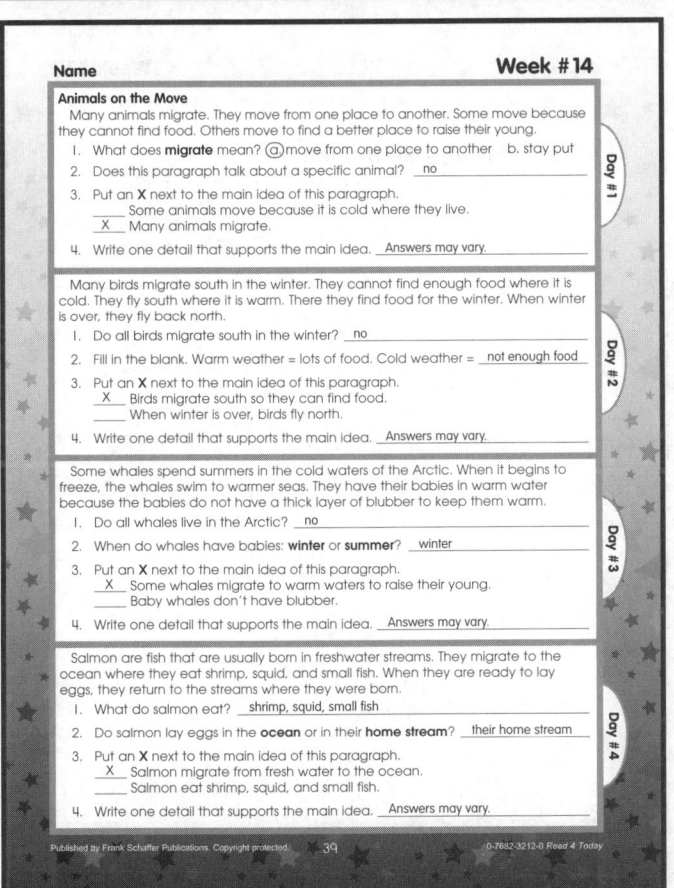

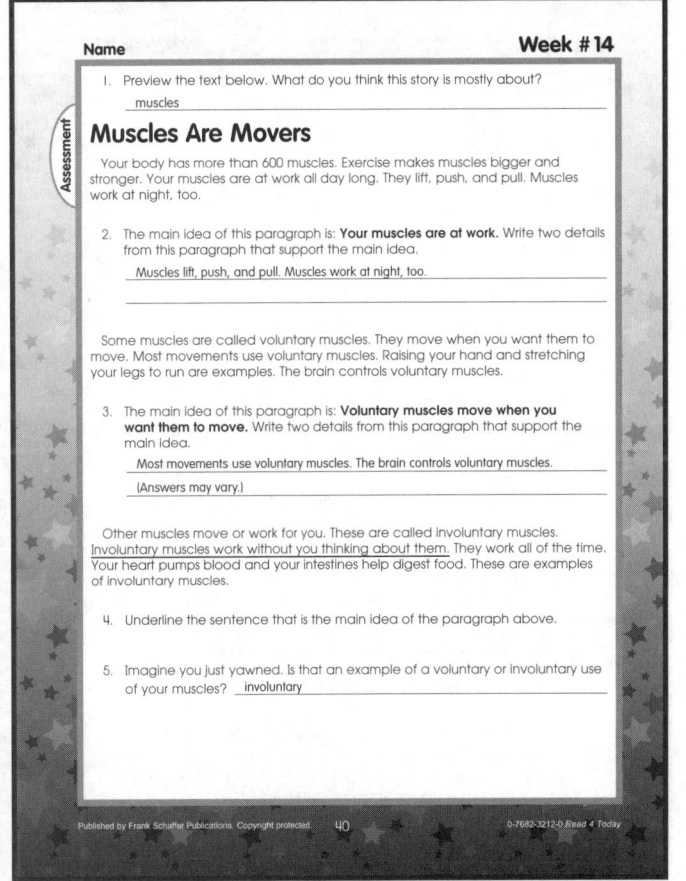

Week #13 — The Loose Tooth Diaries

I have a loose tooth! This is my very first loose tooth! Today I spent a lot of time wiggling my very first loose tooth. I can't wait for it to come out!

Day #1
1. Does the **oo** in **loose** have the same sound as the **oo** in **tooth**? _yes_
2. How do you wiggle a tooth: **move it back and forth** or **blow on it**? _move it back and forth_
3. How much time did Carly spend wiggling her tooth? _a lot_
4. Circle **True** or **False**. Carly is scared to lose her tooth. True (False)
   Underline the sentence you used to figure this out.

I can wiggle my tooth with my tongue! It is getting really loose! Today I tried to eat an apple. My loose tooth made it impossible! It really hurt. My mom cut the apple up into pieces for me.

Day #2
1. What word rhymes with **tongue**: **song** or **sung**? _sung_
2. What does **impossible** mean? _not possible, can't happen_
3. What is this paragraph mostly about: **Carly's tooth has come out** or **Carly's tooth is getting really loose**? _Carly's tooth is getting really loose._
4. Underline one sentence that helped you answer #3.

Today I took a bite of my sandwich, and my tooth popped out! It hurt a little bit. I went into the bathroom. I rinsed my mouth with water. When I touch my space with my tongue, it feels funny! Tonight, I will put my tooth under my pillow. I can't wait!

Day #3
1. Find one other word that has the same **i** sound as in **bite**. Write it. _I, tonight_
2. When you rinse your mouth, do you **drink the water** or **spit it out**? _spit it out_
3. What is this paragraph mostly about: **how Carly's tooth came out** or **how to eat a sandwich**? _how Carly's tooth came out_
4. Underline one sentence that helped you answer #3.

I woke up this morning and found a note under my pillow! It was from the Tooth Fairy! It said my tooth is nice and shiny. She also left me some money! I could get rich if I lose all of my teeth!

Day #4
1. Does the **i** in **shiny** sound the same as the **i** in **nice** or the **i** in **rich**? _i in nice_
2. In the story, what other word could you use instead of **shiny**? _bright (Answers may vary.)_
3. What is this paragraph mostly about: **what the Tooth Fairy leaves every child** or **what the Tooth Fairy left for Carly**? _what the Tooth Fairy left for Carly_
4. Do you think Carly will get rich from her teeth falling out? _no_ Why or why not? _She won't get much money for her teeth._

Week #13 — Assessment — Who Comes for the Teeth?

Many children around the world believe that a mouse comes to take their teeth when they lose them.

In South Africa, the children put their teeth in a slipper. They believe that a mouse comes into their room when they are sleeping. The mouse takes the tooth and leaves a small gift.

In Venezuela, children leave their teeth under their pillow. They believe that a mouse called El Ratón Miguelito takes the tooth and leaves money.

In Spain, children also put their teeth under their pillows. They believe that a mouse named Ratoncita Perez takes the teeth and leaves money or candy.

In Russia, mothers put the teeth in a mouse hole.

There are many customs around the world that use mice instead of a tooth fairy. Do you think a mouse comes for your teeth, too?

1. Circle the words where the letters in bold sound the same as the **i** in **into**.
   (gift)   (in)   mice   (slipper)
2. What word from the story means "more than one mouse"? _mice_
3. What is the main idea of this story?
   (a.) Many children think that a mouse comes for their teeth.
   b. Some children put their teeth in a slipper.
   c. Some mothers put teeth in a mouse hole.
4. Which countries believe the rat or mouse will bring you money? _Venezuela, Spain_
5. Circle true or false. America is the only country where kids get presents for lost teeth. True (False)

Week #14 — Animals on the Move

Many animals migrate. They move from one place to another. Some move because they cannot find food. Others move to find a better place to raise their young.

Day #1
1. What does **migrate** mean? (a.) move from one place to another   b. stay put
2. Does this paragraph talk about a specific animal? _no_
3. Put an **X** next to the main idea of this paragraph.
   ___ Some animals move because it is cold where they live.
   _X_ Many animals migrate.
4. Write one detail that supports the main idea. _Answers may vary._

Many birds migrate south in the winter. They cannot find enough food where it is cold. They fly south where it is warm. There they find food for the winter. When winter is over, they fly back north.

Day #2
1. Do all birds migrate south in the winter? _no_
2. Fill in the blank. Warm weather = lots of food. Cold weather = _not enough food_
3. Put an **X** next to the main idea of this paragraph.
   _X_ Birds migrate south so they can find food.
   ___ When winter is over, birds fly north.
4. Write one detail that supports the main idea. _Answers may vary._

Some whales spend summers in the cold waters of the Arctic. When it begins to freeze, the whales swim to warmer seas. They have their babies in warm water because the babies do not have a thick layer of blubber to keep them warm.

Day #3
1. Do all whales live in the Arctic? _no_
2. When do whales have babies: **winter** or **summer**? _winter_
3. Put an **X** next to the main idea of this paragraph.
   _X_ Some whales migrate to warm waters to raise their young.
   ___ Baby whales don't have blubber.
4. Write one detail that supports the main idea. _Answers may vary._

Salmon are fish that are usually born in freshwater streams. They migrate to the ocean where they eat shrimp, squid, and small fish. When they are ready to lay eggs, they return to the streams where they were born.

Day #4
1. What do salmon eat? _shrimp, squid, small fish_
2. Do salmon lay eggs in the **ocean** or in their **home stream**? _their home stream_
3. Put an **X** next to the main idea of this paragraph.
   _X_ Salmon migrate from fresh water to the ocean.
   ___ Salmon eat shrimp, squid, and small fish.
4. Write one detail that supports the main idea. _Answers may vary._

Week #14 — Assessment — Muscles Are Movers

1. Preview the text below. What do you think this story is mostly about? _muscles_

Your body has more than 600 muscles. Exercise makes muscles bigger and stronger. Your muscles are at work all day long. They lift, push, and pull. Muscles work at night, too.

2. The main idea of this paragraph is: **Your muscles are at work.** Write two details from this paragraph that support the main idea.
   Muscles lift, push, and pull. Muscles work at night, too.

Some muscles are called voluntary muscles. They move when you want them to move. Most movements use voluntary muscles. Raising your hand and stretching your legs to run are examples. The brain controls voluntary muscles.

3. The main idea of this paragraph is: **Voluntary muscles move when you want them to move.** Write two details from this paragraph that support the main idea.
   Most movements use voluntary muscles. The brain controls voluntary muscles.
   (Answers may vary.)

Other muscles move or work for you. These are called involuntary muscles. Involuntary muscles work without you thinking about them. They work all of the time. Your heart pumps blood and your intestines help digest food. These are examples of involuntary muscles.

4. Underline the sentence that is the main idea of the paragraph above.
5. Imagine you just yawned. Is that an example of a voluntary or involuntary use of your muscles? _involuntary_

Answer Key

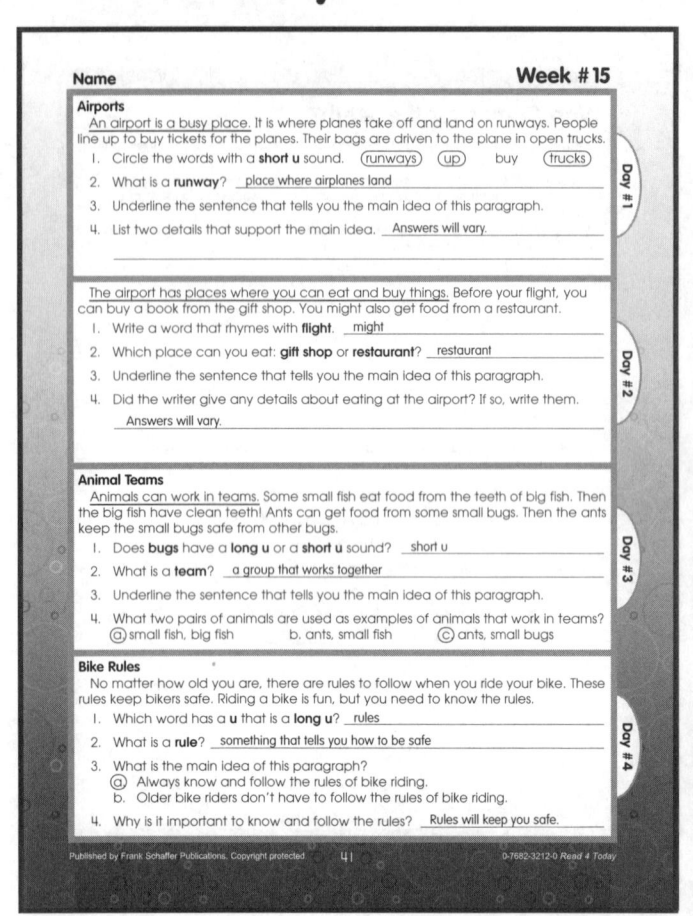

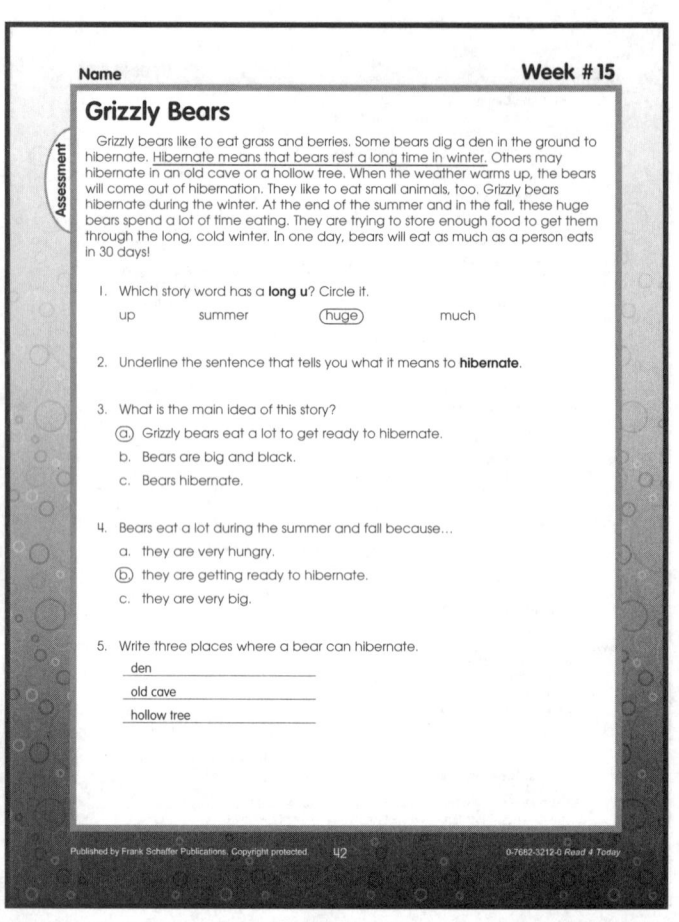

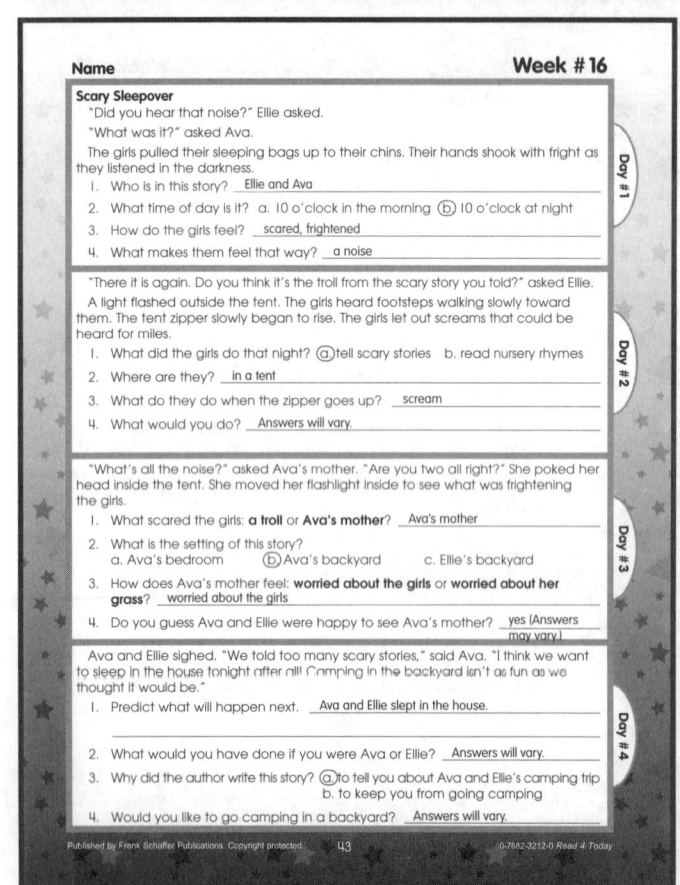

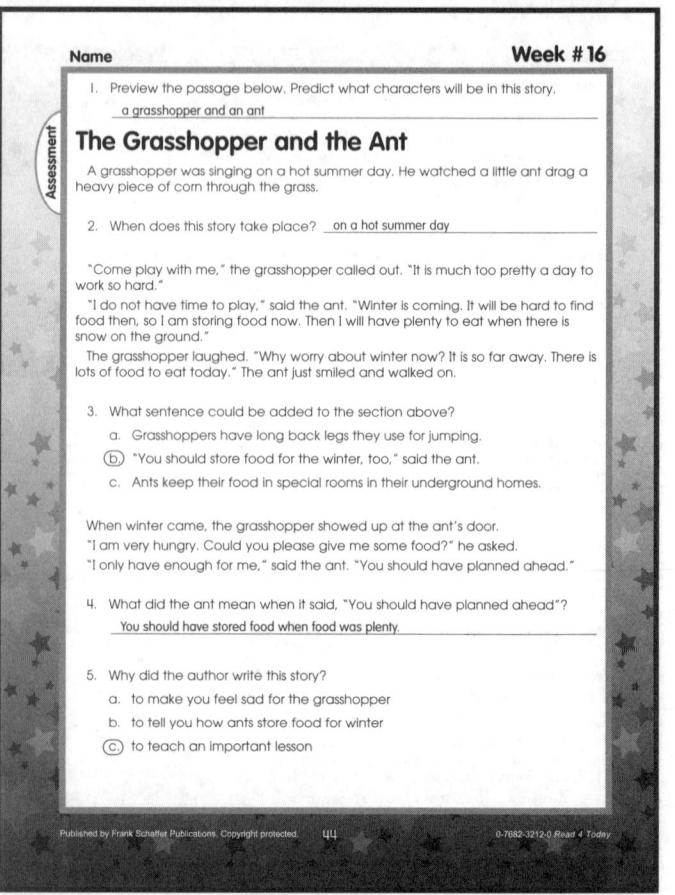

Week #15 — Airports

Day #1
An airport is a busy place. It is where planes take off and land on runways. People line up to buy tickets for the planes. Their bags are driven to the plane in open trucks.
1. Circle the words with a **short u** sound. (runways) (up) buy (trucks)
2. What is a **runway**? _place where airplanes land_
3. Underline the sentence that tells you the main idea of this paragraph.
4. List two details that support the main idea. _Answers will vary._

Day #2
The airport has places where you can eat and buy things. Before your flight, you can buy a book from the gift shop. You might also get food from a restaurant.
1. Write a word that rhymes with **flight**. _might_
2. Which place can you eat: **gift shop** or **restaurant**? _restaurant_
3. Underline the sentence that tells you the main idea of this paragraph.
4. Did the writer give any details about eating at the airport? If so, write them. _Answers will vary._

Day #3 — Animal Teams
Animals can work in teams. Some small fish eat food from the teeth of big fish. Then the big fish have clean teeth! Ants can get food from some small bugs. Then the ants keep the small bugs safe from other bugs.
1. Does **bugs** have a **long u** or a **short u** sound? _short u_
2. What is a **team**? _a group that works together_
3. Underline the sentence that tells you the main idea of this paragraph.
4. What two pairs of animals are used as examples of animals that work in teams?
   a. small fish, big fish   b. ants, small fish   (c.) ants, small bugs

Day #4 — Bike Rules
No matter how old you are, there are rules to follow when you ride your bike. These rules keep bikers safe. Riding a bike is fun, but you need to know the rules.
1. Which word has a **u** that is a **long u**? _rules_
2. What is a **rule**? _something that tells you how to be safe_
3. What is the main idea of this paragraph?
   (a.) Always know and follow the rules of bike riding.
   b. Older bike riders don't have to follow the rules of bike riding.
4. Why is it important to know and follow the rules? _Rules will keep you safe._

Week #15 Assessment — Grizzly Bears

Grizzly bears like to eat grass and berries. Some bears dig a den in the ground to hibernate. Hibernate means that bears rest a long time in winter. Others may hibernate in an old cave or a hollow tree. When the weather warms up, the bears will come out of hibernation. They like to eat small animals, too. Grizzly bears hibernate during the winter. At the end of the summer and in the fall, these huge bears spend a lot of time eating. They are trying to store enough food to get them through the long, cold winter. In one day, bears will eat as much as a person eats in 30 days!

1. Which story word has a **long u**? Circle it.
   up   summer   (huge)   much
2. Underline the sentence that tells you what it means to **hibernate**.
3. What is the main idea of this story?
   (a.) Grizzly bears eat a lot to get ready to hibernate.
   b. Bears are big and black.
   c. Bears hibernate.
4. Bears eat a lot during the summer and fall because…
   a. they are very hungry.
   (b.) they are getting ready to hibernate.
   c. they are very big.
5. Write three places where a bear can hibernate.
   den
   old cave
   hollow tree

Week #16 — Scary Sleepover

Day #1
"Did you hear that noise?" Ellie asked.
"What was it?" asked Ava.
The girls pulled their sleeping bags up to their chins. Their hands shook with fright as they listened in the darkness.
1. Who is in this story? _Ellie and Ava_
2. What time of day is it? a. 10 o'clock in the morning (b.) 10 o'clock at night
3. How do the girls feel? _scared, frightened_
4. What makes them feel that way? _a noise_

Day #2
"There it is again. Do you think it's the troll from the scary story you told?" asked Ellie.
A light flashed outside the tent. The girls heard footsteps walking slowly toward them. The tent zipper slowly began to rise. The girls let out screams that could be heard for miles.
1. What did the girls do that night? (a.) tell scary stories   b. read nursery rhymes
2. Where are they? _in a tent_
3. What do they do when the zipper goes up? _scream_
4. What would you do? _Answers will vary._

Day #3
"What's all the noise?" asked Ava's mother. "Are you two all right?" She poked her head inside the tent. She moved her flashlight inside to see what was frightening the girls.
1. What scared the girls: **a troll** or **Ava's mother**? _Ava's mother_
2. What is the setting of this story?
   a. Ava's bedroom   (b.) Ava's backyard   c. Ellie's backyard
3. How does Ava's mother feel: **worried about the girls** or **worried about her grass**? _worried about the girls_
4. Do you guess Ava and Ellie were happy to see Ava's mother? _yes (Answers may vary.)_

Day #4
Ava and Ellie sighed. "We told too many scary stories," said Ava. "I think we want to sleep in the house tonight after all. Camping in the backyard isn't as fun as we thought it would be."
1. Predict what will happen next. _Ava and Ellie slept in the house._
2. What would you have done if you were Ava or Ellie? _Answers will vary._
3. Why did the author write this story? (a.) to tell you about Ava and Ellie's camping trip
   b. to keep you from going camping
4. Would you like to go camping in a backyard? _Answers will vary._

Week #16 Assessment — The Grasshopper and the Ant

1. Preview the passage below. Predict what characters will be in this story.
   a grasshopper and an ant

A grasshopper was singing on a hot summer day. He watched a little ant drag a heavy piece of corn through the grass.

2. When does this story take place? _on a hot summer day_

"Come play with me," the grasshopper called out. "It is much too pretty a day to work so hard."
"I do not have time to play," said the ant. "Winter is coming. It will be hard to find food then, so I am storing food now. Then I will have plenty to eat when there is snow on the ground."
The grasshopper laughed. "Why worry about winter now? It is so far away. There is lots of food to eat today." The ant just smiled and walked on.

3. What sentence could be added to the section above?
   a. Grasshoppers have long back legs they use for jumping.
   (b.) "You should store food for the winter, too," said the ant.
   c. Ants keep their food in special rooms in their underground homes.

When winter came, the grasshopper showed up at the ant's door.
"I am very hungry. Could you please give me some food?" he asked.
"I only have enough for me," said the ant. "You should have planned ahead."

4. What did the ant mean when it said, "You should have planned ahead"?
   You should have stored food when food was plenty.

5. Why did the author write this story?
   a. to make you feel sad for the grasshopper
   b. to tell you how ants store food for winter
   (c.) to teach an important lesson

Answer Key

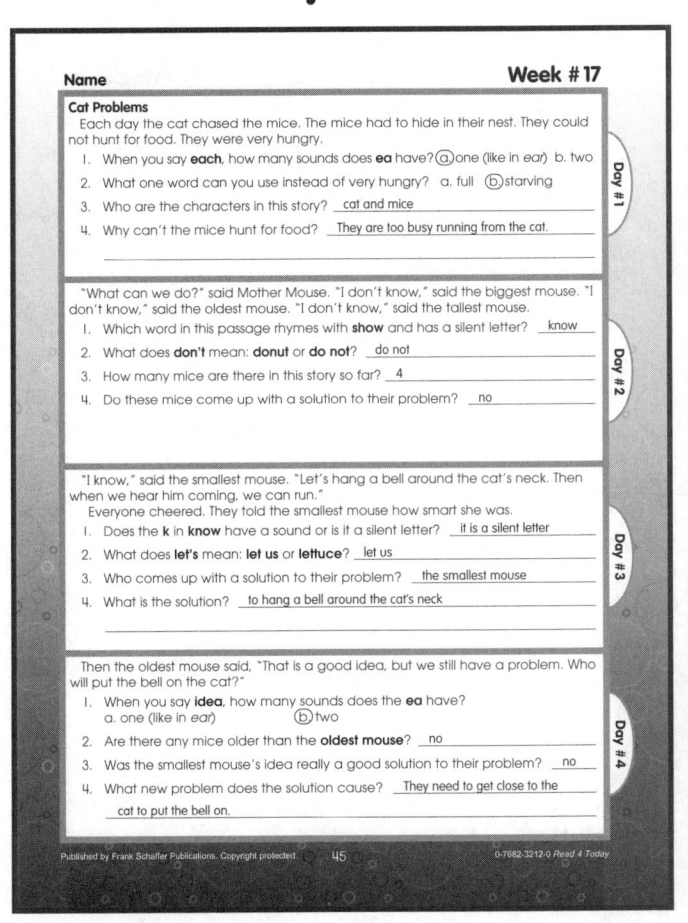

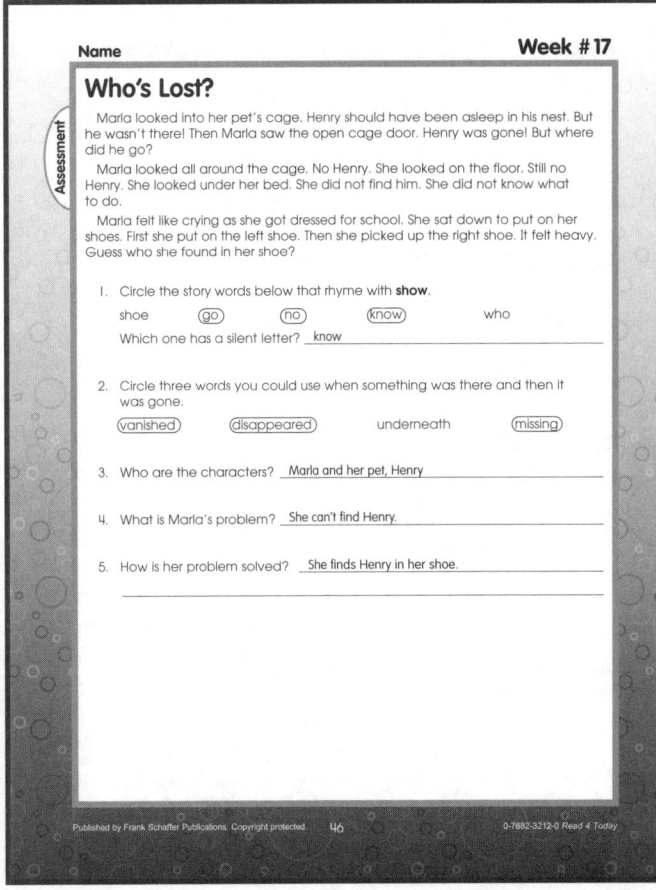

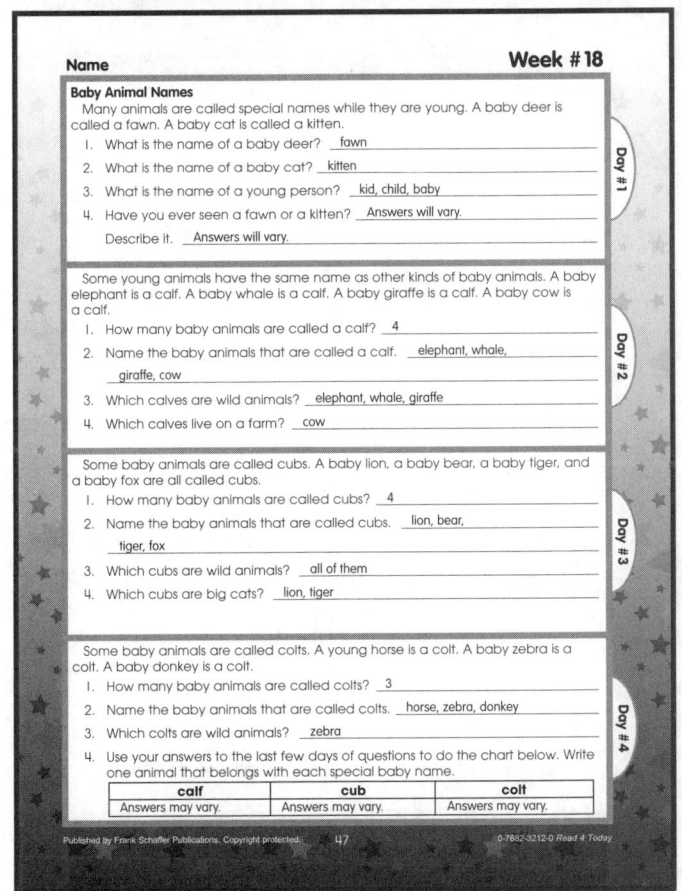

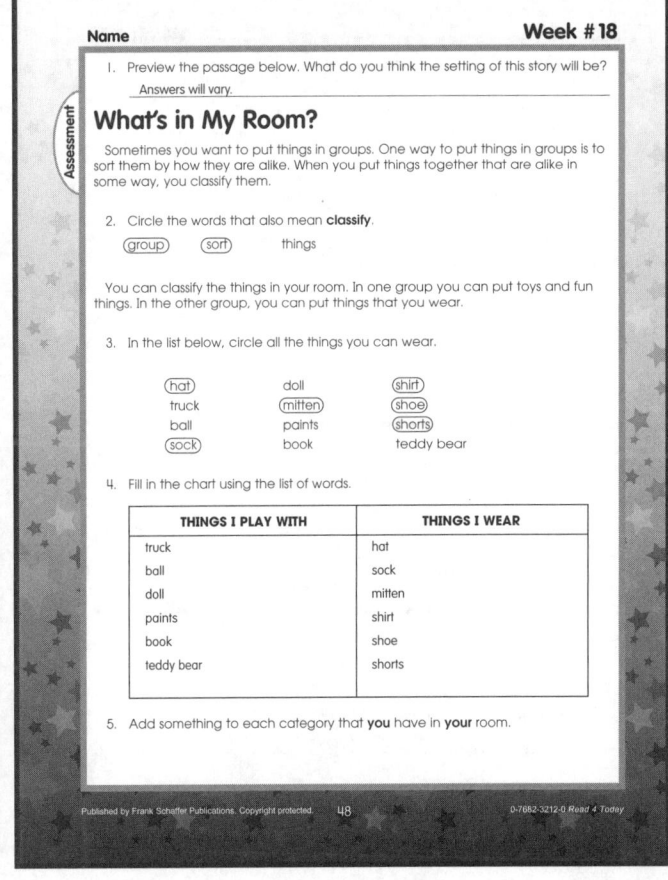

Week #17 — Cat Problems

Each day the cat chased the mice. The mice had to hide in their nest. They could not hunt for food. They were very hungry.

Day #1
1. When you say **each**, how many sounds does **ea** have? (a) one (like in *ear*) b. two
2. What one word can you use instead of very hungry? a. full (b) starving
3. Who are the characters in this story? __cat and mice__
4. Why can't the mice hunt for food? __They are too busy running from the cat.__

"What can we do?" said Mother Mouse. "I don't know," said the biggest mouse. "I don't know," said the oldest mouse. "I don't know," said the tallest mouse.

Day #2
1. Which word in this passage rhymes with **show** and has a silent letter? __know__
2. What does **don't** mean: **donut** or **do not**? __do not__
3. How many mice are there in this story so far? __4__
4. Do these mice come up with a solution to their problem? __no__

"I know," said the smallest mouse. "Let's hang a bell around the cat's neck. Then when we hear him coming, we can run."
Everyone cheered. They told the smallest mouse how smart she was.

Day #3
1. Does the **k** in **know** have a sound or is it a silent letter? __it is a silent letter__
2. What does **let's** mean: **let us** or **lettuce**? __let us__
3. Who comes up with a solution to their problem? __the smallest mouse__
4. What is the solution? __to hang a bell around the cat's neck__

Then the oldest mouse said, "That is a good idea, but we still have a problem. Who will put the bell on the cat?"

Day #4
1. When you say **idea**, how many sounds does the **ea** have?
   a. one (like in *ear*) (b) two
2. Are there any mice older than the **oldest mouse**? __no__
3. Was the smallest mouse's idea really a good solution to their problem? __no__
4. What new problem does the solution cause? __They need to get close to the cat to put the bell on.__

Week #17 — Assessment

Who's Lost?

Marla looked into her pet's cage. Henry should have been asleep in his nest. But he wasn't there! Then Marla saw the open cage door. Henry was gone! But where did he go?

Marla looked all around the cage. No Henry. She looked on the floor. Still no Henry. She looked under her bed. She did not find him. She did not know what to do.

Marla felt like crying as she got dressed for school. She sat down to put on her shoes. First she put on the left shoe. Then she picked up the right shoe. It felt heavy. Guess who she found in her shoe?

1. Circle the story words below that rhyme with **show**.
   shoe (go) (no) (know) who
   Which one has a silent letter? __know__

2. Circle three words you could use when something was there and then it was gone.
   (vanished) (disappeared) underneath (missing)

3. Who are the characters? __Marla and her pet, Henry__
4. What is Marla's problem? __She can't find Henry.__
5. How is her problem solved? __She finds Henry in her shoe.__

Week #18 — Baby Animal Names

Many animals are called special names while they are young. A baby deer is called a fawn. A baby cat is called a kitten.

Day #1
1. What is the name of a baby deer? __fawn__
2. What is the name of a baby cat? __kitten__
3. What is the name of a young person? __kid, child, baby__
4. Have you ever seen a fawn or a kitten? __Answers will vary.__
   Describe it. __Answers will vary.__

Some young animals have the same name as other kinds of baby animals. A baby elephant is a calf. A baby whale is a calf. A baby giraffe is a calf. A baby cow is a calf.

Day #2
1. How many baby animals are called a calf? __4__
2. Name the baby animals that are called a calf. __elephant, whale, giraffe, cow__
3. Which calves are wild animals? __elephant, whale, giraffe__
4. Which calves live on a farm? __cow__

Some baby animals are called cubs. A baby lion, a baby bear, a baby tiger, and a baby fox are all called cubs.

Day #3
1. How many baby animals are called cubs? __4__
2. Name the baby animals that are called cubs. __lion, bear, tiger, fox__
3. Which cubs are wild animals? __all of them__
4. Which cubs are big cats? __lion, tiger__

Some baby animals are called colts. A young horse is a colt. A baby zebra is a colt. A baby donkey is a colt.

Day #4
1. How many baby animals are called colts? __3__
2. Name the baby animals that are called colts. __horse, zebra, donkey__
3. Which colts are wild animals? __zebra__
4. Use your answers to the last few days of questions to do the chart below. Write one animal that belongs with each special baby name.

calf	cub	colt
Answers may vary.	Answers may vary.	Answers may vary.

Week #18 — Assessment

1. Preview the passage below. What do you think the setting of this story will be? __Answers will vary.__

What's in My Room?

Sometimes you want to put things in groups. One way to put things in groups is to sort them by how they are alike. When you put things together that are alike in some way, you classify them.

2. Circle the words that also mean **classify**.
   (group) (sort) things

You can classify the things in your room. In one group you can put toys and fun things. In the other group, you can put things that you wear.

3. In the list below, circle all the things you can wear.

   (hat)   doll   (shirt)
   truck   (mitten) (shoe)
   ball   paints (shorts)
   (sock)   book   teddy bear

4. Fill in the chart using the list of words.

THINGS I PLAY WITH	THINGS I WEAR
truck	hat
ball	sock
doll	mitten
paints	shirt
book	shoe
teddy bear	shorts

5. Add something to each category that **you** have in **your** room.

Answer Key

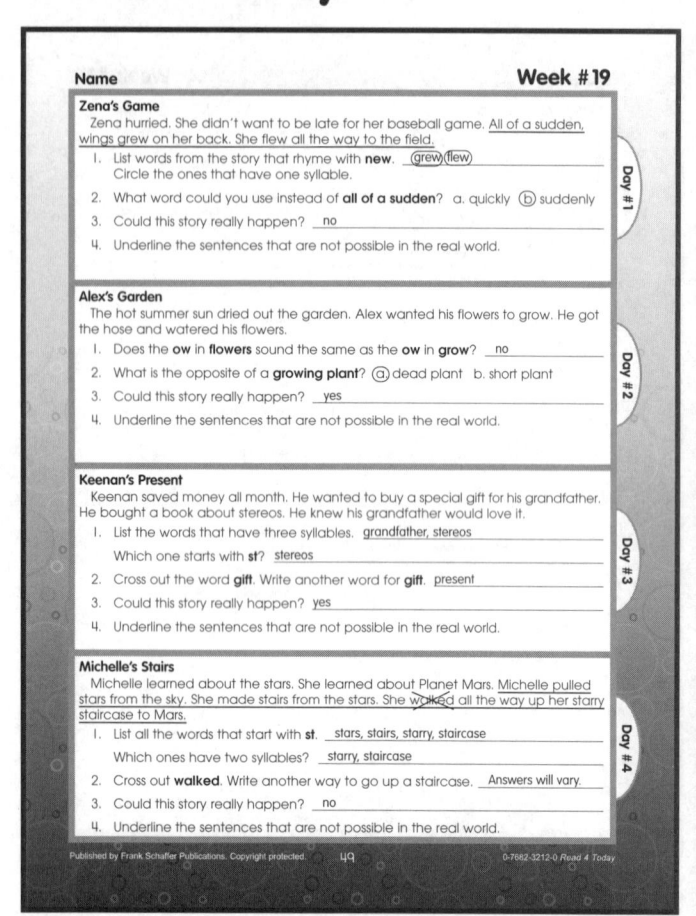

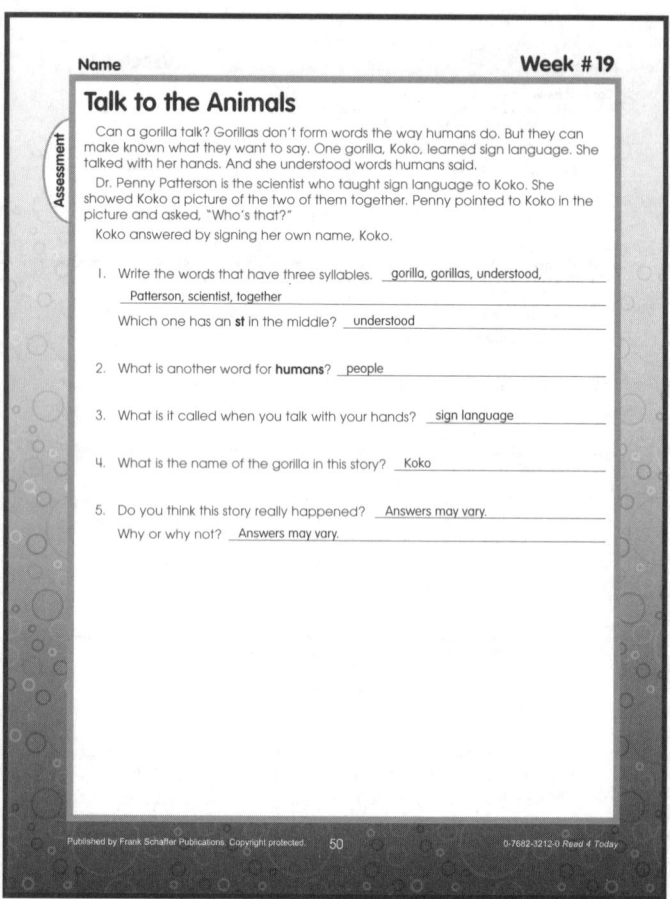

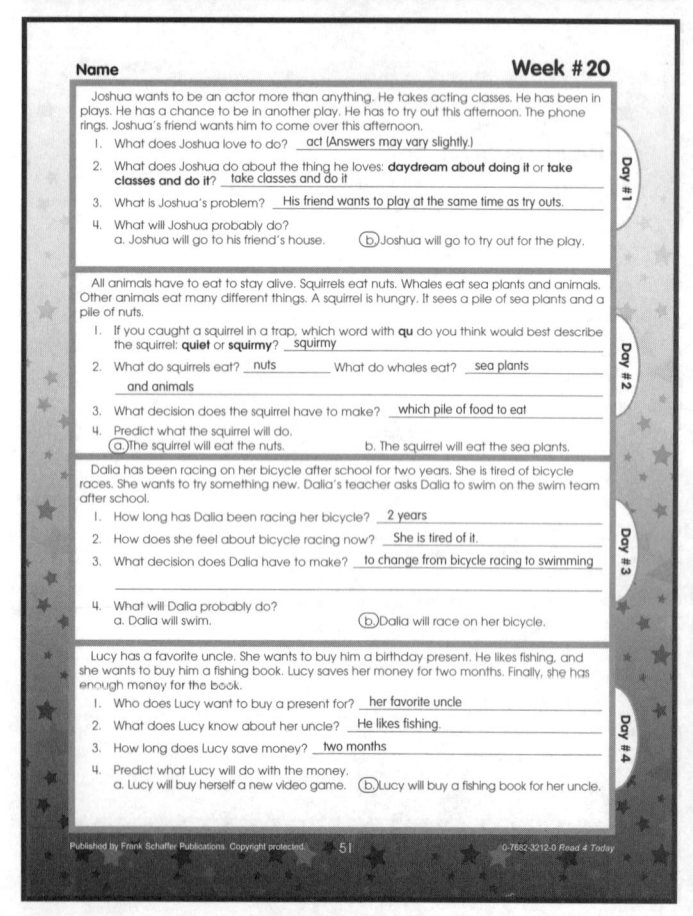

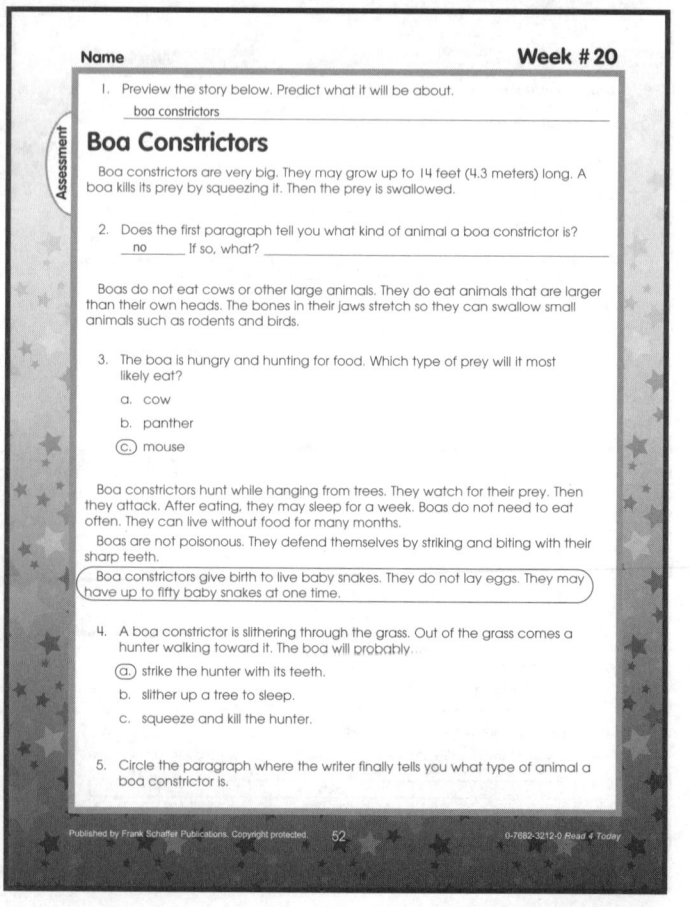

Week #19

Zena's Game
Zena hurried. She didn't want to be late for her baseball game. All of a sudden, wings grew on her back. She flew all the way to the field.

Day #1
1. List words from the story that rhyme with **new**.   grew, flew (grew and flew circled)
   Circle the ones that have one syllable.
2. What word could you use instead of **all of a sudden**?   a. quickly   (b.) suddenly
3. Could this story really happen?   no
4. Underline the sentences that are not possible in the real world.

Alex's Garden
The hot summer sun dried out the garden. Alex wanted his flowers to grow. He got the hose and watered his flowers.

Day #2
1. Does the **ow** in **flowers** sound the same as the **ow** in **grow**?   no
2. What is the opposite of a **growing plant**?   (a.) dead plant   b. short plant
3. Could this story really happen?   yes
4. Underline the sentences that are not possible in the real world.

Keenan's Present
Keenan saved money all month. He wanted to buy a special gift for his grandfather. He bought a book about stereos. He knew his grandfather would love it.

Day #3
1. List the words that have three syllables.   grandfather, stereos
   Which one starts with **st**?   stereos
2. Cross out the word **gift**. Write another word for **gift**.   present
3. Could this story really happen?   yes
4. Underline the sentences that are not possible in the real world.

Michelle's Stairs
Michelle learned about the stars. She learned about Planet Mars. Michelle pulled stars from the sky. She made stairs from the stars. She walked all the way up her starry staircase to Mars.

Day #4
1. List all the words that start with **st**.   stars, stairs, starry, staircase
   Which ones have two syllables?   starry, staircase
2. Cross out **walked**. Write another way to go up a staircase.   Answers will vary.
3. Could this story really happen?   no
4. Underline the sentences that are not possible in the real world.

Week #19 — Assessment

Talk to the Animals
Can a gorilla talk? Gorillas don't form words the way humans do. But they can make known what they want to say. One gorilla, Koko, learned sign language. She talked with her hands. And she understood words humans said.
Dr. Penny Patterson is the scientist who taught sign language to Koko. She showed Koko a picture of the two of them together. Penny pointed to Koko in the picture and asked, "Who's that?"
Koko answered by signing her own name, Koko.

1. Write the words that have three syllables.   gorilla, gorillas, understood, Patterson, scientist, together
   Which one has an **st** in the middle?   understood
2. What is another word for **humans**?   people
3. What is it called when you talk with your hands?   sign language
4. What is the name of the gorilla in this story?   Koko
5. Do you think this story really happened?   Answers may vary.
   Why or why not?   Answers may vary.

Week #20

Joshua wants to be an actor more than anything. He takes acting classes. He has been in plays. He has a chance to be in another play. He has to try out this afternoon. The phone rings. Joshua's friend wants him to come over this afternoon.

Day #1
1. What does Joshua love to do?   act (Answers may vary slightly.)
2. What does Joshua do about the thing he loves: daydream about doing it or take classes and do it?   take classes and do it
3. What is Joshua's problem?   His friend wants to play at the same time as try outs.
4. What will Joshua probably do?
   a. Joshua will go to his friend's house.   (b.) Joshua will go to try out for the play.

All animals have to eat to stay alive. Squirrels eat nuts. Whales eat sea plants and animals. Other animals eat many different things. A squirrel is hungry. It sees a pile of sea plants and a pile of nuts.

Day #2
1. If you caught a squirrel in a trap, which word with **qu** do you think would best describe the squirrel: quiet or squirmy?   squirmy
2. What do squirrels eat?   nuts   What do whales eat?   sea plants and animals
3. What decision does the squirrel have to make?   which pile of food to eat
4. Predict what the squirrel will do.
   (a.) The squirrel will eat the nuts.   b. The squirrel will eat the sea plants.

Dalia has been racing on her bicycle after school for two years. She is tired of bicycle races. She wants to try something new. Dalia's teacher asks Dalia to swim on the swim team after school.

Day #3
1. How long has Dalia been racing her bicycle?   2 years
2. How does she feel about bicycle racing now?   She is tired of it.
3. What decision does Dalia have to make?   to change from bicycle racing to swimming
4. What will Dalia probably do?
   a. Dalia will swim.   (b.) Dalia will race on her bicycle.

Lucy has a favorite uncle. She wants to buy him a birthday present. He likes fishing, and she wants to buy him a fishing book. Lucy saves her money for two months. Finally, she has enough money for the book.

Day #4
1. Who does Lucy want to buy a present for?   her favorite uncle
2. What does Lucy know about her uncle?   He likes fishing.
3. How long does Lucy save money?   two months
4. Predict what Lucy will do with the money.
   a. Lucy will buy herself a new video game.   (b.) Lucy will buy a fishing book for her uncle.

Week #20 — Assessment

1. Preview the story below. Predict what it will be about.   boa constrictors

Boa Constrictors
Boa constrictors are very big. They may grow up to 14 feet (4.3 meters) long. A boa kills its prey by squeezing it. Then the prey is swallowed.

2. Does the first paragraph tell you what kind of animal a boa constrictor is?
   no   If so, what?

Boas do not eat cows or other large animals. They do eat animals that are larger than their own heads. The bones in their jaws stretch so they can swallow small animals such as rodents and birds.

3. The boa is hungry and hunting for food. Which type of prey will it most likely eat?
   a. cow
   b. panther
   (c.) mouse

Boa constrictors hunt while hanging from trees. They watch for their prey. Then they attack. After eating, they may sleep for a week. Boas do not need to eat often. They can live without food for many months.
Boas are not poisonous. They defend themselves by striking and biting with their sharp teeth.
(Boa constrictors give birth to live baby snakes. They do not lay eggs. They may have up to fifty baby snakes at one time.) — circled

4. A boa constrictor is slithering through the grass. Out of the grass comes a hunter walking toward it. The boa will probably
   (a.) strike the hunter with its teeth.
   b. slither up a tree to sleep.
   c. squeeze and kill the hunter.

5. Circle the paragraph where the writer finally tells you what type of animal a boa constrictor is.

Answer Key

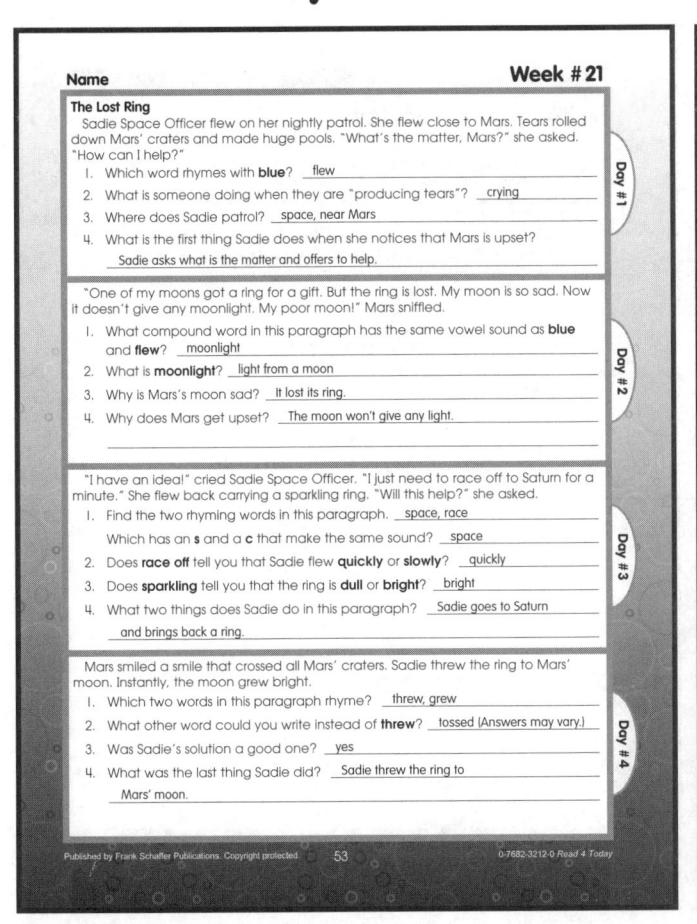

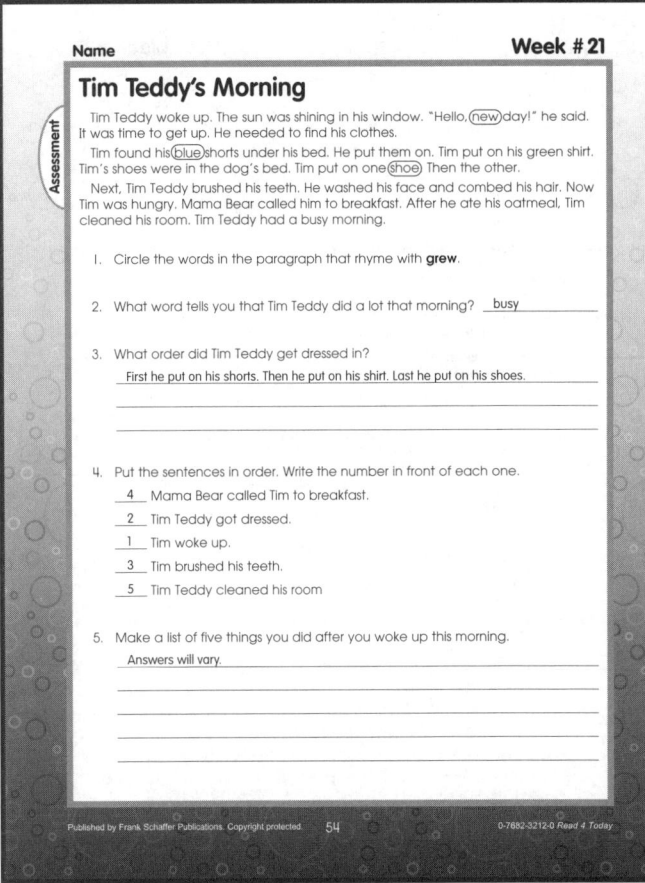

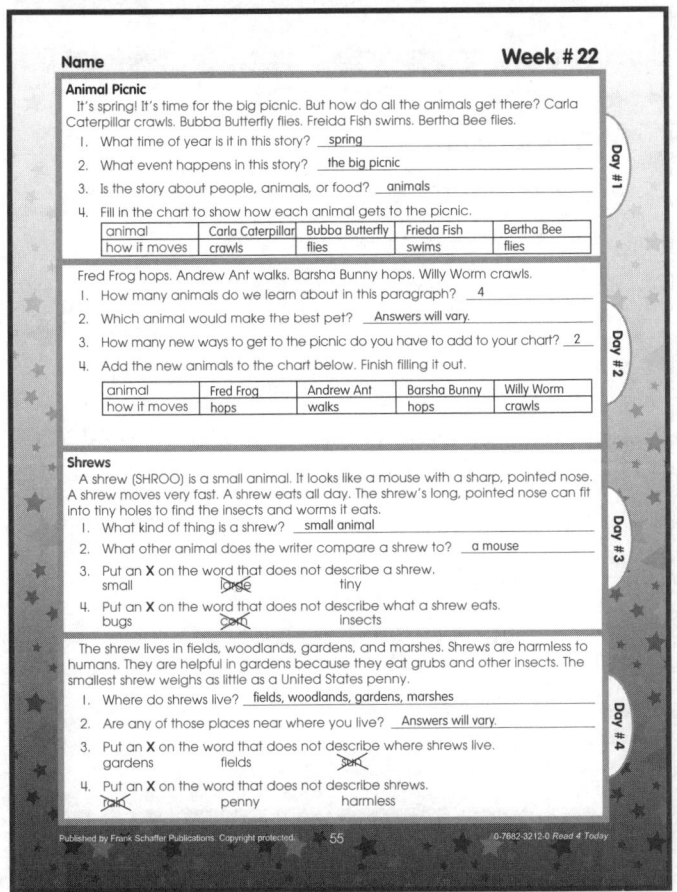

Week #21 — The Lost Ring

Sadie Space Officer flew on her nightly patrol. She flew close to Mars. Tears rolled down Mars' craters and made huge pools. "What's the matter, Mars?" she asked. "How can I help?"

Day #1
1. Which word rhymes with **blue**? flew
2. What is someone doing when they are "producing tears"? crying
3. Where does Sadie patrol? space, near Mars
4. What is the first thing Sadie does when she notices that Mars is upset? Sadie asks what is the matter and offers to help.

"One of my moons got a ring for a gift. But the ring is lost. My moon is so sad. Now it doesn't give any moonlight. My poor moon!" Mars sniffled.

Day #2
1. What compound word in this paragraph has the same vowel sound as **blue** and **flew**? moonlight
2. What is **moonlight**? light from a moon
3. Why is Mars's moon sad? It lost its ring.
4. Why does Mars get upset? The moon won't give any light.

"I have an idea!" cried Sadie Space Officer. "I just need to race off to Saturn for a minute." She flew back carrying a sparkling ring. "Will this help?" she asked.

Day #3
1. Find the two rhyming words in this paragraph. space, race
   Which has an **s** and a **c** that make the same sound? space
2. Does **race off** tell you that Sadie flew **quickly** or **slowly**? quickly
3. Does **sparkling** tell you that the ring is **dull** or **bright**? bright
4. What two things does Sadie do in this paragraph? Sadie goes to Saturn and brings back a ring.

Mars smiled a smile that crossed all Mars' craters. Sadie threw the ring to Mars' moon. Instantly, the moon grew bright.

Day #4
1. Which two words in this paragraph rhyme? threw, grew
2. What other word could you write instead of **threw**? tossed (Answers may vary.)
3. Was Sadie's solution a good one? yes
4. What was the last thing Sadie did? Sadie threw the ring to Mars' moon.

Week #21 — Tim Teddy's Morning (Assessment)

Tim Teddy woke up. The sun was shining in his window. "Hello, (new) day!" he said. It was time to get up. He needed to find his clothes.
Tim found his (blue) shorts under his bed. He put them on. Tim put on his green shirt. Tim's shoes were in the dog's bed. Tim put on one (shoe) Then the other.
Next, Tim Teddy brushed his teeth. He washed his face and combed his hair. Now Tim was hungry. Mama Bear called him to breakfast. After he ate his oatmeal, Tim cleaned his room. Tim Teddy had a busy morning.

1. Circle the words in the paragraph that rhyme with **grew**.
2. What word tells you that Tim Teddy did a lot that morning? busy
3. What order did Tim Teddy get dressed in? First he put on his shorts. Then he put on his shirt. Last he put on his shoes.
4. Put the sentences in order. Write the number in front of each one.
   - 4 Mama Bear called Tim to breakfast.
   - 2 Tim Teddy got dressed.
   - 1 Tim woke up.
   - 3 Tim brushed his teeth.
   - 5 Tim Teddy cleaned his room.
5. Make a list of five things you did after you woke up this morning. Answers will vary.

Week #22 — Animal Picnic

It's spring! It's time for the big picnic. But how do all the animals get there? Carla Caterpillar crawls. Bubba Butterfly flies. Freida Fish swims. Bertha Bee flies.

Day #1
1. What time of year is it in this story? spring
2. What event happens in this story? the big picnic
3. Is the story about people, animals, or food? animals
4. Fill in the chart to show how each animal gets to the picnic.

animal	Carla Caterpillar	Bubba Butterfly	Freida Fish	Bertha Bee
how it moves	crawls	flies	swims	flies

Fred Frog hops. Andrew Ant walks. Barsha Bunny hops. Willy Worm crawls.

Day #2
1. How many animals do we learn about in this paragraph? 4
2. Which animal would make the best pet? Answers will vary.
3. How many new ways to get to the picnic do you have to add to your chart? 2
4. Add the new animals to the chart below. Finish filling it out.

animal	Fred Frog	Andrew Ant	Barsha Bunny	Willy Worm
how it moves	hops	walks	hops	crawls

Shrews
A shrew (SHROO) is a small animal. It looks like a mouse with a sharp, pointed nose. A shrew moves very fast. A shrew eats all day. The shrew's long, pointed nose can fit into tiny holes to find the insects and worms it eats.

Day #3
1. What kind of thing is a shrew? small animal
2. What other animal does the writer compare a shrew to? a mouse
3. Put an **X** on the word that does not describe a shrew.
   small   ~~large~~   tiny
4. Put an **X** on the word that does not describe what a shrew eats.
   bugs   ~~worms~~   insects

The shrew lives in fields, woodlands, gardens, and marshes. Shrews are harmless to humans. They are helpful in gardens because they eat grubs and other insects. The smallest shrew weighs as little as a United States penny.

Day #4
1. Where do shrews live? fields, woodlands, gardens, marshes
2. Are any of those places near where you live? Answers will vary.
3. Put an **X** on the word that does not describe where shrews live.
   gardens   fields   ~~woods~~
4. Put an **X** on the word that does not describe shrews.
   ~~mean~~   penny   harmless

Week #22 — Apple Picking Time (Assessment)

1. Preview the story. What do you think the characters will be sorting? apples

Apple Picking Time

This family picks apples.
"This year, let's sort the apples by size," says Mom.
"Great idea," answers Jamie, "Then we can count them to see how many we have of each size."
"I bet there will be more big apples than any other size," says Dad.

2. Who is picking apples in this story? a family (Mom, Dad, and Jamie)
3. How do they decide to sort the apples they have picked? by size

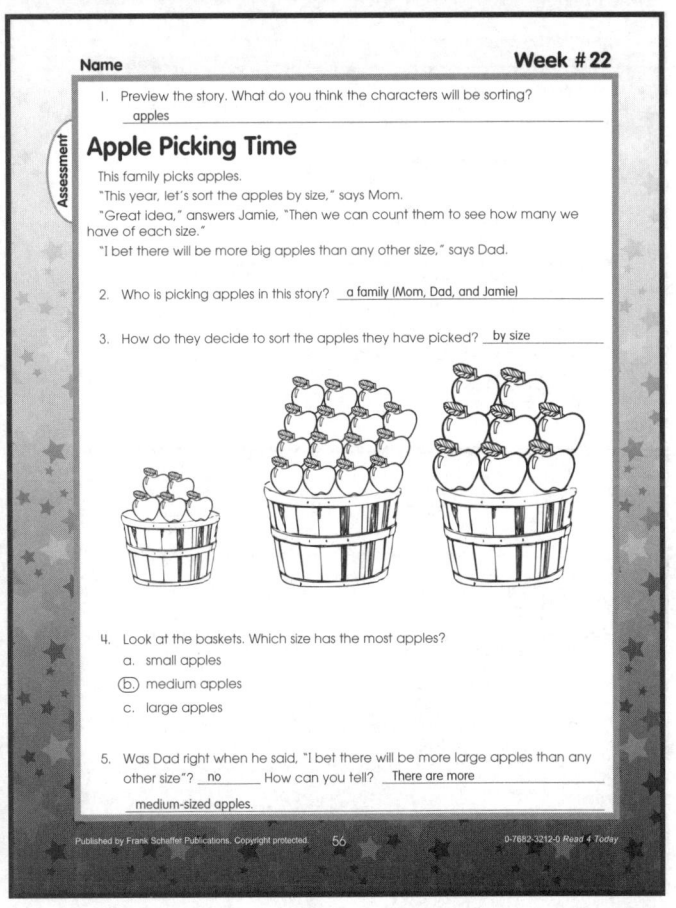

4. Look at the baskets. Which size has the most apples?
   a. small apples
   (b.) medium apples
   c. large apples
5. Was Dad right when he said, "I bet there will be more large apples than any other size"? no   How can you tell? There are more medium-sized apples.

Answer Key

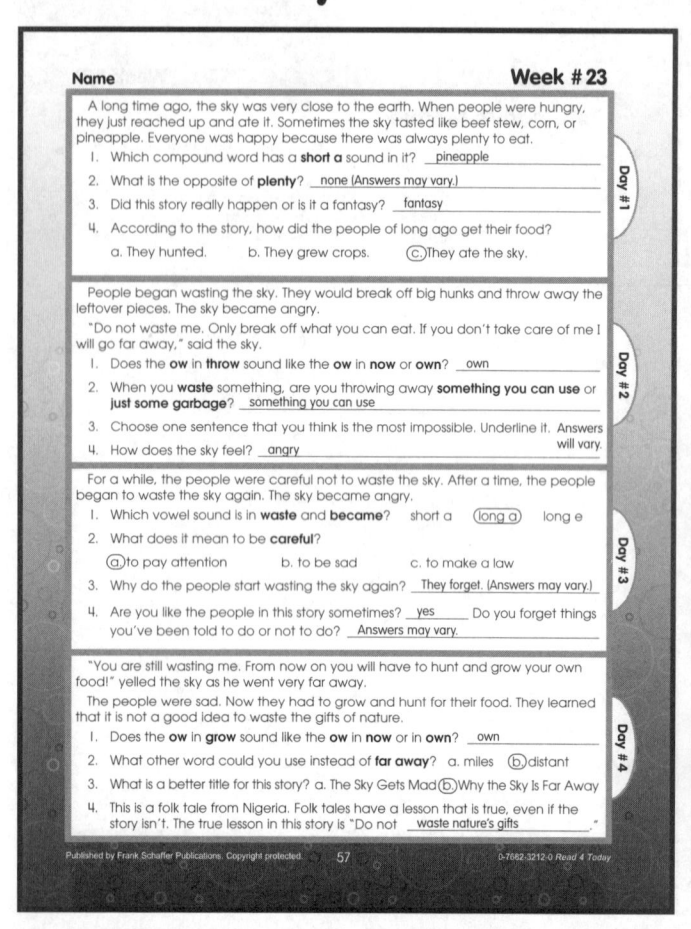

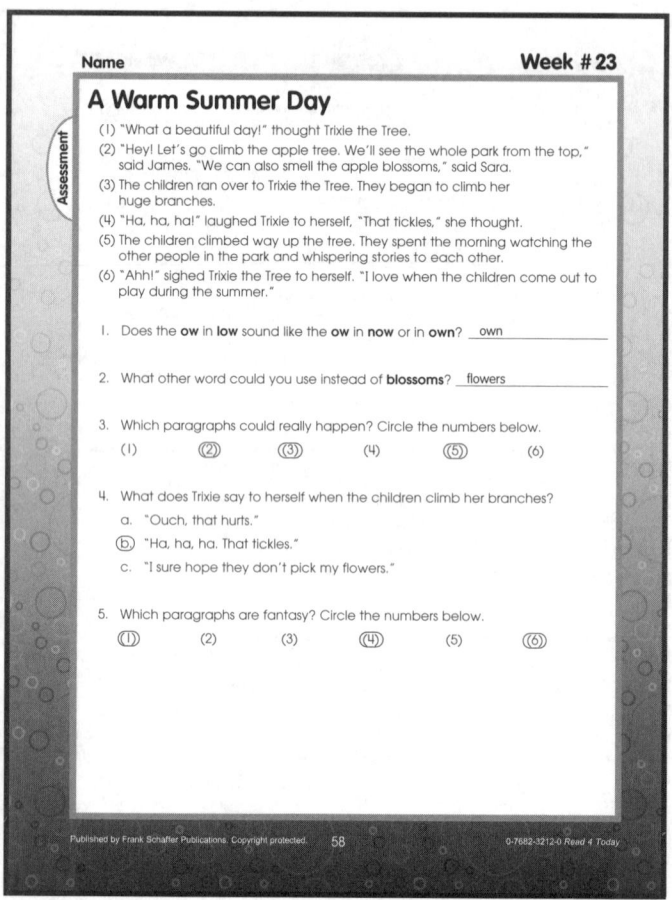

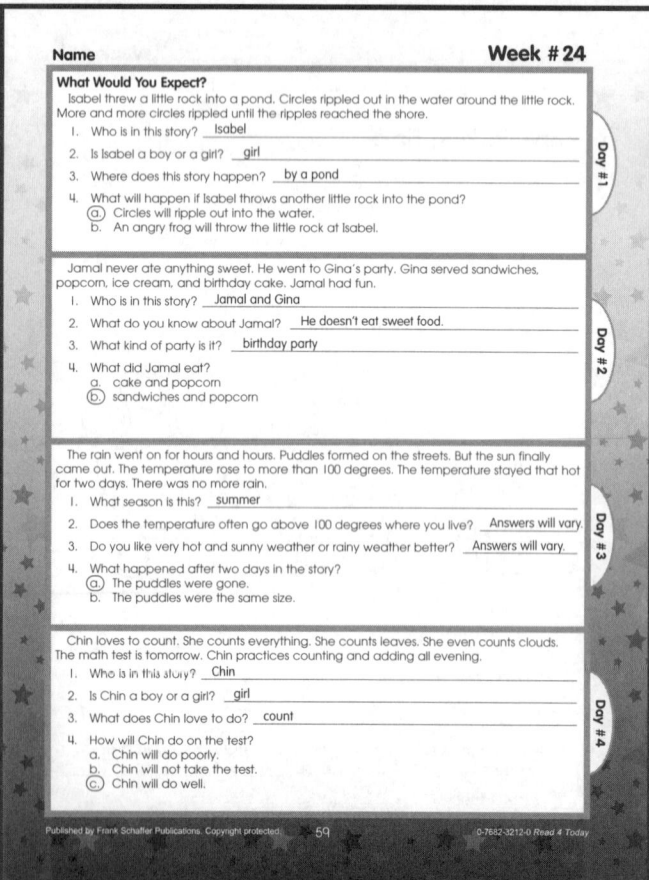

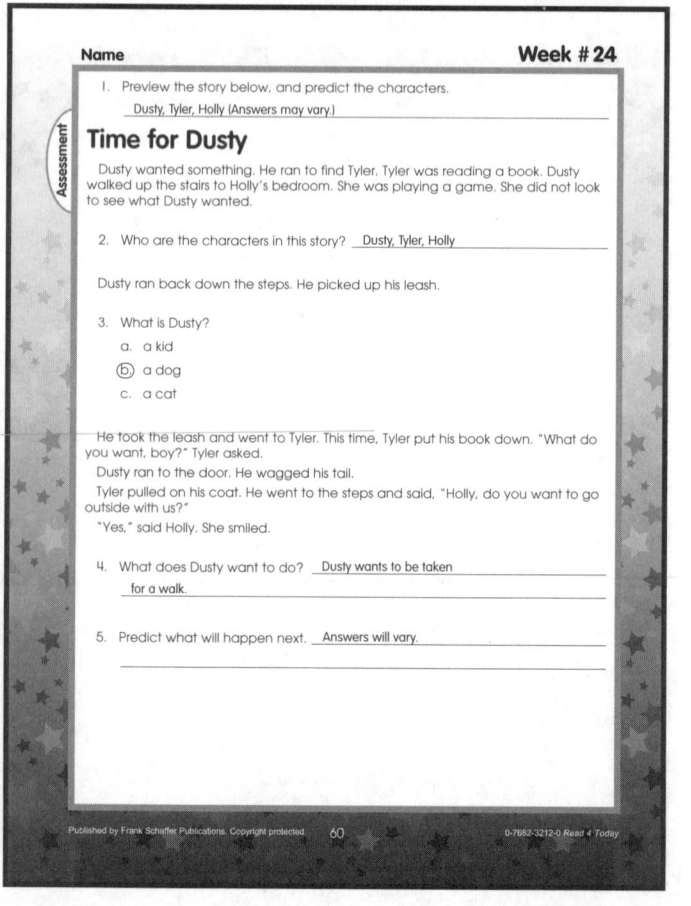

Week #23 — Day #1–#4

A long time ago, the sky was very close to the earth. When people were hungry, they just reached up and ate it. Sometimes the sky tasted like beef stew, corn, or pineapple. Everyone was happy because there was always plenty to eat.
1. Which compound word has a **short a** sound in it? __pineapple__
2. What is the opposite of **plenty**? __none (Answers may vary.)__
3. Did this story really happen or is it a fantasy? __fantasy__
4. According to the story, how did the people of long ago get their food?
   a. They hunted.   b. They grew crops.   (c.) They ate the sky.

People began wasting the sky. They would break off big hunks and throw away the leftover pieces. The sky became angry.
"Do not waste me. Only break off what you can eat. If you don't take care of me I will go far away," said the sky.
1. Does the **ow** in **throw** sound like the **ow** in **now** or **own**? __own__
2. When you **waste** something, are you throwing away **something you can use** or **just some garbage**? __something you can use__
3. Choose one sentence that you think is the most impossible. Underline it. __Answers will vary.__
4. How does the sky feel? __angry__

For a while, the people were careful not to waste the sky. After a time, the people began to waste the sky again. The sky became angry.
1. Which vowel sound is in **waste** and **became**?   short a   (long a)   long e
2. What does it mean to be **careful**?
   (a.) to pay attention   b. to be sad   c. to make a law
3. Why do the people start wasting the sky again? __They forget. (Answers may vary.)__
4. Are you like the people in this story sometimes? __yes__ Do you forget things you've been told to do or not to do? __Answers may vary.__

"You are still wasting me. From now on you will have to hunt and grow your own food!" yelled the sky as he went very far away.
The people were sad. Now they had to grow and hunt for their food. They learned that it is not a good idea to waste the gifts of nature.
1. Does the **ow** in **grow** sound like the **ow** in **now** or in **own**? __own__
2. What other word could you use instead of **far away**?   a. miles   (b.) distant
3. What is a better title for this story?   a. The Sky Gets Mad   (b.) Why the Sky Is Far Away
4. This is a folk tale from Nigeria. Folk tales have a lesson that is true, even if the story isn't. The true lesson in this story is "Do not __waste nature's gifts__."

Week #23 — Assessment

A Warm Summer Day

(1) "What a beautiful day!" thought Trixie the Tree.
(2) "Hey! Let's go climb the apple tree. We'll see the whole park from the top," said James. "We can also smell the apple blossoms," said Sara.
(3) The children ran over to Trixie the Tree. They began to climb her huge branches.
(4) "Ha, ha, ha!" laughed Trixie to herself, "That tickles," she thought.
(5) The children climbed way up the tree. They spent the morning watching the other people in the park and whispering stories to each other.
(6) "Ahh!" sighed Trixie the Tree to herself. "I love when the children come out to play during the summer."

1. Does the **ow** in **low** sound like the **ow** in **now** or in **own**? __own__
2. What other word could you use instead of **blossoms**? __flowers__
3. Which paragraphs could really happen? Circle the numbers below.
   (1)   (②)   (③)   (4)   (⑤)   (6)
4. What does Trixie say to herself when the children climb her branches?
   a. "Ouch, that hurts."
   (b.) "Ha, ha, ha. That tickles."
   c. "I sure hope they don't pick my flowers."
5. Which paragraphs are fantasy? Circle the numbers below.
   (①)   (2)   (3)   (④)   (5)   (⑥)

Week #24 — Day #1–#4

What Would You Expect?
Isabel threw a little rock into a pond. Circles rippled out in the water around the little rock. More and more circles rippled until the ripples reached the shore.
1. Who is in this story? __Isabel__
2. Is Isabel a boy or a girl? __girl__
3. Where does this story happen? __by a pond__
4. What will happen if Isabel throws another little rock into the pond?
   (a.) Circles will ripple out into the water.
   b. An angry frog will throw the little rock at Isabel.

Jamal never ate anything sweet. He went to Gina's party. Gina served sandwiches, popcorn, ice cream, and birthday cake. Jamal had fun.
1. Who is in this story? __Jamal and Gina__
2. What do you know about Jamal? __He doesn't eat sweet food.__
3. What kind of party is it? __birthday party__
4. What did Jamal eat?
   a. cake and popcorn
   (b.) sandwiches and popcorn

The rain went on for hours and hours. Puddles formed on the streets. But the sun finally came out. The temperature rose to more than 100 degrees. The temperature stayed that hot for two days. There was no more rain.
1. What season is this? __summer__
2. Does the temperature often go above 100 degrees where you live? __Answers will vary.__
3. Do you like very hot and sunny weather or rainy weather better? __Answers will vary.__
4. What happened after two days in the story?
   (a.) The puddles were gone.
   b. The puddles were the same size.

Chin loves to count. She counts everything. She counts leaves. She even counts clouds. The math test is tomorrow. Chin practices counting and adding all evening.
1. Who is in this story? __Chin__
2. Is Chin a boy or a girl? __girl__
3. What does Chin love to do? __count__
4. How will Chin do on the test?
   a. Chin will do poorly.
   b. Chin will not take the test.
   (c.) Chin will do well.

Week #24 — Assessment

1. Preview the story below, and predict the characters.
   __Dusty, Tyler, Holly (Answers may vary.)__

Time for Dusty

Dusty wanted something. He ran to find Tyler. Tyler was reading a book. Dusty walked up the stairs to Holly's bedroom. She was playing a game. She did not look to see what Dusty wanted.

2. Who are the characters in this story? __Dusty, Tyler, Holly__

Dusty ran back down the steps. He picked up his leash.

3. What is Dusty?
   a. a kid
   (b.) a dog
   c. a cat

He took the leash and went to Tyler. This time, Tyler put his book down. "What do you want, boy?" Tyler asked.
Dusty ran to the door. He wagged his tail.
Tyler pulled on his coat. He went to the steps and said, "Holly, do you want to go outside with us?"
"Yes," said Holly. She smiled.

4. What does Dusty want to do? __Dusty wants to be taken for a walk.__

5. Predict what will happen next. __Answers will vary.__

Published by Frank Schaffer Publications. Copyright protected. 104 0-7682-3212-0 Read 4 Today

Answer Key

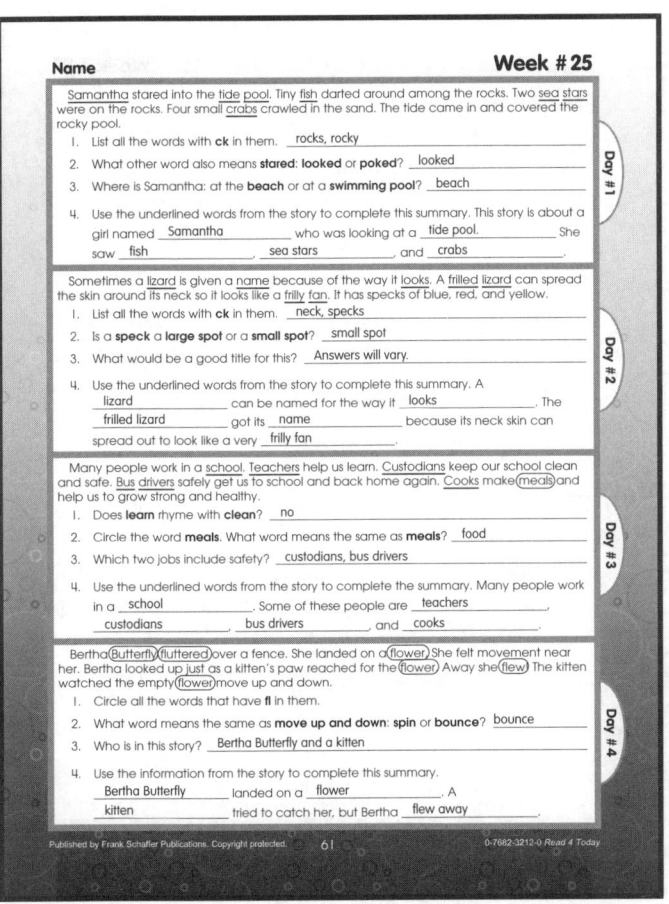

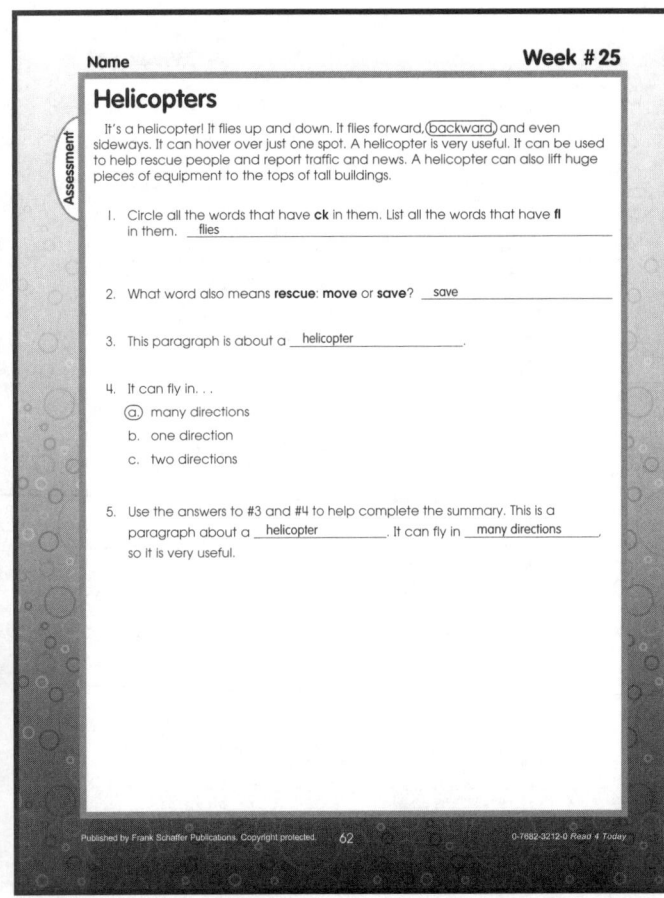

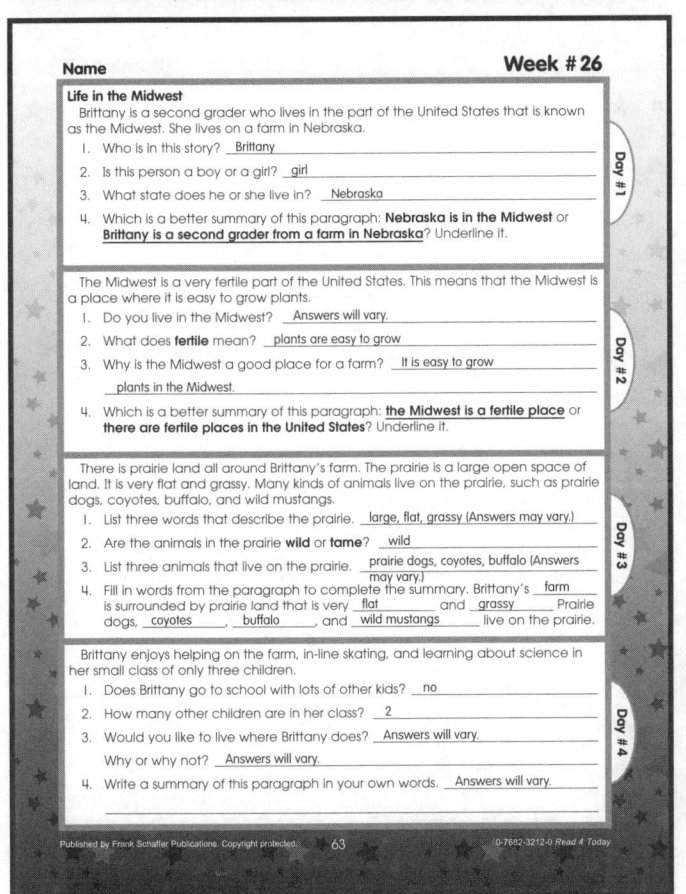

Week #25 — Day #1

Samantha stared into the tide pool. Tiny fish darted around among the rocks. Two sea stars were on the rocks. Four small crabs crawled in the sand. The tide came in and covered the rocky pool.

1. List all the words with **ck** in them. __rocks, rocky__
2. What other word also means **stared**: **looked** or **poked**? __looked__
3. Where is Samantha: at the **beach** or at a **swimming pool**? __beach__
4. Use the underlined words from the story to complete this summary. This story is about a girl named __Samantha__ who was looking at a __tide pool__. She saw __fish__, __sea stars__, and __crabs__.

Week #25 — Day #2

Sometimes a lizard is given a name because of the way it looks. A frilled lizard can spread the skin around its neck so it looks like a frilly fan. It has specks of blue, red, and yellow.

1. List all the words with **ck** in them. __neck, specks__
2. Is a **speck** a **large spot** or a **small spot**? __small spot__
3. What would be a good title for this? __Answers will vary.__
4. Use the underlined words from the story to complete this summary. A __lizard__ can be named for the way it __looks__. The __frilled lizard__ got its __name__ because its neck skin can spread out to look like a very __frilly fan__.

Week #25 — Day #3

Many people work in a school. Teachers help us learn. Custodians keep our school clean and safe. Bus drivers safely get us to school and back home again. Cooks make (meals) and help us to grow strong and healthy.

1. Does **learn** rhyme with **clean**? __no__
2. Circle the word **meals**. What word means the same as **meals**? __food__
3. Which two jobs include safety? __custodians, bus drivers__
4. Use the underlined words from the story to complete the summary. Many people work in a __school__. Some of these people are __teachers__, __custodians__, __bus drivers__, and __cooks__.

Week #25 — Day #4

Bertha (Butterfly) (fluttered) over a fence. She landed on a (flower). She felt movement near her. Bertha looked up just as a kitten's paw reached for the (flower). Away she (flew). The kitten watched the empty (flower) move up and down.

1. Circle all the words that have **fl** in them.
2. What word means the same as **move up and down**: **spin** or **bounce**? __bounce__
3. Who is in this story? __Bertha Butterfly and a kitten__
4. Use the information from the story to complete this summary. __Bertha Butterfly__ landed on a __flower__. A __kitten__ tried to catch her, but Bertha __flew away__.

Week #25 — Assessment

Helicopters

It's a helicopter! It flies up and down. It flies forward, (backward), and even sideways. It can hover over just one spot. A helicopter is very useful. It can be used to help rescue people and report traffic and news. A helicopter can also lift huge pieces of equipment to the tops of tall buildings.

1. Circle all the words that have **ck** in them. List all the words that have **fl** in them. __flies__
2. What word also means **rescue**: **move** or **save**? __save__
3. This paragraph is about a __helicopter__.
4. It can fly in. . .
   a. many directions
   b. one direction
   c. two directions
5. Use the answers to #3 and #4 to help complete the summary. This is a paragraph about a __helicopter__. It can fly in __many directions__, so it is very useful.

Week #26 — Day #1

Life in the Midwest

Brittany is a second grader who lives in the part of the United States that is known as the Midwest. She lives on a farm in Nebraska.

1. Who is in this story? __Brittany__
2. Is this person a boy or a girl? __girl__
3. What state does he or she live in? __Nebraska__
4. Which is a better summary of this paragraph: **Nebraska is in the Midwest** or **Brittany is a second grader from a farm in Nebraska**? Underline it.

Week #26 — Day #2

The Midwest is a very fertile part of the United States. This means that the Midwest is a place where it is easy to grow plants.

1. Do you live in the Midwest? __Answers will vary.__
2. What does **fertile** mean? __plants are easy to grow__
3. Why is the Midwest a good place for a farm? __It is easy to grow plants in the Midwest.__
4. Which is a better summary of this paragraph: **the Midwest is a fertile place** or **there are fertile places in the United States**? Underline it.

Week #26 — Day #3

There is prairie land all around Brittany's farm. The prairie is a large open space of land. It is very flat and grassy. Many kinds of animals live on the prairie, such as prairie dogs, coyotes, buffalo, and wild mustangs.

1. List three words that describe the prairie. __large, flat, grassy (Answers may vary.)__
2. Are the animals in the prairie **wild** or **tame**? __wild__
3. List three animals that live on the prairie. __prairie dogs, coyotes, buffalo (Answers may vary.)__
4. Fill in words from the paragraph to complete the summary. Brittany's __farm__ is surrounded by prairie land that is very __flat__ and __grassy__. Prairie dogs, __coyotes__, __buffalo__, and __wild mustangs__ live on the prairie.

Week #26 — Day #4

Brittany enjoys helping on the farm, in-line skating, and learning about science in her small class of only three children.

1. Does Brittany go to school with lots of other kids? __no__
2. How many other children are in her class? __2__
3. Would you like to live where Brittany does? __Answers will vary.__ Why or why not? __Answers will vary.__
4. Write a summary of this paragraph in your own words. __Answers will vary.__

Week #26 — Assessment

1. Preview the story. What kind of writing is this? __a poem__

A Rabbit Poem

2. What will the poem be about? __a rabbit__

The rabbit is small and fast,
With a short and fluffy tail.
He has long ears that let him hear
Scary animals without fail.

3. Write a sentence to tell what rabbits look like. __Rabbits are small animals with short fluffy tails and long ears. (Answers may vary.)__

Rabbits love to eat and eat!
They love the green, green grass.
They love to munch on vegetables
In a farmer's garden patch.

4. What two things do rabbits love to eat? __grass and vegetables__
5. Write one sentence to summarize the whole poem. __Rabbits are small animals that eat grass and vegetables. (Answers may vary.)__

Answer Key

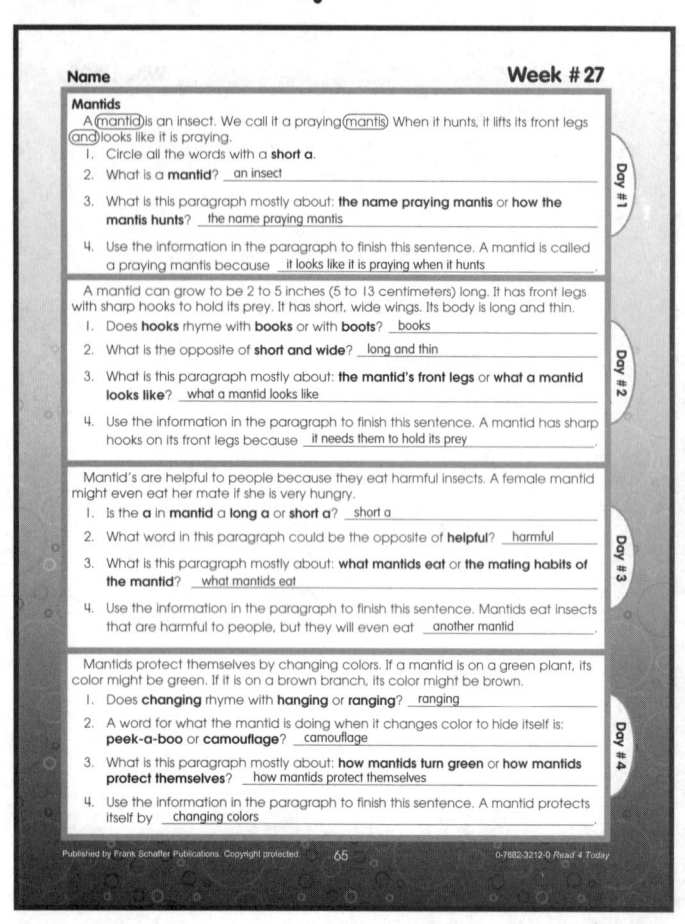

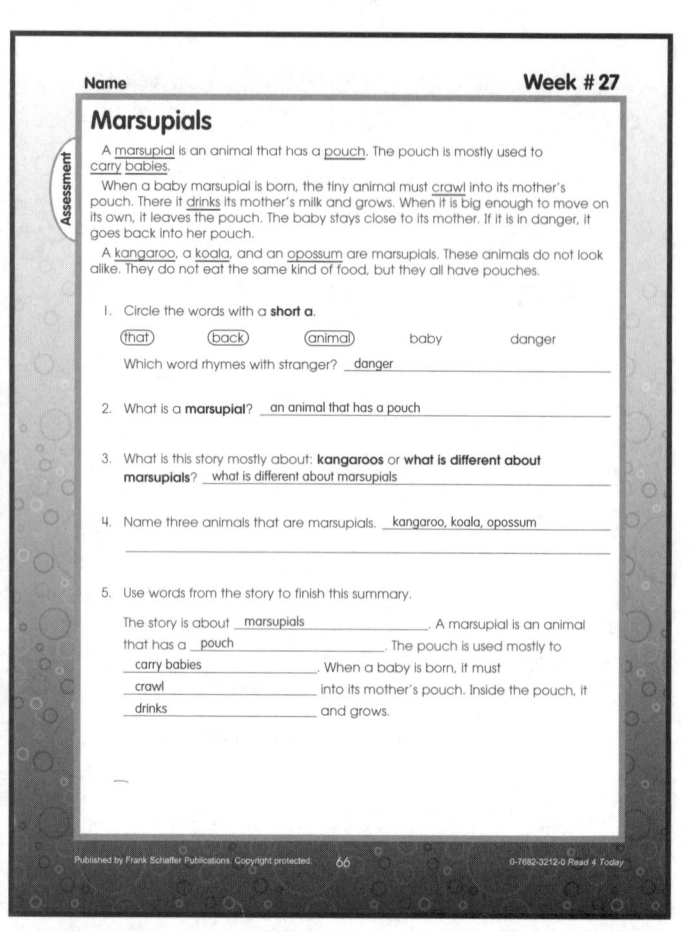

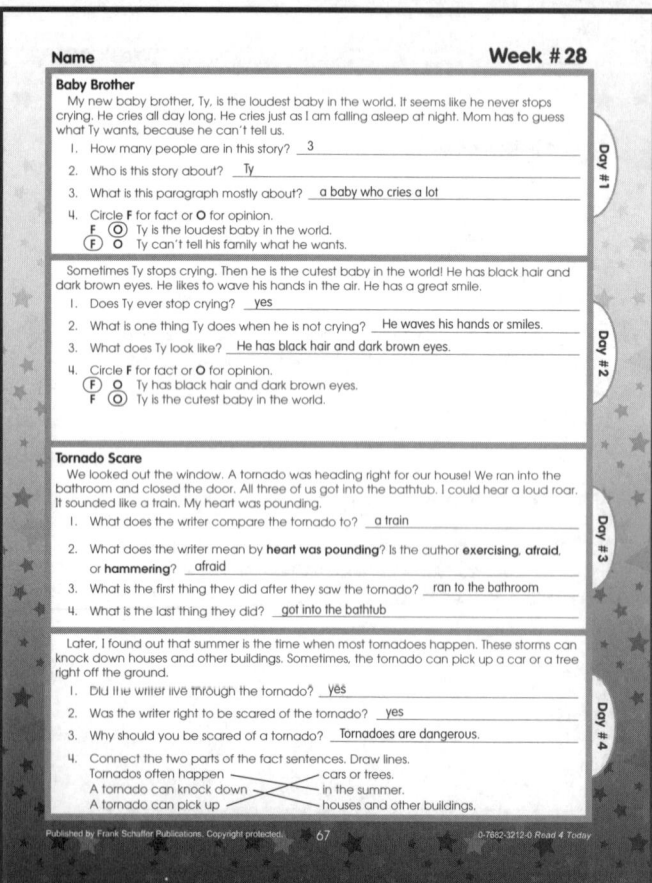

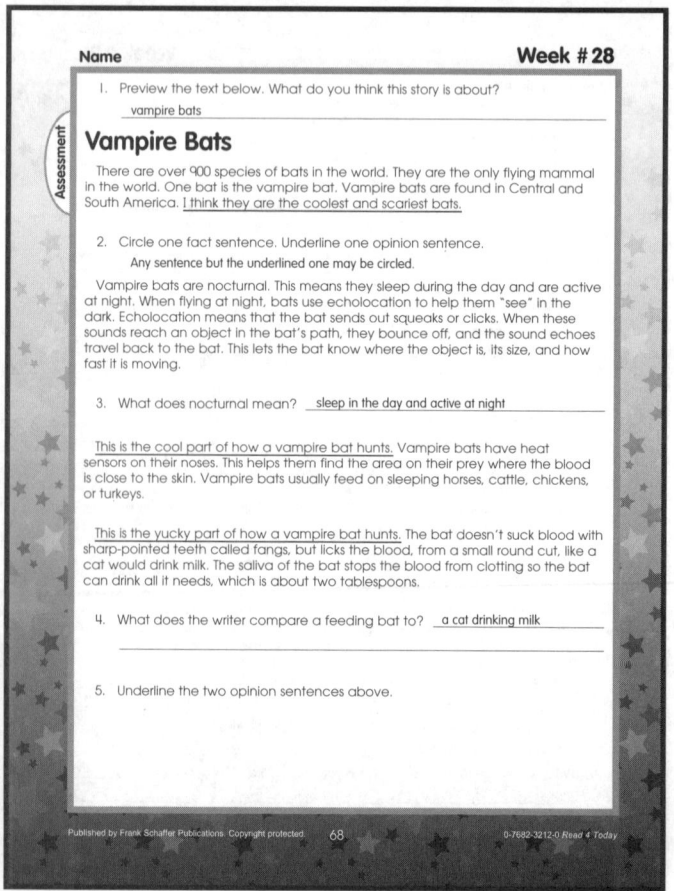

Week #27 — Mantids

Mantids
A (mantid) is an insect. We call it a praying (mantis.) When it hunts, it lifts its front legs (and) looks like it is praying.

Day #1
1. Circle all the words with a **short a**.
2. What is a **mantid**? _an insect_
3. What is this paragraph mostly about: **the name praying mantis** or **how the mantis hunts**? _the name praying mantis_
4. Use the information in the paragraph to finish this sentence. A mantid is called a praying mantis because _it looks like it is praying when it hunts_

A mantid can grow to be 2 to 5 inches (5 to 13 centimeters) long. It has front legs with sharp hooks to hold its prey. It has short, wide wings. Its body is long and thin.

Day #2
1. Does **hooks** rhyme with **books** or with **boots**? _books_
2. What is the opposite of **short and wide**? _long and thin_
3. What is this paragraph mostly about: **the mantid's front legs** or **what a mantid looks like**? _what a mantid looks like_
4. Use the information in the paragraph to finish this sentence. A mantid has sharp hooks on its front legs because _it needs them to hold its prey_

Mantid's are helpful to people because they eat harmful insects. A female mantid might even eat her mate if she is very hungry.

Day #3
1. Is the **a** in **mantid** a **long a** or **short a**? _short a_
2. What word in this paragraph could be the opposite of **helpful**? _harmful_
3. What is this paragraph mostly about: **what mantids eat** or **the mating habits of the mantid**? _what mantids eat_
4. Use the information in the paragraph to finish this sentence. Mantids eat insects that are harmful to people, but they will even eat _another mantid_

Mantids protect themselves by changing colors. If a mantid is on a green plant, its color might be green. If it is on a brown branch, its color might be brown.

Day #4
1. Does **changing** rhyme with **hanging** or **ranging**? _ranging_
2. A word for what the mantid is doing when it changes color to hide itself is: **peek-a-boo** or **camouflage**? _camouflage_
3. What is this paragraph mostly about: **how mantids turn green** or **how mantids protect themselves**? _how mantids protect themselves_
4. Use the information in the paragraph to finish this sentence. A mantid protects itself by _changing colors_

Week #27 — Marsupials (Assessment)

Marsupials
A _marsupial_ is an animal that has a _pouch_. The pouch is mostly used to _carry babies_.

When a baby marsupial is born, the tiny animal must _crawl_ into its mother's pouch. There it _drinks_ its mother's milk and grows. When it is big enough to move on its own, it leaves the pouch. The baby stays close to its mother. If it is in danger, it goes back into her pouch.

A _kangaroo_, a _koala_, and an _opossum_ are marsupials. These animals do not look alike. They do not eat the same kind of food, but they all have pouches.

1. Circle the words with a **short a**.
   (that)   (back)   (animal)   baby   danger
   Which word rhymes with stranger? _danger_

2. What is a **marsupial**? _an animal that has a pouch_

3. What is this story mostly about: **kangaroos** or **what is different about marsupials**? _what is different about marsupials_

4. Name three animals that are marsupials. _kangaroo, koala, opossum_

5. Use words from the story to finish this summary.
   The story is about _marsupials_ . A marsupial is an animal that has a _pouch_ . The pouch is used mostly to _carry babies_ . When a baby is born, it must _crawl_ into its mother's pouch. Inside the pouch, it _drinks_ and grows.

Week #28 — Baby Brother / Tornado Scare

Baby Brother
My new baby brother, Ty, is the loudest baby in the world. It seems like he never stops crying. He cries all day long. He cries just as I am falling asleep at night. Mom has to guess what Ty wants, because he can't tell us.

Day #1
1. How many people are in this story? _3_
2. Who is this story about? _Ty_
3. What is this paragraph mostly about? _a baby who cries a lot_
4. Circle **F** for fact or **O** for opinion.
   F (O) Ty is the loudest baby in the world.
   (F) O Ty can't tell his family what he wants.

Sometimes Ty stops crying. Then he is the cutest baby in the world! He has black hair and dark brown eyes. He likes to wave his hands in the air. He has a great smile.

Day #2
1. Does Ty ever stop crying? _yes_
2. What is one thing Ty does when he is not crying? _He waves his hands or smiles._
3. What does Ty look like? _He has black hair and dark brown eyes._
4. Circle **F** for fact or **O** for opinion.
   (F) O Ty has black hair and dark brown eyes.
   F (O) Ty is the cutest baby in the world.

Tornado Scare
We looked out the window. A tornado was heading right for our house! We ran into the bathroom and closed the door. All three of us got into the bathtub. I could hear a loud roar. It sounded like a train. My heart was pounding.

Day #3
1. What does the writer compare the tornado to? _a train_
2. What does the writer mean by **heart was pounding**? Is the author **exercising**, **afraid**, or **hammering**? _afraid_
3. What is the first thing they did after they saw the tornado? _ran to the bathroom_
4. What is the last thing they did? _got into the bathtub_

Later, I found out that summer is the time when most tornadoes happen. These storms can knock down houses and other buildings. Sometimes, the tornado can pick up a car or a tree right off the ground.

Day #4
1. Did the writer live through the tornado? _yes_
2. Was the writer right to be scared of the tornado? _yes_
3. Why should you be scared of a tornado? _Tornadoes are dangerous._
4. Connect the two parts of the fact sentences. Draw lines.
   Tornadoes often happen — in the summer.
   A tornado can knock down — houses and other buildings.
   A tornado can pick up — cars or trees.

Week #28 — Vampire Bats (Assessment)

1. Preview the text below. What do you think this story is about? _vampire bats_

Vampire Bats
There are over 900 species of bats in the world. They are the only flying mammal in the world. One bat is the vampire bat. Vampire bats are found in Central and South America. I think they are the coolest and scariest bats.

2. Circle one fact sentence. Underline one opinion sentence.
   Any sentence but the underlined one may be circled.

Vampire bats are nocturnal. This means they sleep during the day and are active at night. When flying at night, bats use echolocation to help them "see" in the dark. Echolocation means that the bat sends out squeaks or clicks. When these sounds reach an object in the bat's path, they bounce off, and the sound echoes travel back to the bat. This lets the bat know where the object is, its size, and how fast it is moving.

3. What does nocturnal mean? _sleep in the day and active at night_

This is the cool part of how a vampire bat hunts. Vampire bats have heat sensors on their noses. This helps them find the area on their prey where the blood is close to the skin. Vampire bats usually feed on sleeping horses, cattle, chickens, or turkeys.

This is the yucky part of how a vampire bat hunts. The bat doesn't suck blood with sharp-pointed teeth called fangs, but licks the blood, from a small round cut, like a cat would drink milk. The saliva of the bat stops the blood from clotting so the bat can drink all it needs, which is about two tablespoons.

4. What does the writer compare a feeding bat to? _a cat drinking milk_

5. Underline the two opinion sentences above.

Answer Key

Week #29 — Figs

Figs
Fig is the name of a fruit and the plant the fruit grows on. The plant can look like a bush or like a tree. Fig plants grow where it is warm all year long.

1. List all the words that start with a **hard g** sound. _grows, grow_
2. Which word describes a place where it is warm all year long? a. frosty (b.) tropical
3. Which word does **fruit** rhyme with: **hit** or **toot**? _toot_
4. Circle the sentence that is a fact. Underline the sentence that is an opinion.
   (A fig is a plant and a fruit.) The fig tree is very pretty.

Day #1

The fig fruit grows in bunches on the stems of fig plants. Some figs can be picked two times each year.

1. List all the words that have a **hard g** sound. _fig, grows, figs_
2. What word could you write instead of **bunches**? a. singles (b.) groups
3. What is the main idea of this paragraph: **how figs grow** or **what figs look like**? _how figs grow_
4. Circle the sentence that is a fact. Underline the sentence that is an opinion.
   Figs remind me of a bunch of balloons. (Figs grow in a bunch.)

Day #2

They (can) be (picked) from old branches in June or July. They (can) be (picked) from new branches in August or September.

1. Circle all the words that have a **hard c** sound.
2. What other word could you write instead of **picked**? (a.) plucked b. bitten
3. How many months can you pick figs? _4_
4. Circle the sentence that is a fact. Underline the sentence that is an opinion.
   Figs are hard to pick. (You can pick figs mostly in the summer.)

Day #3

Many people like to eat figs. They (can) be eaten in fig (cookies) or in fig bars. They (can) be (canned) or eaten fresh. Sometimes figs are dried.

1. Circle all the words that start with a **hard c**.
2. What other word could you use instead of **many**: **all** or **lots**? _lots_
3. What other food can be eaten fresh, canned, or dried? (a.) cherries b. broccoli
4. Circle the sentence that is a fact. Underline the sentence that is an opinion.
   The best way to eat a fig is in a fig cookie. (You can eat figs in many ways.)

Day #4

Week #29 — Pilots (Assessment)

Pilots
A pilot is a person who can fly an airplane. Pilots go to special schools to learn how to fly planes. Some pilots fly planes for fun. Other pilots fly planes as their job. They carry people or cargo from city to city. Pilots have to learn how to fly in all kinds of weather. They have to work with people on the ground to land planes safely. Being a pilot is an important job.

1. List the story words that start with a **hard c**. _can, carry, cargo_

   List the story words that start with a **hard g**. _go, ground_

2. What is a **pilot**? _a person who can fly an airplane_

3. Draw lines to connect the two parts of the fact sentences together.
   Pilots go to special schools — for fun.
   Some pilots fly planes — of weather.
   Pilots have to fly in all kinds — to learn how to fly planes.

4. Circle the sentence that is a fact.
   a. Pilots must have a lot of fun flying planes.
   b. It must be scary to fly in a storm.
   (c.) Some pilots fly planes as their job.

5. Write your own opinion sentence about pilots. _Answers will vary._

Week #30 — Chain Reaction

Chain Reaction
Terri dropped the marble. It hit the sleeping cat on the nose. The surprised cat jumped on the dog's tail. The dog yipped and chased the cat.

1. What happened first? _Terri dropped the marble._
2. What happened second? _The marble hit the cat on the nose._
3. What happened third? _The cat jumped on the dog's tail._
4. What happened fourth? _The dog chased the cat._

Day #1

The cat ran under the fish tank. The fish tank wobbled back and forth. Water and one small fish splashed out onto the floor. The happy cat ate the fish. The thirsty dog lapped up the water.

1. What was the last effect on the dog? _The dog drank water._
2. What was the last effect on the cat? _The cat ate a fish._
3. What caused the chain reaction? _Terri dropped a marble._
4. Do you think Terri dropped the marble on the cat's nose **on purpose** or **by accident**? _by accident (Answers may vary.)_

Day #2

The Food Chain
Predators are animals that eat other animals. The animals they eat are called prey. Predators and prey do important jobs in nature. Prey animals are food for the animals that hunt them. But predators also help prey.

1. What do you call an animal that eats other animals? _predator_
2. What do you call an animal that is eaten by other animals? _prey_
3. How does the prey help the predator? _It is food for the predator._
4. Are people predators or prey? _predators_

Day #3

Coyotes hunt rabbits. If coyotes did not eat some rabbits, there would be too many rabbits hopping around. There would not be enough food for all the rabbits to eat. Then the hungry rabbits would grow weak and sick. Some might even die.

1. Coyotes are called _predators_ because they eat other animals.
2. Rabbits are called _prey_ because they are animals that coyotes eat.
3. What would the effect be if coyotes stopped eating rabbits? _Too many rabbits for their food and some would die._
4. Does this paragraph tell you what rabbits eat? _no_

Day #4

Week #30 — Science Magic (Assessment)

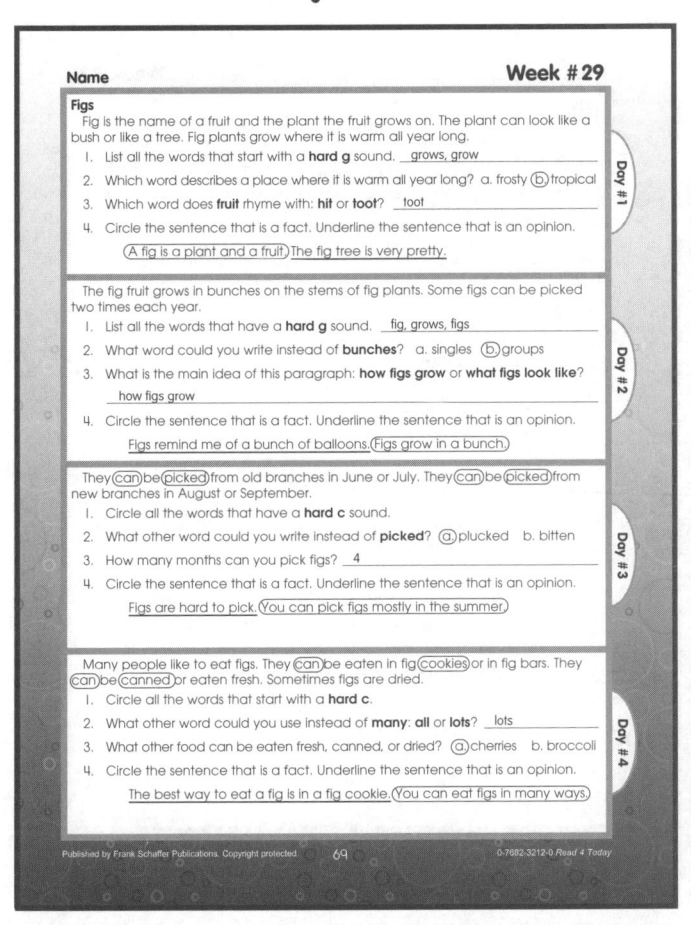

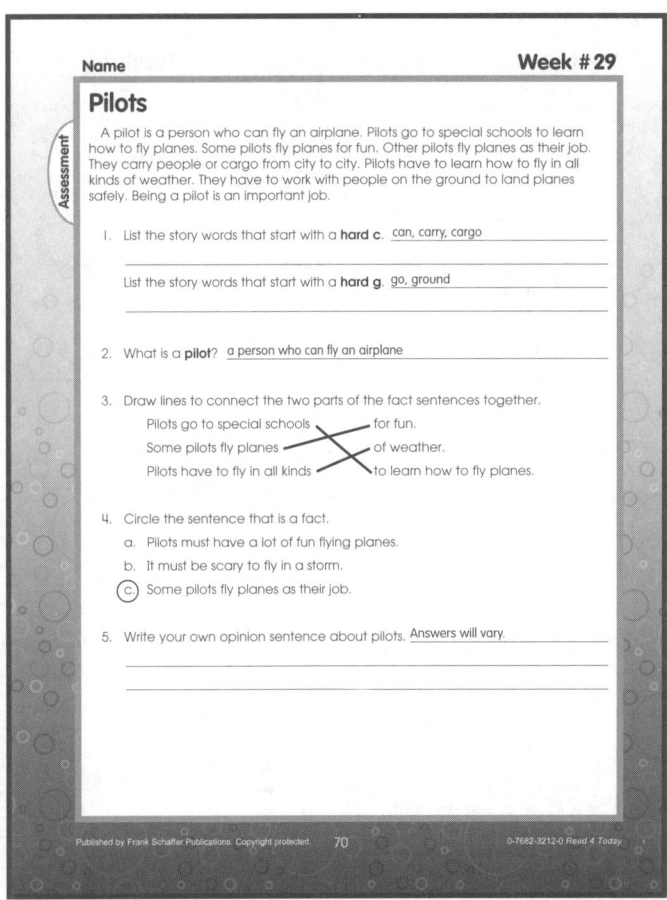

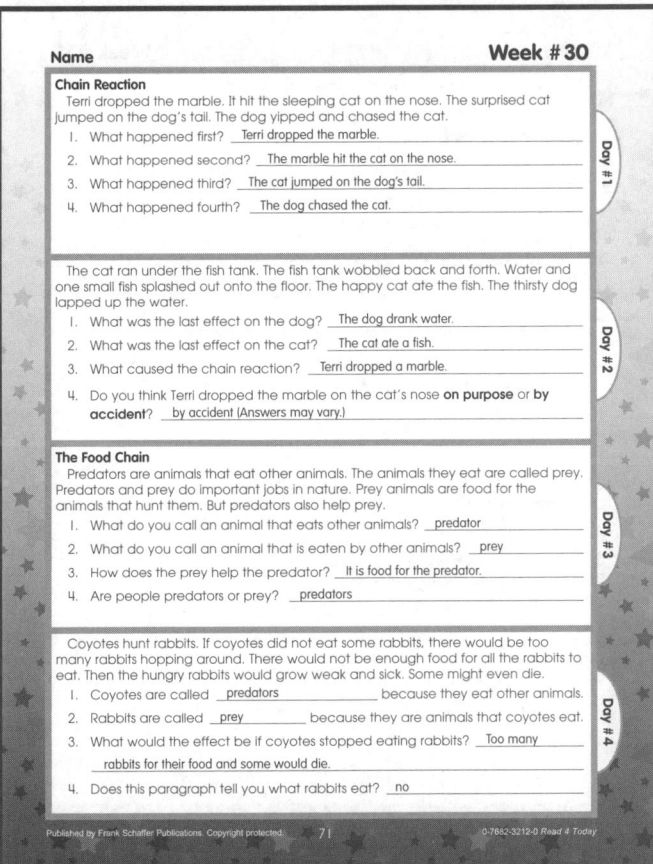

1. Based on the title below, predict what the story will be about.
   Answers will vary.

Science Magic
Joe shared a magic science trick with his class. He said, "How can you tell a raw egg from a hard-boiled egg without cracking it open?"
Marta asked, "Shake it?"
"No," said Joe. "Watch this. One of these eggs is hard-boiled. The other one is raw."
Joe put the eggs on the table. He made each egg spin like a top. Then he gently touched the top of each egg with two fingers. One egg stopped. The other one kept spinning. Joe picked up the egg that stopped spinning.

2. What does Joe do first? _Joe asks the class a question._

3. How are the two eggs different? _One is hard-boiled and the other one is raw._

"This is the hard-boiled egg," Joe said. "The raw egg inside the shell keeps moving. That makes the raw egg keep spinning. The hard-boiled egg stops because nothing inside the shell is moving."

4. The raw egg kept moving because _the egg inside the shell keeps moving_

5. Why did Joe do this trick for his class? _Answers will vary._

Published by Frank Schaffer Publications. Copyright protected.   107   0-7682-3212-0 Read 4 Today

Answer Key

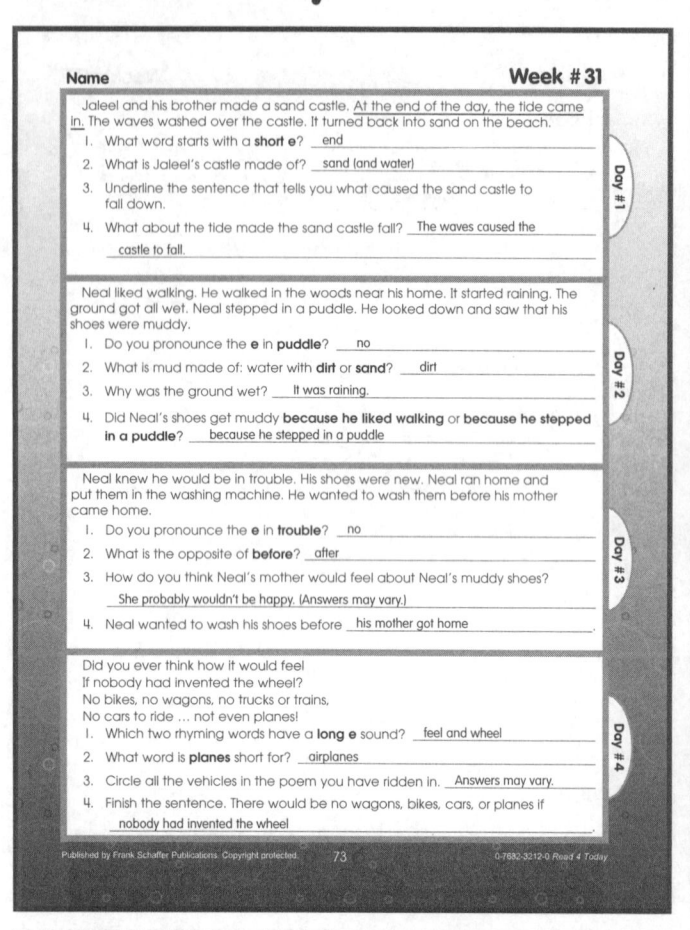

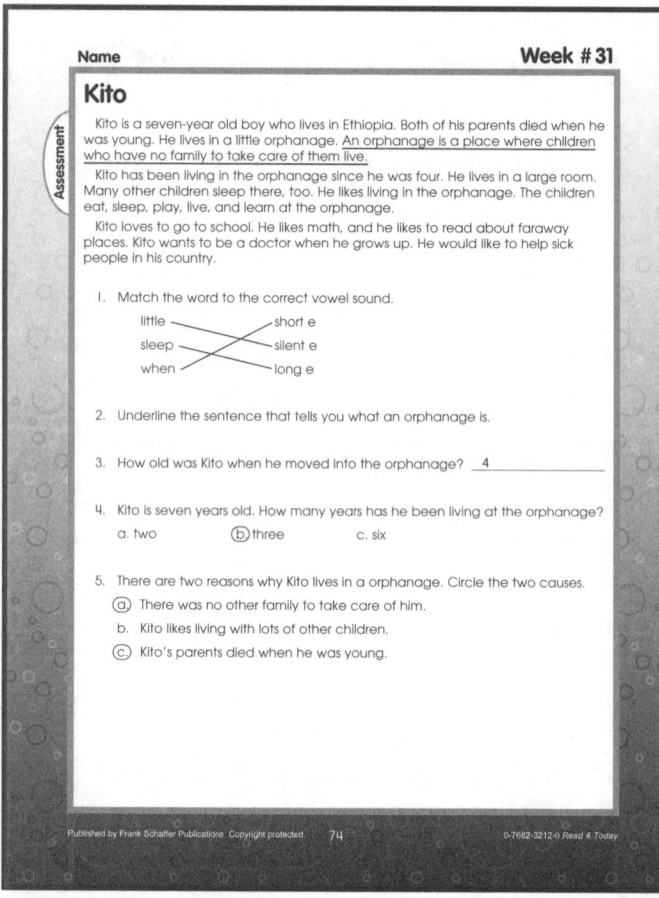

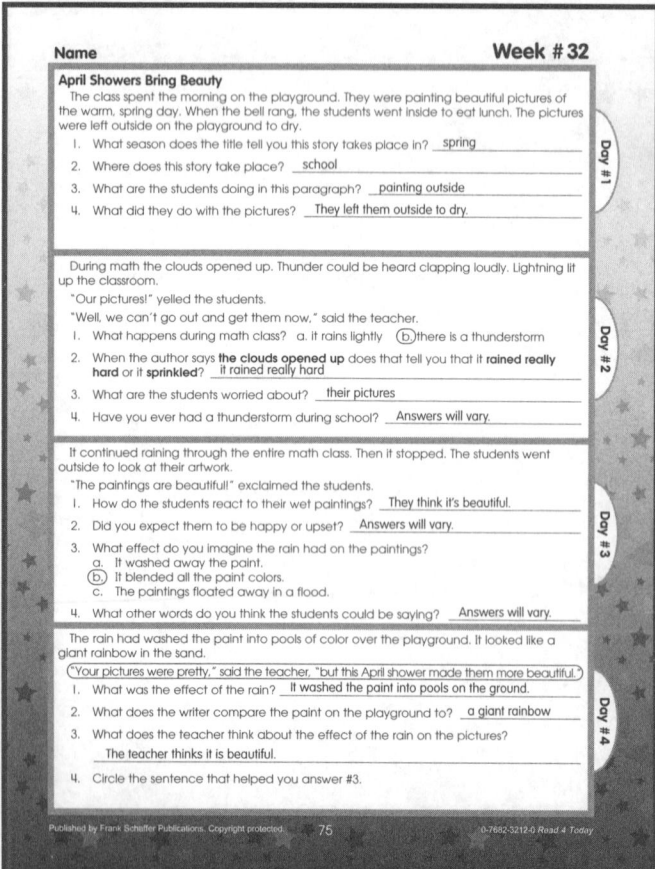

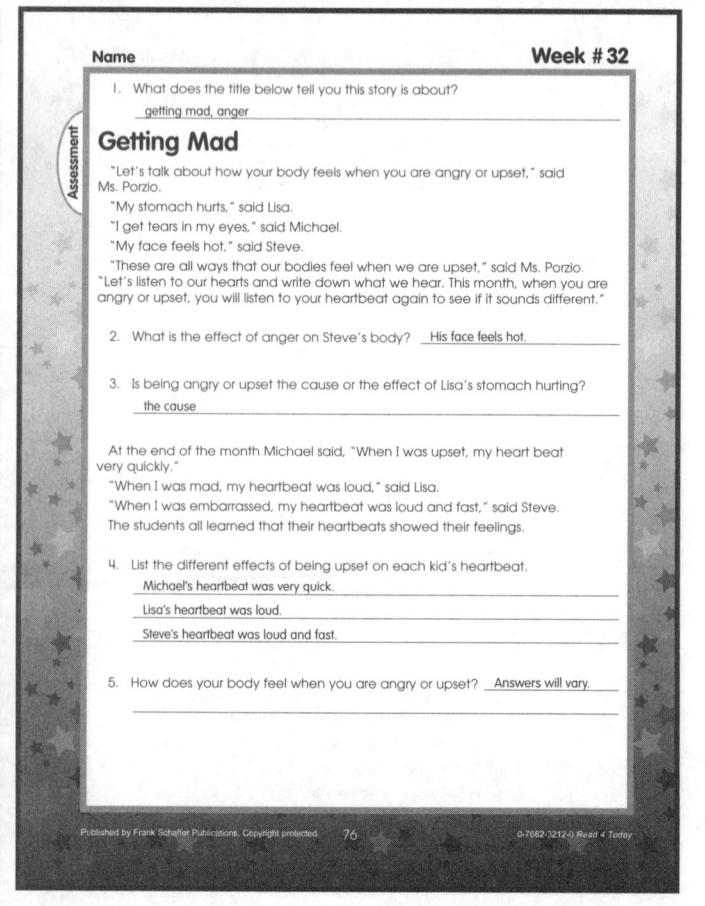

Week #31 — Day #1
Jaleel and his brother made a sand castle. <u>At the end of the day, the tide came in.</u> The waves washed over the castle. It turned back into sand on the beach.
1. What word starts with a **short e**? __end__
2. What is Jaleel's castle made of? __sand (and water)__
3. Underline the sentence that tells you what caused the sand castle to fall down.
4. What about the tide made the sand castle fall? __The waves caused the castle to fall.__

Week #31 — Day #2
Neal liked walking. He walked in the woods near his home. It started raining. The ground got all wet. Neal stepped in a puddle. He looked down and saw that his shoes were muddy.
1. Do you pronounce the **e** in **puddle**? __no__
2. What is mud made of: water with **dirt** or **sand**? __dirt__
3. Why was the ground wet? __It was raining.__
4. Did Neal's shoes get muddy **because he liked walking** or **because he stepped in a puddle**? __because he stepped in a puddle__

Week #31 — Day #3
Neal knew he would be in trouble. His shoes were new. Neal ran home and put them in the washing machine. He wanted to wash them before his mother came home.
1. Do you pronounce the **e** in **trouble**? __no__
2. What is the opposite of **before**? __after__
3. How do you think Neal's mother would feel about Neal's muddy shoes? __She probably wouldn't be happy. (Answers may vary.)__
4. Neal wanted to wash his shoes before __his mother got home__.

Week #31 — Day #4
Did you ever think how it would feel
If nobody had invented the wheel?
No bikes, no wagons, no trucks or trains,
No cars to ride ... not even planes!
1. Which two rhyming words have a **long e** sound? __feel and wheel__
2. What word is **planes** short for? __airplanes__
3. Circle all the vehicles in the poem you have ridden in. __Answers may vary.__
4. Finish the sentence. There would be no wagons, bikes, cars, or planes if __nobody had invented the wheel__.

Week #31 — Assessment
Kito
Kito is a seven-year old boy who lives in Ethiopia. Both of his parents died when he was young. He lives in a little orphanage. <u>An orphanage is a place where children who have no family to take care of them live.</u>
Kito has been living in the orphanage since he was four. He lives in a large room. Many other children sleep there, too. He likes living in the orphanage. The children eat, sleep, play, live, and learn at the orphanage.
Kito loves to go to school. He likes math, and he likes to read about faraway places. Kito wants to be a doctor when he grows up. He would like to help sick people in his country.

1. Match the word to the correct vowel sound.
   little → short e
   sleep → long e
   when → silent e
2. Underline the sentence that tells you what an orphanage is.
3. How old was Kito when he moved into the orphanage? __4__
4. Kito is seven years old. How many years has he been living at the orphanage?
   a. two   (b.) three   c. six
5. There are two reasons why Kito lives in a orphanage. Circle the two causes.
   (a.) There was no other family to take care of him.
   b. Kito likes living with lots of other children.
   (c.) Kito's parents died when he was young.

Week #32 — Day #1
April Showers Bring Beauty
The class spent the morning on the playground. They were painting beautiful pictures of the warm, spring day. When the bell rang, the students went inside to eat lunch. The pictures were left outside on the playground to dry.
1. What season does the title tell you this story takes place in? __spring__
2. Where does this story take place? __school__
3. What are the students doing in this paragraph? __painting outside__
4. What did they do with the pictures? __They left them outside to dry.__

Week #32 — Day #2
During math the clouds opened up. Thunder could be heard clapping loudly. Lightning lit up the classroom.
"Our pictures!" yelled the students.
"Well, we can't go out and get them now," said the teacher.
1. What happens during math class? a. it rains lightly (b.) there is a thunderstorm
2. When the author says **the clouds opened up** does that tell you that it **rained really hard** or it **sprinkled**? __it rained really hard__
3. What are the students worried about? __their pictures__
4. Have you ever had a thunderstorm during school? __Answers will vary.__

Week #32 — Day #3
It continued raining through the entire math class. Then it stopped. The students went outside to look at their artwork.
"The paintings are beautiful!" exclaimed the students.
1. How do the students react to their wet paintings? __They think it's beautiful.__
2. Did you expect them to be happy or upset? __Answers will vary.__
3. What effect do you imagine the rain had on the paintings?
   a. It washed away the paint.
   (b.) It blended all the paint colors.
   c. The paintings floated away in a flood.
4. What other words do you think the students could be saying? __Answers will vary.__

Week #32 — Day #4
The rain had washed the paint into pools of color over the playground. It looked like a giant rainbow in the sand.
<u>"Your pictures were pretty," said the teacher, "but this April shower made them more beautiful."</u>
1. What was the effect of the rain? __It washed the paint into pools on the ground.__
2. What does the writer compare the paint on the playground to? __a giant rainbow__
3. What does the teacher think about the effect of the rain on the pictures? __The teacher thinks it is beautiful.__
4. Circle the sentence that helped you answer #3.

Week #32 — Assessment
1. What does the title below tell you this story is about? __getting mad, anger__

Getting Mad
"Let's talk about how your body feels when you are angry or upset," said Ms. Porzio.
"My stomach hurts," said Lisa.
"I get tears in my eyes," said Michael.
"My face feels hot," said Steve.
"These are all ways that our bodies feel when we are upset," said Ms. Porzio. "Let's listen to our hearts and write down what we hear. This month, when you are angry or upset, you will listen to your heartbeat again to see if it sounds different."

2. What is the effect of anger on Steve's body? __His face feels hot.__
3. Is being angry or upset the cause or the effect of Lisa's stomach hurting? __the cause__

At the end of the month Michael said, "When I was upset, my heart beat very quickly."
"When I was mad, my heartbeat was loud," said Lisa.
"When I was embarrassed, my heartbeat was loud and fast," said Steve.
The students all learned that their heartbeats showed their feelings.

4. List the different effects of being upset on each kid's heartbeat.
   __Michael's heartbeat was very quick.__
   __Lisa's heartbeat was loud.__
   __Steve's heartbeat was loud and fast.__
5. How does your body feel when you are angry or upset? __Answers will vary.__

Answer Key

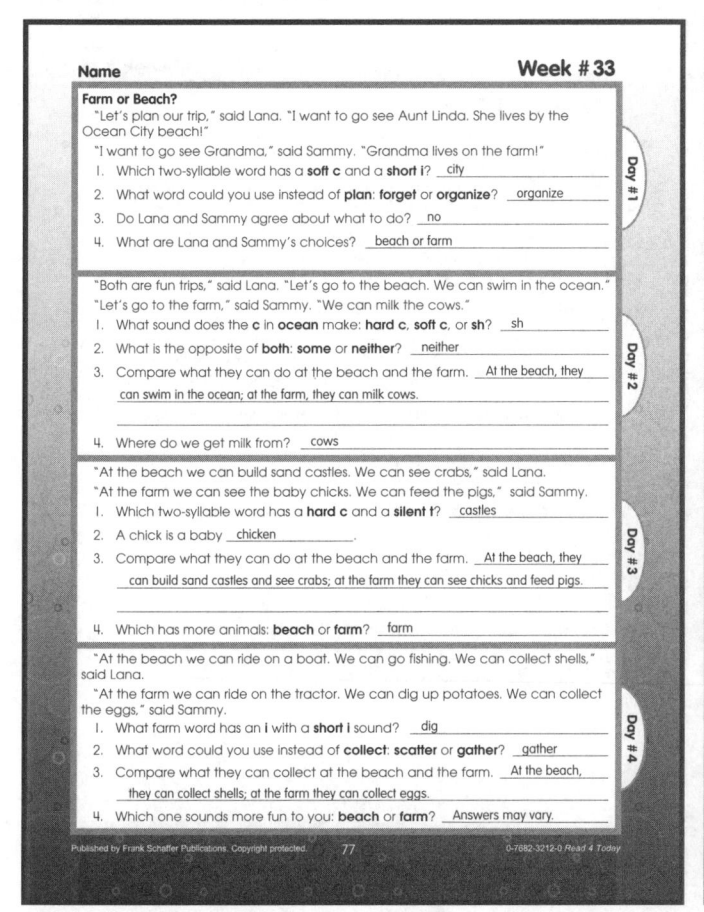

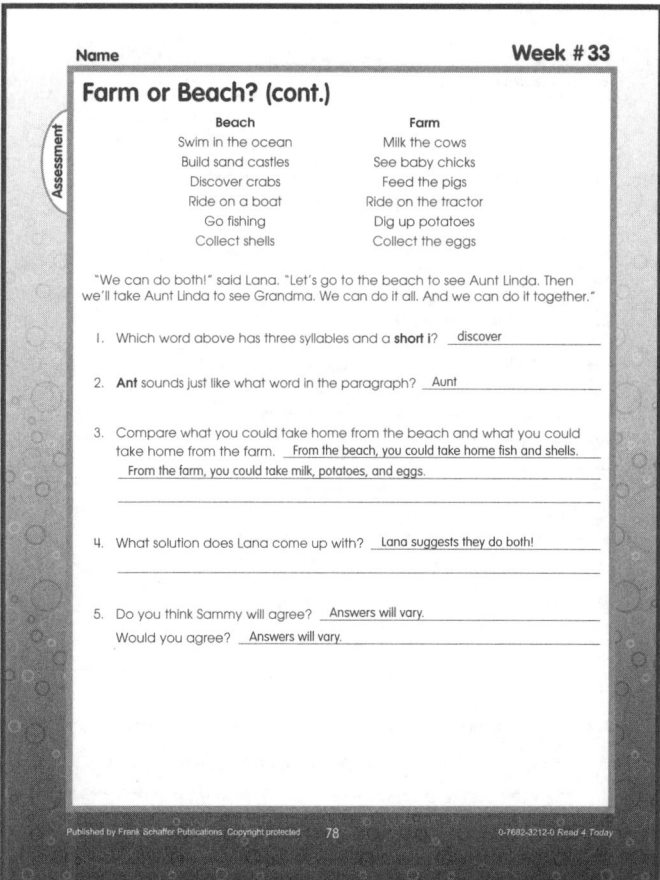

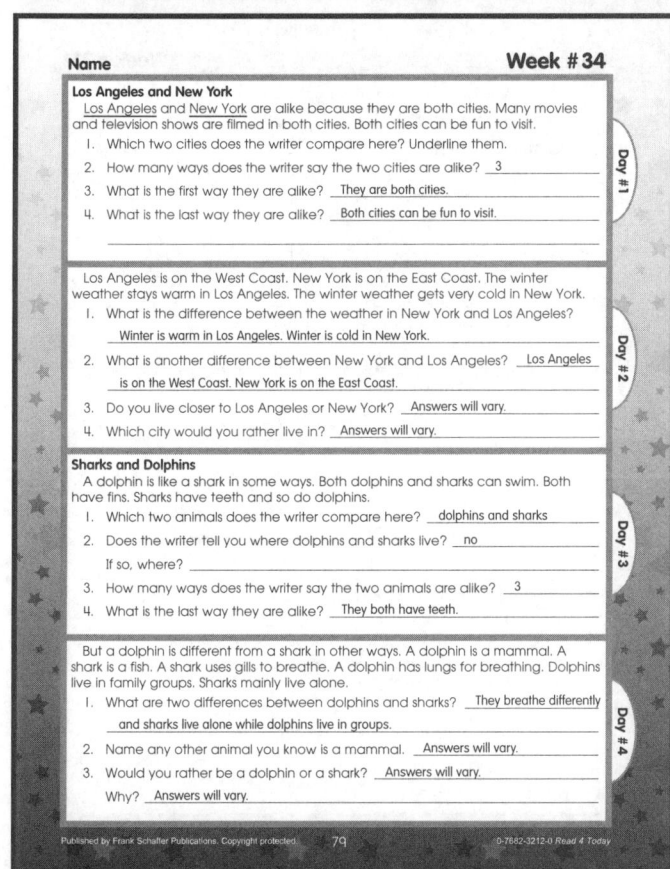

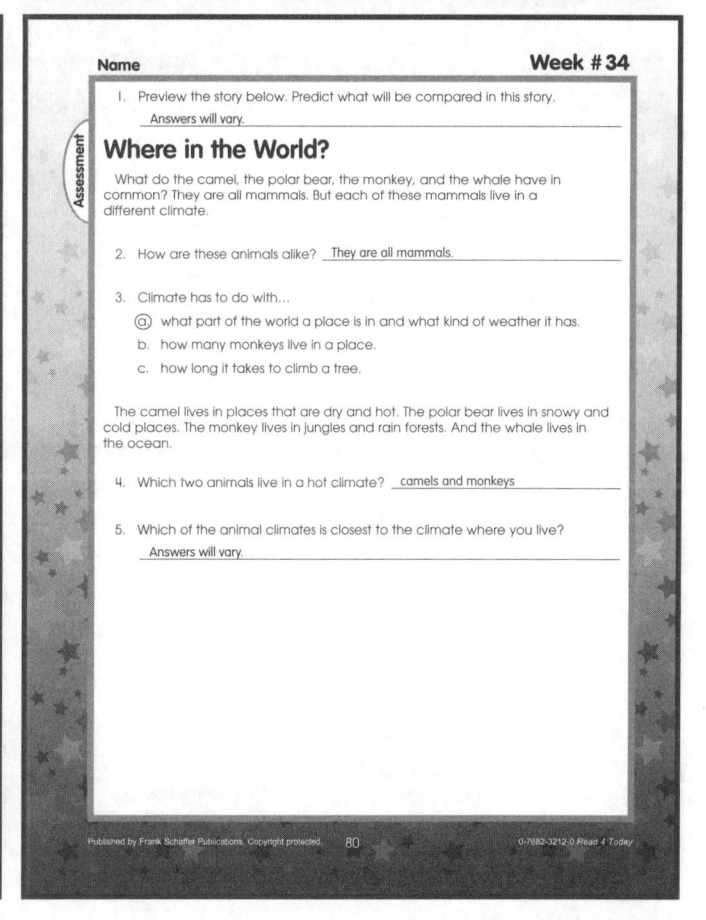

Week #33 — Farm or Beach?

"Let's plan our trip," said Lana. "I want to go see Aunt Linda. She lives by the Ocean City beach!"
"I want to go see Grandma," said Sammy. "Grandma lives on the farm!"

Day #1
1. Which two-syllable word has a **soft c** and a **short i**? _city_
2. What word could you use instead of **plan**: **forget** or **organize**? _organize_
3. Do Lana and Sammy agree about what to do? _no_
4. What are Lana and Sammy's choices? _beach or farm_

"Both are fun trips," said Lana. "Let's go to the beach. We can swim in the ocean."
"Let's go to the farm," said Sammy. "We can milk the cows."

Day #2
1. What sound does the **c** in **ocean** make: **hard c**, **soft c**, or **sh**? _sh_
2. What is the opposite of **both**: **some** or **neither**? _neither_
3. Compare what they can do at the beach and the farm. _At the beach, they can swim in the ocean; at the farm, they can milk cows._
4. Where do we get milk from? _cows_

"At the beach we can build sand castles. We can see crabs," said Lana.
"At the farm we can see the baby chicks. We can feed the pigs," said Sammy.

Day #3
1. Which two-syllable word has a **hard c** and a **silent t**? _castles_
2. A chick is a baby _chicken_.
3. Compare what they can do at the beach and the farm. _At the beach, they can build sand castles and see crabs; at the farm they can see chicks and feed pigs._
4. Which has more animals: **beach** or **farm**? _farm_

"At the beach we can ride on a boat. We can go fishing. We can collect shells," said Lana.
"At the farm we can ride on the tractor. We can dig up potatoes. We can collect the eggs," said Sammy.

Day #4
1. What farm word has an **i** with a **short i** sound? _dig_
2. What word could you use instead of **collect**: **scatter** or **gather**? _gather_
3. Compare what they can collect at the beach and the farm. _At the beach, they can collect shells; at the farm they can collect eggs._
4. Which one sounds more fun to you: **beach** or **farm**? _Answers may vary._

Week #33 — Farm or Beach? (cont.) — Assessment

Beach	Farm
Swim in the ocean	Milk the cows
Build sand castles	See baby chicks
Discover crabs	Feed the pigs
Ride on a boat	Ride on the tractor
Go fishing	Dig up potatoes
Collect shells	Collect the eggs

"We can do both!" said Lana. "Let's go to the beach to see Aunt Linda. Then we'll take Aunt Linda to see Grandma. We can do it all. And we can do it together."

1. Which word above has three syllables and a **short i**? _discover_
2. **Ant** sounds just like what word in the paragraph? _Aunt_
3. Compare what you could take home from the beach and what you could take home from the farm. _From the beach, you could take home fish and shells. From the farm, you could take milk, potatoes, and eggs._
4. What solution does Lana come up with? _Lana suggests they do both!_
5. Do you think Sammy will agree? _Answers will vary._
   Would you agree? _Answers will vary._

Week #34 — Los Angeles and New York

Los Angeles and New York are alike because they are both cities. Many movies and television shows are filmed in both cities. Both cities can be fun to visit.

Day #1
1. Which two cities does the writer compare here? Underline them.
2. How many ways does the writer say the two cities are alike? _3_
3. What is the first way they are alike? _They are both cities._
4. What is the last way they are alike? _Both cities can be fun to visit._

Los Angeles is on the West Coast. New York is on the East Coast. The winter weather stays warm in Los Angeles. The winter weather gets very cold in New York.

Day #2
1. What is the difference between the weather in New York and Los Angeles? _Winter is warm in Los Angeles. Winter is cold in New York._
2. What is another difference between New York and Los Angeles? _Los Angeles is on the West Coast. New York is on the East Coast._
3. Do you live closer to Los Angeles or New York? _Answers will vary._
4. Which city would you rather live in? _Answers will vary._

Sharks and Dolphins

A dolphin is like a shark in some ways. Both dolphins and sharks can swim. Both have fins. Sharks have teeth and so do dolphins.

Day #3
1. Which two animals does the writer compare here? _dolphins and sharks_
2. Does the writer tell you where dolphins and sharks live? _no_
   If so, where?
3. How many ways does the writer say the two animals are alike? _3_
4. What is the last way they are alike? _They both have teeth._

But a dolphin is different from a shark in other ways. A dolphin is a mammal. A shark is a fish. A shark uses gills to breathe. A dolphin has lungs for breathing. Dolphins live in family groups. Sharks mainly live alone.

Day #4
1. What are two differences between dolphins and sharks? _They breathe differently and sharks live alone while dolphins live in groups._
2. Name any other animal you know is a mammal. _Answers will vary._
3. Would you rather be a dolphin or a shark? _Answers will vary._
   Why? _Answers will vary._

Week #34 — Assessment

1. Preview the story below. Predict what will be compared in this story.
   Answers will vary.

Where in the World?

What do the camel, the polar bear, the monkey, and the whale have in common? They are all mammals. But each of these mammals live in a different climate.

2. How are these animals alike? _They are all mammals._
3. Climate has to do with...
   a. what part of the world a place is in and what kind of weather it has. ✓
   b. how many monkeys live in a place.
   c. how long it takes to climb a tree.

The camel lives in places that are dry and hot. The polar bear lives in snowy and cold places. The monkey lives in jungles and rain forests. And the whale lives in the ocean.

4. Which two animals live in a hot climate? _camels and monkeys_
5. Which of the animal climates is closest to the climate where you live?
   Answers will vary.

Answer Key

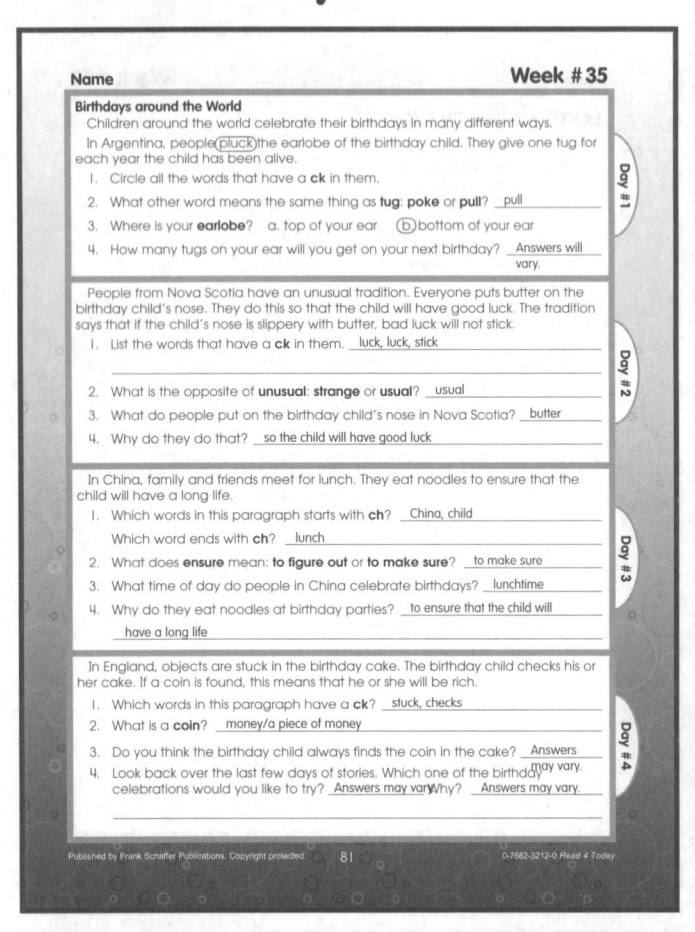

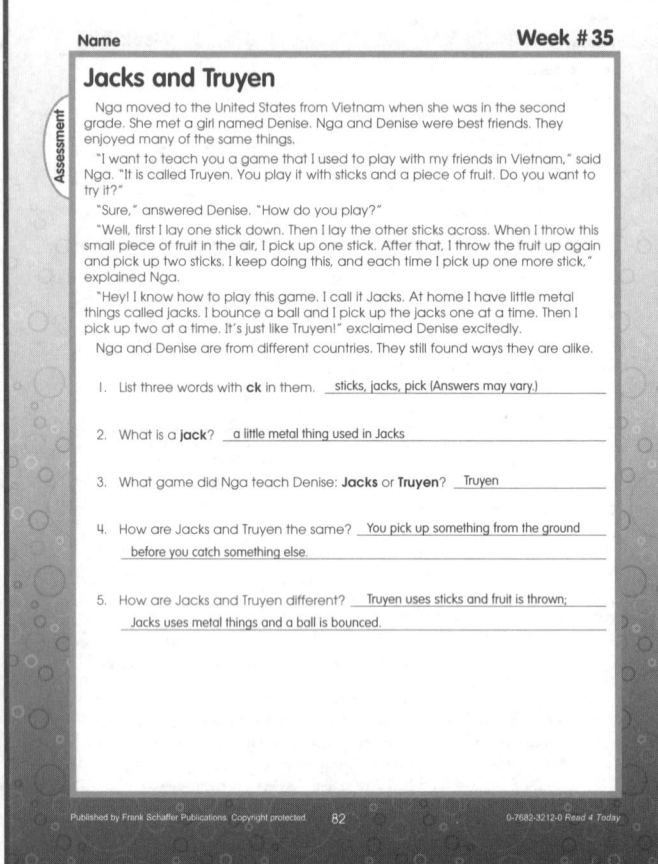

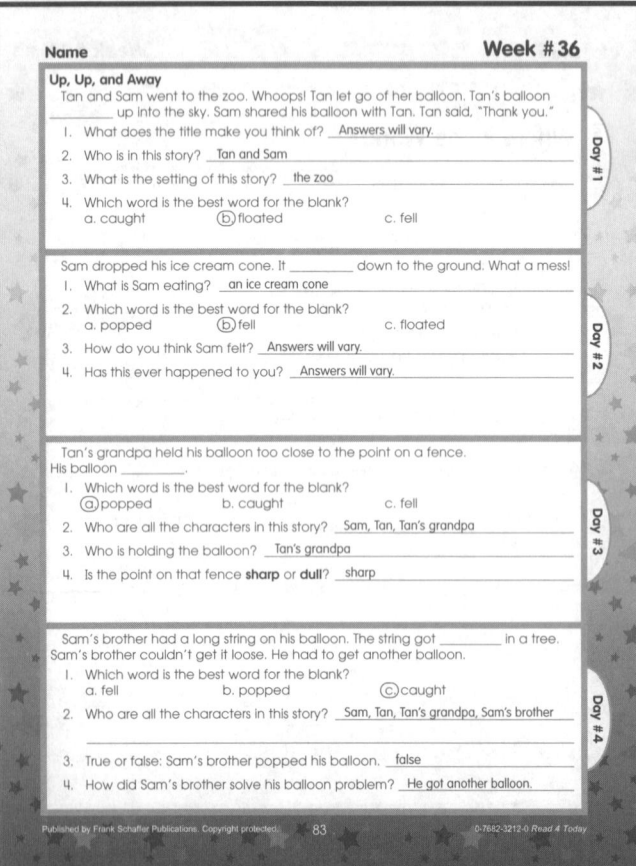

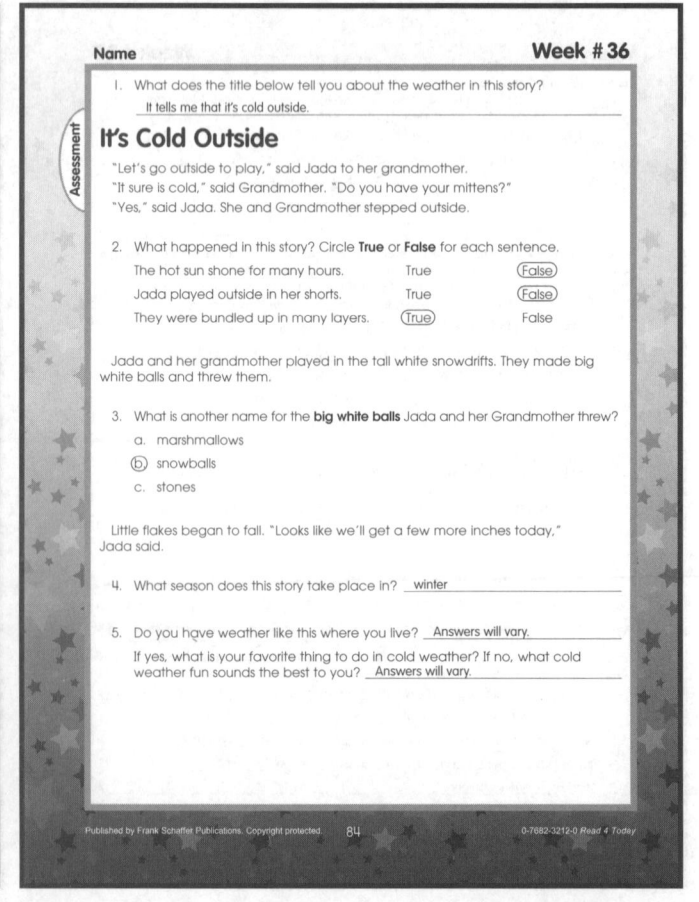

Week #35 — Birthdays around the World

Children around the world celebrate their birthdays in many different ways.

In Argentina, people (pluck) the earlobe of the birthday child. They give one tug for each year the child has been alive.

Day #1
1. Circle all the words that have a **ck** in them.
2. What other word means the same thing as **tug**: poke or **pull**? ___pull___
3. Where is your **earlobe**? a. top of your ear (b) bottom of your ear
4. How many tugs on your ear will you get on your next birthday? ___Answers will vary.___

People from Nova Scotia have an unusual tradition. Everyone puts butter on the birthday child's nose. They do this so that the child will have good luck. The tradition says that if the child's nose is slippery with butter, bad luck will not stick.

Day #2
1. List the words that have a **ck** in them. ___luck, luck, stick___
2. What is the opposite of **unusual**: strange or **usual**? ___usual___
3. What do people put on the birthday child's nose in Nova Scotia? ___butter___
4. Why do they do that? ___so the child will have good luck___

In China, family and friends meet for lunch. They eat noodles to ensure that the child will have a long life.

Day #3
1. Which words in this paragraph starts with **ch**? ___China, child___
   Which word ends with **ch**? ___lunch___
2. What does **ensure** mean: to figure out or **to make sure**? ___to make sure___
3. What time of day do people in China celebrate birthdays? ___lunchtime___
4. Why do they eat noodles at birthday parties? ___to ensure that the child will have a long life___

In England, objects are stuck in the birthday cake. The birthday child checks his or her cake. If a coin is found, this means that he or she will be rich.

Day #4
1. Which words in this paragraph have a **ck**? ___stuck, checks___
2. What is a **coin**? ___money/a piece of money___
3. Do you think the birthday child always finds the coin in the cake? ___Answers may vary.___
4. Look back over the last few days of stories. Which one of the birthday celebrations would you like to try? ___Answers may vary___ Why? ___Answers may vary.___

Week #35 — Jacks and Truyen (Assessment)

Nga moved to the United States from Vietnam when she was in the second grade. She met a girl named Denise. Nga and Denise were best friends. They enjoyed many of the same things.

"I want to teach you a game that I used to play with my friends in Vietnam," said Nga. "It is called Truyen. You play it with sticks and a piece of fruit. Do you want to try it?"

"Sure," answered Denise. "How do you play?"

"Well, first I lay one stick down. Then I lay the other sticks across. When I throw this small piece of fruit in the air, I pick up one stick. After that, I throw the fruit up again and pick up two sticks. I keep doing this, and each time I pick up one more stick," explained Nga.

"Hey! I know how to play this game. I call it Jacks. At home I have little metal things called jacks. I bounce a ball and I pick up the jacks one at a time. Then I pick up two at a time. It's just like Truyen!" exclaimed Denise excitedly.

Nga and Denise are from different countries. They still found ways they are alike.

1. List three words with **ck** in them. ___sticks, jacks, pick (Answers may vary.)___
2. What is a **jack**? ___a little metal thing used in Jacks___
3. What game did Nga teach Denise: **Jacks** or **Truyen**? ___Truyen___
4. How are Jacks and Truyen the same? ___You pick up something from the ground before you catch something else.___
5. How are Jacks and Truyen different? ___Truyen uses sticks and fruit is thrown; Jacks uses metal things and a ball is bounced.___

Week #36 — Up, Up, and Away

Tan and Sam went to the zoo. Whoops! Tan let go of her balloon. Tan's balloon _____ up into the sky. Sam shared his balloon with Tan. Tan said, "Thank you."

Day #1
1. What does the title make you think of? ___Answers will vary.___
2. Who is in this story? ___Tan and Sam___
3. What is the setting of this story? ___the zoo___
4. Which word is the best word for the blank?
   a. caught (b) floated c. fell

Sam dropped his ice cream cone. It _____ down to the ground. What a mess!

Day #2
1. What is Sam eating? ___an ice cream cone___
2. Which word is the best word for the blank?
   a. popped (b) fell c. floated
3. How do you think Sam felt? ___Answers will vary.___
4. Has this ever happened to you? ___Answers will vary.___

Tan's grandpa held his balloon too close to the point on a fence. His balloon _____.

Day #3
1. Which word is the best word for the blank?
   (a) popped b. caught c. fell
2. Who are all the characters in this story? ___Sam, Tan, Tan's grandpa___
3. Who is holding the balloon? ___Tan's grandpa___
4. Is the point on that fence **sharp** or **dull**? ___sharp___

Sam's brother had a long string on his balloon. The string got _____ in a tree. Sam's brother couldn't get it loose. He had to get another balloon.

Day #4
1. Which word is the best word for the blank?
   a. fell b. popped (c) caught
2. Who are all the characters in this story? ___Sam, Tan, Tan's grandpa, Sam's brother___
3. True or false: Sam's brother popped his balloon. ___false___
4. How did Sam's brother solve his balloon problem? ___He got another balloon.___

Week #36 — It's Cold Outside (Assessment)

1. What does the title below tell you about the weather in this story? ___It tells me that it's cold outside.___

"Let's go outside to play," said Jada to her grandmother.
"It sure is cold," said Grandmother. "Do you have your mittens?"
"Yes," said Jada. She and Grandmother stepped outside.

2. What happened in this story? Circle **True** or **False** for each sentence.
   - The hot sun shone for many hours. True (False)
   - Jada played outside in her shorts. True (False)
   - They were bundled up in many layers. (True) False

Jada and her grandmother played in the tall white snowdrifts. They made big white balls and threw them.

3. What is another name for the **big white balls** Jada and her Grandmother threw?
   a. marshmallows
   (b) snowballs
   c. stones

Little flakes began to fall. "Looks like we'll get a few more inches today," Jada said.

4. What season does this story take place in? ___winter___
5. Do you have weather like this where you live? ___Answers will vary.___
   If yes, what is your favorite thing to do in cold weather? If no, what cold weather fun sounds the best to you? ___Answers will vary.___

Answer Key

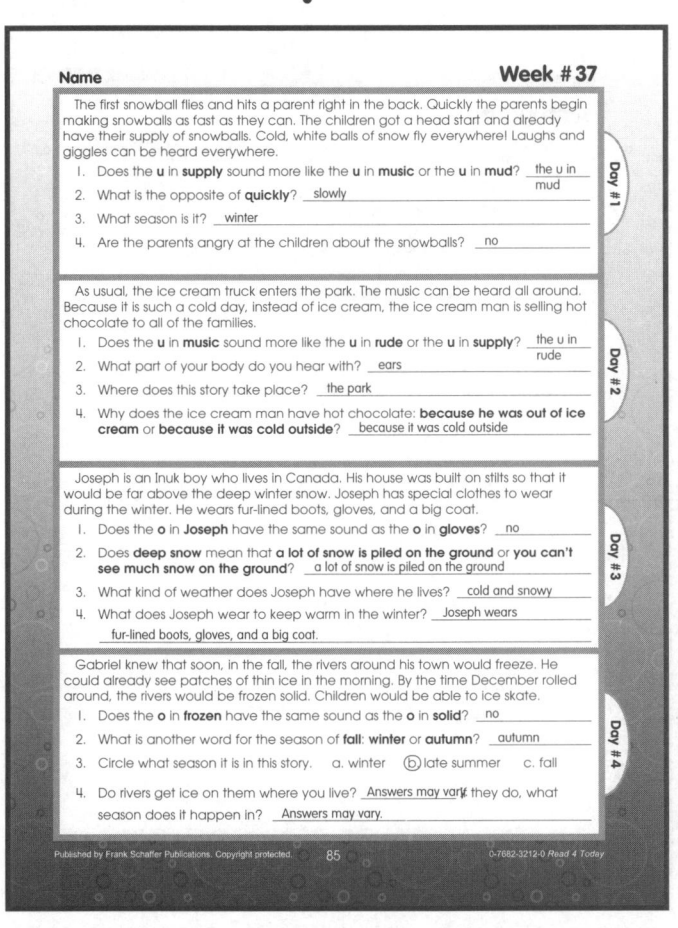

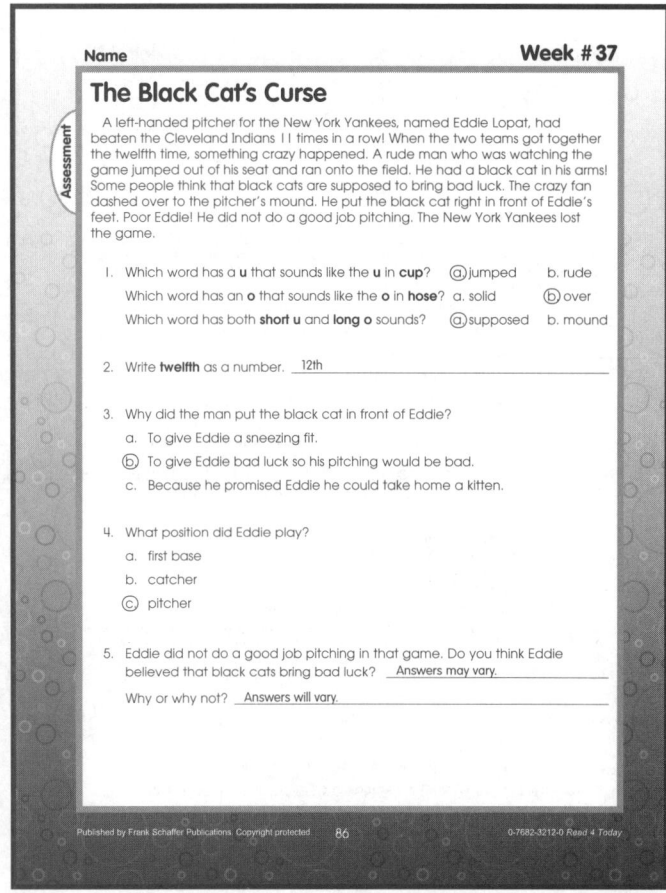

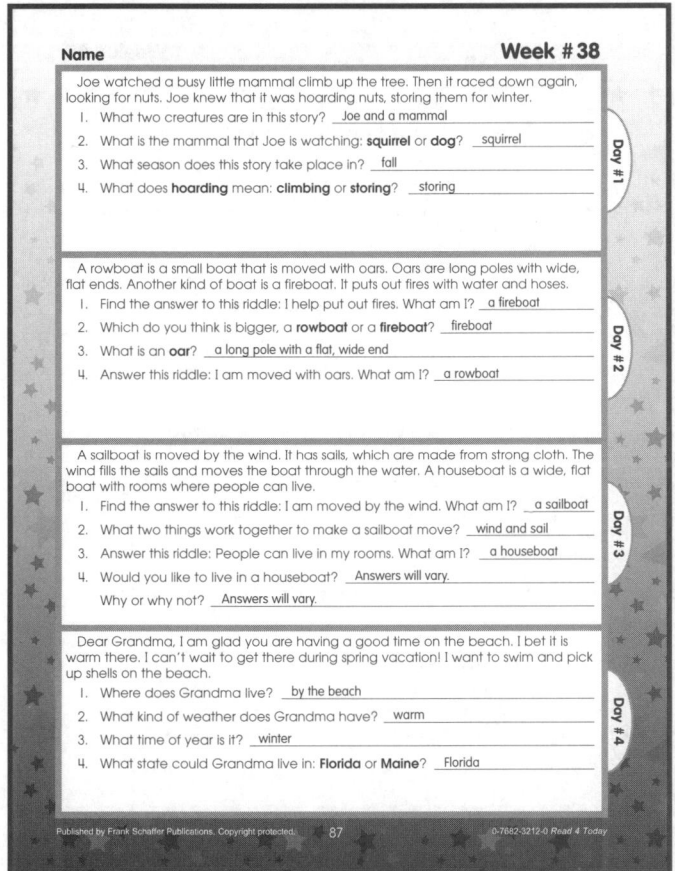

Week #37 — Day #1–#4

The first snowball flies and hits a parent right in the back. Quickly the parents begin making snowballs as fast as they can. The children got a head start and already have their supply of snowballs. Cold, white balls of snow fly everywhere! Laughs and giggles can be heard everywhere.

1. Does the **u** in **supply** sound more like the **u** in **music** or the **u** in **mud**? _the u in mud_
2. What is the opposite of **quickly**? _slowly_
3. What season is it? _winter_
4. Are the parents angry at the children about the snowballs? _no_

As usual, the ice cream truck enters the park. The music can be heard all around. Because it is such a cold day, instead of ice cream, the ice cream man is selling hot chocolate to all of the families.

1. Does the **u** in **music** sound more like the **u** in **rude** or the **u** in **supply**? _the u in rude_
2. What part of your body do you hear with? _ears_
3. Where does this story take place? _the park_
4. Why does the ice cream man have hot chocolate: **because he was out of ice cream** or **because it was cold outside**? _because it was cold outside_

Joseph is an Inuk boy who lives in Canada. His house was built on stilts so that it would be far above the deep winter snow. Joseph has special clothes to wear during the winter. He wears fur-lined boots, gloves, and a big coat.

1. Does the **o** in **Joseph** have the same sound as the **o** in **gloves**? _no_
2. Does **deep snow** mean that **a lot of snow is piled on the ground** or **you can't see much snow on the ground**? _a lot of snow is piled on the ground_
3. What kind of weather does Joseph have where he lives? _cold and snowy_
4. What does Joseph wear to keep warm in the winter? _Joseph wears fur-lined boots, gloves, and a big coat._

Gabriel knew that soon, in the fall, the rivers around his town would freeze. He could already see patches of thin ice in the morning. By the time December rolled around, the rivers would be frozen solid. Children would be able to ice skate.

1. Does the **o** in **frozen** have the same sound as the **o** in **solid**? _no_
2. What is another word for the season of **fall**: **winter** or **autumn**? _autumn_
3. Circle what season it is in this story. a. winter (b) late summer c. fall
4. Do rivers get ice on them where you live? _Answers may vary._ If they do, what season does it happen in? _Answers may vary._

Week #37 — Assessment

The Black Cat's Curse

A left-handed pitcher for the New York Yankees, named Eddie Lopat, had beaten the Cleveland Indians 11 times in a row! When the two teams got together the twelfth time, something crazy happened. A rude man who was watching the game jumped out of his seat and ran onto the field. He had a black cat in his arms! Some people think that black cats are supposed to bring bad luck. The crazy fan dashed over to the pitcher's mound. He put the black cat right in front of Eddie's feet. Poor Eddie! He did not do a good job pitching. The New York Yankees lost the game.

1. Which word has a **u** that sounds like the **u** in **cup**? (a) jumped b. rude
   Which word has an **o** that sounds like the **o** in **hose**? a. solid (b) over
   Which word has both **short u** and **long o** sounds? (a) supposed b. mound

2. Write **twelfth** as a number. _12th_

3. Why did the man put the black cat in front of Eddie?
   a. To give Eddie a sneezing fit.
   (b) To give Eddie bad luck so his pitching would be bad.
   c. Because he promised Eddie he could take home a kitten.

4. What position did Eddie play?
   a. first base
   b. catcher
   (c) pitcher

5. Eddie did not do a good job pitching in that game. Do you think Eddie believed that black cats bring bad luck? _Answers may vary._
   Why or why not? _Answers will vary._

Week #38 — Day #1–#4

Joe watched a busy little mammal climb up the tree. Then it raced down again, looking for nuts. Joe knew that it was hoarding nuts, storing them for winter.

1. What two creatures are in this story? _Joe and a mammal_
2. What is the mammal that Joe is watching: **squirrel** or **dog**? _squirrel_
3. What season does this story take place in? _fall_
4. What does **hoarding** mean: **climbing** or **storing**? _storing_

A rowboat is a small boat that is moved with oars. Oars are long poles with wide, flat ends. Another kind of boat is a fireboat. It puts out fires with water and hoses.

1. Find the answer to this riddle: I help put out fires. What am I? _a fireboat_
2. Which do you think is bigger, a **rowboat** or a **fireboat**? _fireboat_
3. What is an **oar**? _a long pole with a flat, wide end_
4. Answer this riddle: I am moved with oars. What am I? _a rowboat_

A sailboat is moved by the wind. It has sails, which are made from strong cloth. The wind fills the sails and moves the boat through the water. A houseboat is a wide, flat boat with rooms where people can live.

1. Find the answer to this riddle: I am moved by the wind. What am I? _a sailboat_
2. What two things work together to make a sailboat move? _wind and sail_
3. Answer this riddle: People can live in my rooms. What am I? _a houseboat_
4. Would you like to live in a houseboat? _Answers will vary._
   Why or why not? _Answers will vary._

Dear Grandma, I am glad you are having a good time on the beach. I bet it is warm there. I can't wait to get there during spring vacation! I want to swim and pick up shells on the beach.

1. Where does Grandma live? _by the beach_
2. What kind of weather does Grandma have? _warm_
3. What time of year is it? _winter_
4. What state could Grandma live in: **Florida** or **Maine**? _Florida_

Week #38 — Assessment

1. Only read the title below. Who is the story about? _Samantha_
   What day is the story about? _Samantha's birthday_

Samantha's Birthday

I knew it would be a great day from the minute I woke up. Piled beside my bed was a stack of presents. I jumped out of bed. I was so excited. When I came downstairs carrying the presents, everyone shouted, "Happy birthday!"

2. Who do you think wrote this paragraph?
   a. Samantha's mother
   (b) Samantha
   c. Samantha's brother

Before Samantha woke up, I left her presents beside her bed. I knew she would like the surprise from her father and me. When we saw Samantha on the stairs, we surprised her by saying, "Happy birthday!"

3. Who do you think wrote this paragraph?
   (a) Samantha's mother
   b. Samantha
   c. Samantha's brother

I bought Samantha a book about dinosaurs for her birthday. Mom and Dad let me do extra chores to earn the money. I had to wake up early to surprise her but it was worth it to see her face when we all said, "Happy birthday!"

4. Who do you think wrote this paragraph?
   a. Samantha's mother
   b. Samantha
   (c) Samantha's brother

5. Circle true or false: Samantha's family does not make a big deal about birthdays. True (False)

Answer Key

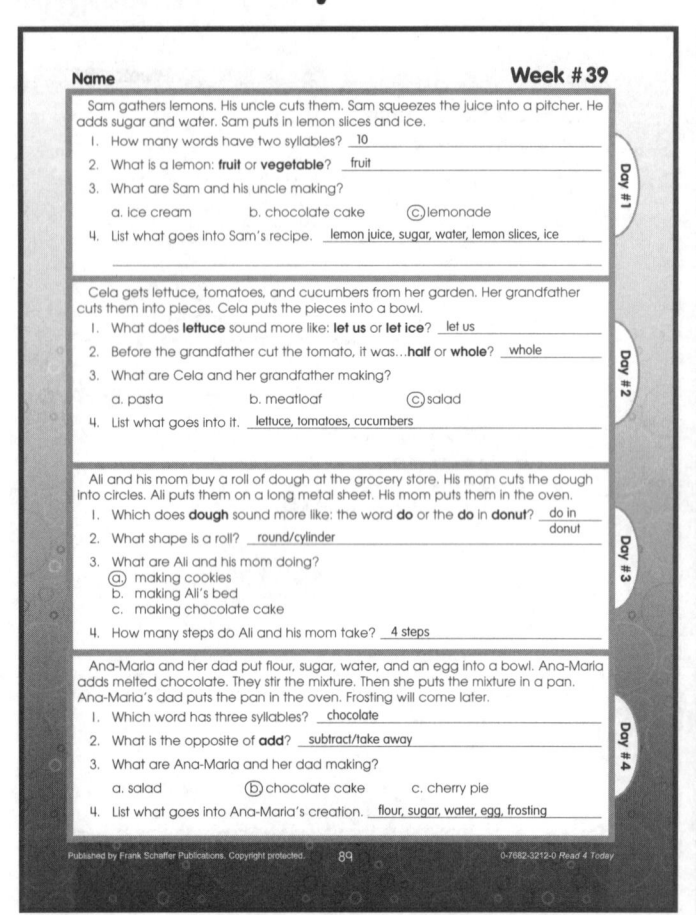

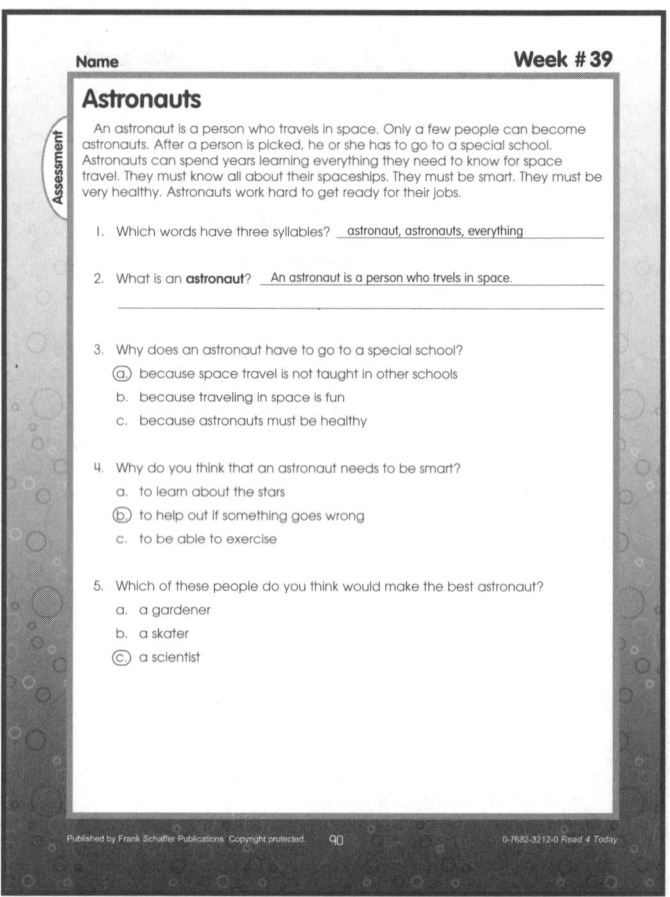

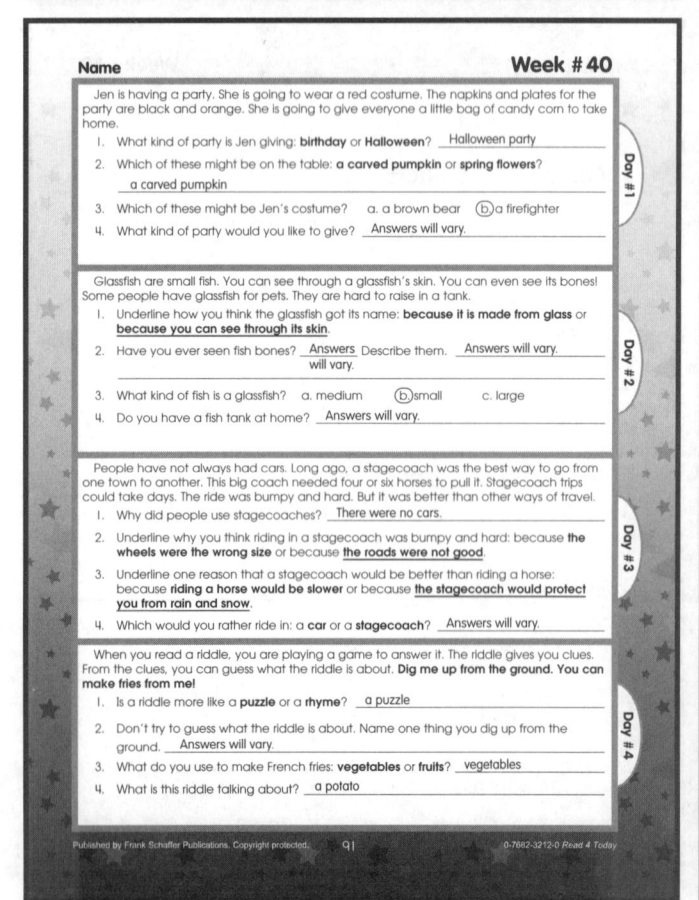

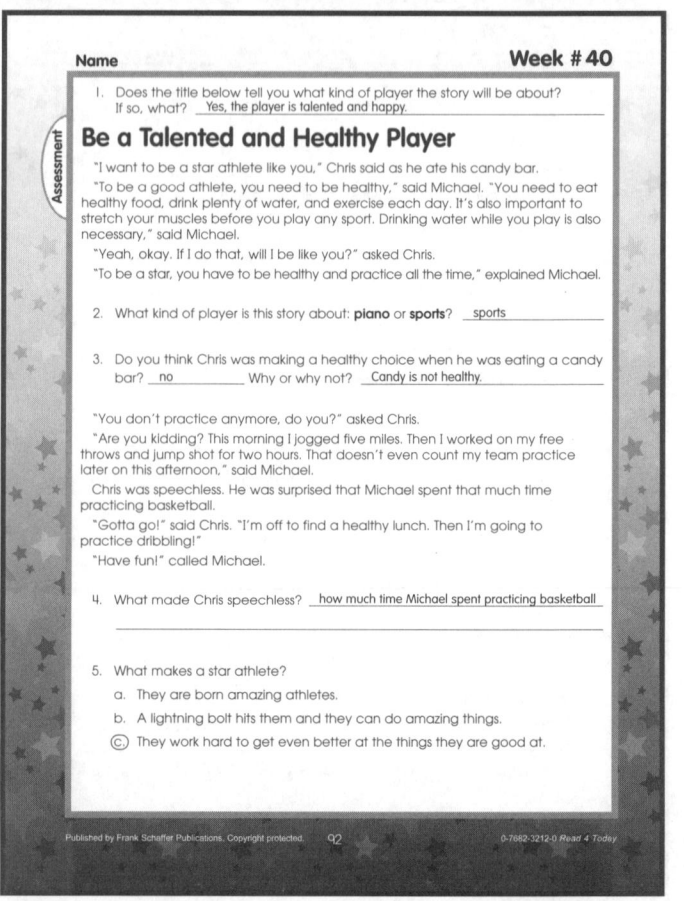

Week #39 — Day #1

Sam gathers lemons. His uncle cuts them. Sam squeezes the juice into a pitcher. He adds sugar and water. Sam puts in lemon slices and ice.

1. How many words have two syllables? __10__
2. Is a lemon: **fruit** or **vegetable**? __fruit__
3. What are Sam and his uncle making?
   a. ice cream   b. chocolate cake   (c) lemonade
4. List what goes into Sam's recipe. __lemon juice, sugar, water, lemon slices, ice__

Day #2

Cela gets lettuce, tomatoes, and cucumbers from her garden. Her grandfather cuts them into pieces. Cela puts the pieces into a bowl.

1. What does **lettuce** sound more like: **let us** or **let ice**? __let us__
2. Before the grandfather cut the tomato, it was…**half** or **whole**? __whole__
3. What are Cela and her grandfather making?
   a. pasta   b. meatloaf   (c) salad
4. List what goes into it. __lettuce, tomatoes, cucumbers__

Day #3

Ali and his mom buy a roll of dough at the grocery store. His mom cuts the dough into circles. Ali puts them on a long metal sheet. His mom puts them in the oven.

1. Which does **dough** sound more like: the word **do** or the **do** in **donut**? __do in donut__
2. What shape is a roll? __round/cylinder__
3. What are Ali and his mom doing?
   (a) making cookies
   b. making Ali's bed
   c. making chocolate cake
4. How many steps do Ali and his mom take? __4 steps__

Day #4

Ana-Maria and her dad put flour, sugar, water, and an egg into a bowl. Ana-Maria adds melted chocolate. They stir the mixture. Then she puts the mixture in a pan. Ana-Maria's dad puts the pan in the oven. Frosting will come later.

1. Which word has three syllables? __chocolate__
2. What is the opposite of **add**? __subtract/take away__
3. What are Ana-Maria and her dad making?
   a. salad   (b) chocolate cake   c. cherry pie
4. List what goes into Ana-Maria's creation. __flour, sugar, water, egg, frosting__

Week #39 — Assessment

Astronauts

An astronaut is a person who travels in space. Only a few people can become astronauts. After a person is picked, he or she has to go to a special school. Astronauts can spend years learning everything they need to know for space travel. They must know all about their spaceships. They must be smart. They must be very healthy. Astronauts work hard to get ready for their jobs.

1. Which words have three syllables? __astronaut, astronauts, everything__
2. What is an **astronaut**? __An astronaut is a person who trvels in space.__
3. Why does an astronaut have to go to a special school?
   (a) because space travel is not taught in other schools
   b. because traveling in space is fun
   c. because astronauts must be healthy
4. Why do you think that an astronaut needs to be smart?
   a. to learn about the stars
   (b) to help out if something goes wrong
   c. to be able to exercise
5. Which of these people do you think would make the best astronaut?
   a. a gardener
   b. a skater
   (c) a scientist

Week #40 — Day #1

Jen is having a party. She is going to wear a red costume. The napkins and plates for the party are black and orange. She is going to give everyone a little bag of candy corn to take home.

1. What kind of party is Jen giving: **birthday** or **Halloween**? __Halloween party__
2. Which of these might be on the table: **a carved pumpkin** or **spring flowers**? __a carved pumpkin__
3. Which of these might be Jen's costume?   a. a brown bear   (b) a firefighter
4. What kind of party would you like to give? __Answers will vary.__

Day #2

Glassfish are small fish. You can see through a glassfish's skin. You can even see its bones! Some people have glassfish for pets. They are hard to raise in a tank.

1. Underline how you think the glassfish got its name: **because it is made from glass** or **because you can see through its skin**.
2. Have you ever seen fish bones? __Answers will vary.__ Describe them. __Answers will vary.__
3. What kind of fish is a glassfish?   a. medium   (b) small   c. large
4. Do you have a fish tank at home? __Answers will vary.__

Day #3

People have not always had cars. Long ago, a stagecoach was the best way to go from one town to another. This big coach needed four or six horses to pull it. Stagecoach trips could take days. The ride was bumpy and hard. But it was better than other ways of travel.

1. Why did people use stagecoaches? __There were no cars.__
2. Underline why you think riding in a stagecoach was bumpy and hard: because **the wheels were the wrong size** or because **the roads were not good**.
3. Underline one reason that a stagecoach would be better than riding a horse: because **riding a horse would be slower** or because **the stagecoach would protect you from rain and snow**.
4. Which would you rather ride in: **a car** or **a stagecoach**? __Answers will vary.__

Day #4

When you read a riddle, you are playing a game to answer it. The riddle gives you clues. From the clues, you can guess what the riddle is about. Dig me up from the ground. You can make fries from me!

1. Is a riddle more like a **puzzle** or a **rhyme**? __a puzzle__
2. Don't try to guess what the riddle is about. Name one thing you dig up from the ground. __Answers will vary.__
3. What do you use to make French fries: **vegetables** or **fruits**? __vegetables__
4. What is this riddle talking about? __a potato__

Week #40 — Assessment

1. Does the title below tell you what kind of player the story will be about? If so, what? __Yes, the player is talented and happy.__

Be a Talented and Healthy Player

"I want to be a star athlete like you," Chris said as he ate his candy bar.

"To be a good athlete, you need to be healthy," said Michael. "You need to eat healthy food, drink plenty of water, and exercise each day. It's also important to stretch your muscles before you play any sport. Drinking water while you play is also necessary," said Michael.

"Yeah, okay. If I do that, will I be like you?" asked Chris.

"To be a star, you have to be healthy and practice all the time," explained Michael.

2. What kind of player is this story about: **piano** or **sports**? __sports__
3. Do you think Chris was making a healthy choice when he was eating a candy bar? __no__ Why or why not? __Candy is not healthy.__

"You don't practice anymore, do you?" asked Chris.

"Are you kidding? This morning I jogged five miles. Then I worked on my free throws and jump shot for two hours. That doesn't even count my team practice later on this afternoon," said Michael.

Chris was speechless. He was surprised that Michael spent that much time practicing basketball.

"Gotta go!" said Chris. "I'm off to find a healthy lunch. Then I'm going to practice dribbling!"

"Have fun!" called Michael.

4. What made Chris speechless? __how much time Michael spent practicing basketball__
5. What makes a star athlete?
   a. They are born amazing athletes.
   b. A lightning bolt hits them and they can do amazing things.
   (c) They work hard to get even better at the things they are good at.